THE QUEST TO SUCCEED

K. C. ARORA

ACKNOWLEDGEMENT

I am grateful to my family for encouraging me to write this novel. I often discussed the story and the plot with them which provided an insight into right direction. They read the manuscript and made valuable suggestions. They also aided with the design of cover and my photograph. The cover is designed by pch.vector / Freepik.

This book is dedicated to the memory of my late wife Santosh Rani Arora, devoted wife, loving mother and affectionate grandmother.

OTHER PUBLICATIONS

BY K.C. ARORA

1   *E\qual Opportunities for Ethnic Minorities in Work Related NAFE: Identifying and Developing Good Practice in Colleges* (with others); Inner London Education Authority, 1990.

2   *Indian Nationalist Movement in Britain, 1930-49*; Inter India Publications, New Delhi, 1992

3. *Colonialism and the Decline of the Cotton Industry in 19th Century India*; University of Greenwich, 1993

4. Mahatma Gandhi on Communal Individuality; *The Good Society Review*, July 1993

5. Krishna Menon: A St. Pancras-Councillor; *The Good Society Review*, July 1995

6. *The Steel Frame: Indian Civil Service Since 1860*; Sanchar Publishing House, New Delhi, 1996

K. C. Arora

7. V.K, Krishna Menon: A Brilliant Eccentric; *India Weekly*, 3 May 1996

8. *Imperialism and the Non-Aligned Movement*; Sanchar Publishing House, New Delhi, 1998

9. *V.K. Krishna Menon- A Biography*; Sanchar Publishing House, New Delhi, 1998

10. *A Short Introduction to the Principles of Economics*; Hamilton & Co. Publishers Ltd., London, 2000

11. *The City of Parks: Memories of an Outsider*; Author House, Bloomington, USA, 2016

12. *Stagnation & Change, The Economic Impact of British Raj in India (1757-1947)*; Inter-India Publications, New Delhi, 2018

THE QUEST TO SUCCEED

PREFACE

"The Quest to Succeed" aims to identify the socio-psychological traits leading to the founding elements of human conduct and mental attitude. Certain features are inherited, others develop in course of time, by living in a set of circles. It is, nevertheless, a work of fiction. People should not attempt to identify their experiences and situations with the narrative of this book. If there are any similarities in the knowledge of any person with the present subject, these could be coincidental.

The objective of this novel is to highlight the traditions and customs that prevail in certain countries, and the determination of a group of populaces to create potholes in the lives of simple-minded people, who want to move forward through their own travails. This is, however, a story of an Indian villager Jay (hero of the novel) who had lived in various parts of the country and indeed in other parts of the world. Jay witnessed different lifestyles in villages and cities. He saw that villagers in India had started to

5

migrate to cities in order to seek education and employment. In cities, they encountered enormous problems, especially in finding proper employment and accommodation.

Jay was sincere, polite, and helpful to individuals and groups of people. Even so, he faced problems, not only in his childhood, but also in later life. At times, people misconstrued him and took advantage of his gentleness. Gloomy thinkers attempted to create obstructions in his life. Indeed, he discussed such situations with pragmatics and sought solutions to adversities without confrontation. He had a sharp mind and a piercing memory. Memories represent past events and phenomenon, which are reflected in this novel.

This novel weave together certain traits of human nature, like determination, jealousy, confidence, and challenging work. A person must countenance others in the community and society. Some people have psychological problems such as anti-social nature, superiority, inferiority complexes, jealousy, and narcissistic idiosyncrasy. Others ignore the achievements of successful individuals. They possess an aggressive nature. Childhood habits continue in adolescence.

This novel acknowledges the importance of family life and parental reassurance in advancement. Human beings react to jealousy, hindrance, confrontation, prejudice, discrimination, incomprehension and their social impact on posture and port. They continue to make improvements in social, educational, and economic fields.

Most people tend to reconcile with others without giving up their own essential qualities. A community cannot forcefully be controlled for a prolonged period and must find its own solution. Man is a social being. An individual, a community or a nation would prosper and succeed by acquiring knowledge, wisdom, farsightedness, goodwill, and generosity. They should have inspiration and should be prepared to bring about constructive and productive application of them. The creative flow has been maintained by enlightening the emotions and personality entities. It is, nevertheless, a literary novel in conversational language.

,

<u>1</u>

In the first week of July, on a sunny day, Jay was standing on the roof-terrace of his house. He was close to the top of the stairs, where he could see his family in the open courtyard, as well as the villagers going through the lane. Kalu, who was going to school, raising his head up, asked, "Jay, when would you start going to school?" Jay made no reply and looked at his mother who was standing on the ground floor precinct.

Jay felt that it was time, he started to go to school. He said to his mother, "mom, I would also like to go to school with the children of our vicinity." His mother replied, "three of your siblings are already at the centre of learning, if you join them, you will need an academy for yourselves". Moreover, "you are not yet five years old" and "a child like you should be running after the village cattle and collecting cow-dung."

Next morning, Jay picked up a small bucket and went to the edge of the village, where the owners were leaving their cattle for the shepherds to take them for grazing. He collected about half kg dung and put it in his bucket. The cattle moved on to graze outside the village in the open fields. Jay could not follow them and returned home. He told his mother that "the cattle ran fast. I could not go after them."

(NB: In Indian villages, cow dung was dried in the sun and used as fuel to cook food and boil water and milk. In the 1980s, however, biogas production started, when dairy farming became popular and a large amount of cow dung or Gobar as it is called in Hindi, could be collected at one place. It started to be used for gas extraction. Gobar gas is a renewable energy produced from organic waste like cow dung. Gobar is a clean, sustainable alternative to fossil fuels). (It is also known as biogas. It provides clean fuel to households. Biogas can be used to produce electricity to power farm machinery. It is very safe and does not produce greenhouse gases. Biogas is produced through anaerobic digestion system which breaks down, the organic matter in an oxygen-deprived environment. It is an excellent source of energy. It was first started in India but now it has become popular in many developing countries.)

Jay hardly ever went back to collect cow dung after that. His mother had a strong personality. She was tall and well built. She used to wear a sari rather than a long skirt. Though she kept one for ceremonies. She had it made with ten yards of cloth. It was big and heavy and in a beautiful colour. She could control her children by speaking loudly. None of them questioned her but she was also a caring lady.

When Jay stopped going to collect cow dung, she did not say anything and understood his problem and interest. She was good at helping the villagers with money and often gave poor people old clothes and leftover food. She did not speak much in the presence of Jay's grandmother. After Jay's grandmother's death, his mother started money lending business of her own.

She used to charge an interest on loans and would ask them for some jewellery as a guarantee or collateral. She dealt only with women, who used to come to her house to borrow money and later to pay interest or the whole amount. Often, she allowed them to pay in monthly instalments.

Jay's sisters helped in domestic work, but he never saw them cooking or cleaning dishes or kitchenware. They wore Kurta Salwar (loose shirts and baggy cotton patterned trousers). Always put a large scarf over their shoulders. His eldest sister liked embroidery and weaving sweaters by hand. Once she made a carpet at home and wrote Jay's elder brother Gautam's name on it.

She used assorted colours of cotton thread. It turned out to be a beautiful carpet. Other sisters and brothers also helped in weaving the family carpet, which lasted a few years. The cotton thread for the carpet was spun by family members at home. Cotton was grown in Jay's village and a large amount was used by households to spin thread. Only surplus cotton was sold in the town market.

A great amount of cotton was used by residents in his village and in many other villages in the country. The cotton cloth was being manufactured in India for thousands of years. The raw cotton brought from farms was first dried in the sun by the farmers themselves. It was then sold to households. Jay's father bought raw cotton only for his own family use. Women in the village participated in working in the cotton cottage industry.

The cotton and its seed were separated by a charkhi (wooden wheel). The cotton was then rolled by hand into puny (cotton ball). Charkha (spinning wheel) was used to make thread. Takwa or spindle was attached to clay, which rested on a cowrie shell. Family members did all this work themselves.

The cotton ball (puny) was held in the left hand, while the spindle was revolved by the right hand. The motion stretched the cotton wool into thread and rolled it around the capstan. As soon as a certain quantity of thread was twisted round the pivot, it was removed. The process commenced again. Jay saw his grandmother and mother spinning charkha in the afternoons, after lunch.

11

He wanted to try to make thread and spin the charkha, but he was not allowed to do so. However, he used to make puny with dried cotton. He loved watching the act of cotton thread making and removing the cotton ball from the pin (Takua). There were no weavers in his village. Weavers, however, used to come to his village from a nearby locality. They used to go around the village, asking households, if they had raw thread ready to sell.

They would buy thread and take it to their village, wash it and convert the thread into cloth. They would bring the ready-made cloth to Jay's village to sell in yards. Sometimes, they (the weavers would stitch the cloth into quilt or quilt covers). Raw cotton for quilt was spun by a dhunka (bow like instrument) to convert it into refined and clean cotton. It made the cotton smooth and easy to fill in a cloth conducive to making a quilt, which people needed in winter to keep them warm at night.

When Jay stopped going to collect cow dung, he started to go to his grandfather's shop, where he learned numbers and timetable. He could recount timetable from two to twenty- times ten, which he enjoyed. The fifteen's timetable, he could enumerate within seconds, then laugh at his achievement. He also learned quarters, halves, three quarters, one and a half times and two and a half times of figures, which increased his grasp over oral arithmetic.

He wanted to learn three and a quarter and three and half-times of figures up to twenty. His grandfather, however, suggested to him, "You do not need it, these days". "You can work out all calculations and multiplication with your existing knowledge, by using a slate". Papers were in short supply in his village. His grandfather did a great deal of calculation orally for his accounting. Jay's grandfather was a tall gentleman of about six feet. He used to wear dhoti (lion cloth) and kurta (loose shirt without collar). In the winter he wore white pyjamas (trousers) and wrapped a shawl over his upper body. He also had a woollen coat, which he used to wear when he went out of the village. He wore a white turban in all seasons. He was very fond of riding horses. As a young man he used to allow his horse to run and would jump on it as a sport.

At the age of fourteen, he thought that he would go to university to study Law and become a lawyer. After his father's death at an early age, he gave up his studies and decided to help his elder brother in the family business. After his marriage, he started his own shop in another village and moved to live there with his small family. His family had been traders and businesspeople for at least three hundred years.

He was a kind man, always helped people in need. He often asked them, especially those who were strangers in the village, whether they have had food. He would take them to his house and provide them lunch, milk, or tea. Some persons were reluctant to go to his house, where women and children lived. He used to leave his shop for a few minutes and bring meal from his house for those people. He never charged any money of them. There was no restaurant in the village.

Jay's village did not have a post office of its own. A postman used to come to deliver post from the nearby town. He served five villages and travelled by bicycle. There were not substantial number of posts to be delivered in each village. When he could not go to individual houses to deliver post, he used to leave letters at Jay's grandfather's shop. His grandfather saw many customers from all the communities in the village. They used to collect their post from his shop.

The postal worker also delivered money orders because there were army pensioners in the village. Some villagers, who had gone out to work in cities, sent money to their parents and families. The mail carrier, however, was not allowed to deliver more than one hundred rupees at a time. If there was a money order for more than one hundred rupees, the recipients had to go to the main post office in the town, to collect their money. The main post office was about five miles away from Jay's village. The postal worker had to be present at the time of payment in order to ensure that the right person received his/her money.

Jay's grandfather liked the company of his family. He looked after his grandchildren well. The younger ones were taken to the well to be given a bath. He encouraged them to study and read books. He himself had read books and magazines. He knew all about the Indian epics the *Ramayana* and the *Mahabharat*. He had read the *Ramayana* many times over.

His knowledge of the Indian Epics, and general knowledge was very vast. Still, he did not interfere with the grandchildren's homework, which they were encouraged to do themselves. He, however, used to teach them about social interaction, never to quarrel with anyone, always to live in cooperation and harmony with each other. People should not be jealous of others.

He never compared himself with nearby people or relatives. He did not have any complexes and did not see others as inferior or superior to himself. He lived a peaceful and contented life and believed in the welfare of all. He hoped for their good health. He had a strong willpower. He converted his challenges into opportunities.

The students and shopkeepers used slates to work out their calculations and accounts. Whenever a customer bought goods on credit, Jay's grandfather used to write it on a slate and not on a paper. These customers used to pay back the credit within a week. The barter system was more popular than the use of money in the village.

As a child, Jay played gully Danda with the boys in the village. (Gully or gally is a small stick and Danda is a big stick) Gully is hit by the big stick (Danda) and is thrown as far as possible. The other players had to catch it before it fell on the ground. His father encouraged him to play baseball. The gully Danda (stick) could hurt the players or passersby.

Kabaddi was also a popular game in his village. Young children played as a team. The grown-up young men played separately. Two opposing teams of six boys each were needed in this game. (Kabaddi was like rugby in western countries but it was played without a ball). Jay had good relations with all the boys of his age group in the village. He used to participate in games with them and went out with them.

In the spring season, there was a fair in another village, he went to see that fair with his friend rather than with the family. Jay and his friend returned to the village together. His friend's grandfather, however, did not like him going out of the village. There were only a few occasions when they went out of the village. In the village, however, they were often together and visited each other's house. His friend's parents were always polite to him. His friend received encouragement from him and took interest in his studies. Eventually, he became a Primary School teacher. He did not study for a degree, which was essential to become a High School teacher. While Jay's grandfather looked after the shop, his father dealt with the other side of business. When Jay's dad went to city to buy groceries and other goods for the shop, Gautam used to stay at the shop with grandpa to help him in attending the customers. He used to skip school. It created a gap in his learning. He was almost fifteen years old, when he completed his primary education, compared to most students who finished their primary schooling at the age of eleven.

He was quite old when he wanted to attend the Secondary School. Other students were much younger than him. Jay was in year two of Secondary School, when Gautam was to be admitted in year one. He refused to be in a lower grade than his brother who was four years younger to him. With the result he gave up his studies forever.

17

2

Jay's dad used to help farmers in the sale of their surplus crops of wheat and peas and sometimes barley and chickpeas. He advised them where to go to city market to get the best price. Some farmers could not go to the city. They were always busy with farming or family affairs. Jay's dad used to purchase their products, especially wheat and peas. Sometimes he hoarded these goods in his warehouse for a few months and sold them when the prices started to go up.

He often took the agriculture produce to the city market, the same day or within a couple of days. He never kept his own vehicle but used to hire bullock carts to carry goods. He had contact with two bullock cart owners, Kartar, and Samar. One or the other was always available. Kartar was a farmer, but he did a side business and used to carry Jay's dad's commodities to the city. When Jay's father could not go with him, Kartar was entrusted with the merchandise.

He knew which aadti's (commission agent's) shop to go to. He would sell the goods and bring money to the village. The aadti (commission agent) had a place to park the cart and oxen to rest and eat fodder. There was also a khat (small bed) for Kartar to sit and rest. He had drinking water facilities for both- human beings as well as for animals. Samar was also a dependable ox- drawn cart owner. He was a building worker but would give up his work for a day and take Jay's dad's wheat or peas to the city.

His father used the same aadti (commission agent or intermediary) to sell the crop. If he did not need the money immediately in the village, he used to ask Samar to leave the finance from sales with the aadti. Samar was sometimes given a list of essentials for the shop to purchase. He knew where to buy these items from. He would bring the goods to the village in the afternoon and deliver at the shop.

Jay's father used to go to the bordering villages to find out if farmers wanted to sell their surplus crops and needed money in order to pay their taxes and other bills. He used to take Samar and his bullock cart or Kartar and his bullock cart to those villages. They used to bring the agricultural products to their village and would take them to the town the next day. In such a situation, the bullock cart was parked outside Jay's grandfather's shop, where they could look after it at night. Sometimes Jay and his brother Gautam slept in the cart as security guards. If a cart was available in the other village, Jay's dad would hire it there and take the goods direct to the city.

Jay's father was a good storyteller. When Jay was young, he used to listen to his dad's stories every night. At one stage he thought that he would like to write all his dad's stories and become a story writer himself. He told his sister about his ambition. She said that she would tell him lots of stories, which he could write. His sister was studying in the village primary school.

He, however, could not forget a story which his dad told him and his siblings. It related to humans as well as animals. Jay felt that an animal could be as sensitive and respond like a human being. As in many other stories in village life, it was about a Princess, who lived in her father's palace, but she was not allowed to go out of the building. No visitors were permitted to meet her.

The princess had a boyfriend whom she liked meeting but had to see him outside the castle. She became friendly with a court servant who used to take her, outside the royal residence, hidden in the ear of an elephant. When they reached the outskirts of the town, they would rest under a tree. The Princess would come out of the elephant's ear and the servant would fan the beast. The animal used to fall asleep in the cold breeze under the tree.

The Princess would go walking with her boyfriend. She would return within half an hour before the elephant woke up. She would then enter the elephant's ear and return to the mansion. No one knew about her adventure. Like any other day, the Princess went out hidden in the elephant's ear. On reaching the outskirts of the town, the elephant stopped under a tree, and she got out of its ear. The servant started to fan the animal who fell asleep.

The Princess, however, did not return within the scheduled time of half an hour on that day. The servant realized that the Princess was late, and the elephant was to wake up, he attempted to enter the elephant's ear. However, before he could do so, the elephant woke up. In indignation and rage, it killed the servant.

When the Princess arrived at the scene, she found the servant dead and the elephant was making noise in anger. Her adventure or misadventure was discovered by the king and his ministers. She was not permitted to leave the palace after that incident. Jay reflected that the animals were equally sensitive like human beings.

Because of the underage, Jay was not allowed to go to school. He, however, stayed at home or at his grandfather's shop. He waited for another two years, before he could start his schooling. He was sometimes restless and wanted to do something constructive. One

21

day, he thought of making a cart with mud and straw, which were freely available in the village. He had a design on his mind. His mother, however, discerned that she will instruct a carpenter to make a wood cart for him. She did not realize that Jay wanted to use his talent and skills regarding making a cart. He did not necessarily want to play with it, as a toy.

It was not until when he was almost seven years old, his elder sister left the village primary, Jay started to attend the school. There he learned to read a book and write on a wooden piece called takhti. He already knew the numbers and timetable. The teacher asked him to teach the numbers and timetable to his fellow students. The teacher was so impressed with Jay, he commented, as "if Jay was born with all these skills," and he learned to count numbers and timetable in his mother's womb". He, nevertheless, learned oral arithmetic of his grandfather.

Jay's primary school was co-educational. However, only about ten percent of the students were girls, and the rest were boys. There were only seventy students altogether in the school and they came from five close by villages. Every village did not have a primary school in the 1940s. There was no lady teacher in that village until the 1970s. But the teaching standard of the school, was very high.

22

For Jay there was no distinction between boys and girls. He helped everyone and would not distinguish whether a student was from his village or came from another village. He had good association with them all. The school held sports competitions, especially hurdle races, long-distance race, and long jump. Students used to take part in these sports and in physical exercises.

The boys also staged a play from the epic *Mahabharata*. Jay was particularly fascinated with the drama, when Arjun's son, Abhimanyu faced eight warriors. He continued to fight even when all his armaments were destroyed. At one stage he turned the chariot's wheel into a weapon. Abhimanyu was eventually killed. The spectators had tears in their eyes.

In the drama, boys had to play the role of girls, because the parents did not allow their daughters to take part in the school play. They went to school only to get education, to learn to read and write. For these parents, extracurricular activities were not an essential part of learning. Over a period, however, that outlook and perspective changed.

In his village, he noticed that a dramatic company used to come to perform Ram Leela, based on the life of Hindu god Ram. Ram was the son of King Dasharatha and Queen Kausalya of Ayodhya. The Ram Leela continued for ten days from Ram's birth to education, his exile to forest, kidnapping of his wife Sita and her recovery. Ram, Sita, and brother Laxman returned to Ayodhya, where people celebrated their arrival by lighting Diva. This started the festival of Diwali.

Jay was, however, fascinated with the story about the birth of Ram and how Ram and his brothers were born. King Dashrath and queen Kaushalya had a daughter named Shanta, but they bestowed her to their friend Roma pada, the king of Anga, who had no children. King Dasharatha and Queen Kausalya thought that they would have another child soon. King Dashrath, however, could not have any more children after Shanta. He did not ask king Roma pada to render their daughter to them because she had by now become the Princess of Anga. Dasharatha married twice again but no children were born.

Princess Shanta was a beautiful young lady. Once Rishi Asringa (a scholar and scientist) came to seek help from king Roma pada of Anga. He saw the young Princess and enquired about her siblings. The King said, "we have no other children. The King of Ayodhya bestowed her to us when she was very young".

Rishi (Sage) Asringa said that "he was doing research, on fertility treatment, with his guru Vibhandak Rishi, whom he treated as his father because he, (Sage Vibhandak) brought him up. "If you wish, we can experiment medicine on you and the queen". But his condition was that Shanta should be given to him in marriage after the success of the experiment. Roma Pada could not decide on this request by the sage.

He, therefore, invited his friend Dasharatha and queen Kausalya to Anga. When they arrived, Rishi's proposal was presented to them. The King of Ayodhya did not like the notion that his daughter should be married to a rough looking, forest dweller researcher Rishi. He wanted his daughter to marry a Prince and live in a royal palace. He was, therefore, reluctant to agree to this marriage proposal.

Shanta, nonetheless, agreed to marry Sage Asringa and for a rough life in the forest, if she could have siblings. The rishi and his guru started their medicine experiments. The queen of Anga had a child just after one year and second child, one year after that. The treatment was successful.

After careful consideration and discussion with the queens of Ayodhya, King Dasharatha also agreed to the same experiment in his capital city. Rishi Asringa started the treatment and afforded the medicine mixed in kheer (rice pudding) serving it in a cup, each to queen Kausalya and queen Kaikai. They obtained one more cup. Both the queens poured half of their share of kheer in that cup.

Third cup was given to the middle queen, Sumitra. All three queens had kheer with medicine prepared by the Rishi.

After the maturity time, Queen Kausalya gave birth to Ram. Queen Kaikai gave birth to Bharat and Queen Sumitra gave birth to twins, Laxman, and Shatrughan. Since Kheer was taken by the queens on the same day, they gave birth together at the same hour. But Ram was the first born and was, therefore, treated as the eldest Prince and elder brother of the other three Princes.

Jay maintained that it was important to recognize the birth of King Dasharatha's sons and to acknowledge that fertility treatment existed in ancient India. In the treta yug (during the period of Dashrath's reign) it was conducted first in the kingdom of Anga and then in the kingdom of Ayodhya. Treta in Sanskrit means a collection of three. According to Hindu Puranas, three Avatars (incarnation) of Lord Vishnu took place. The first was Vaman, the second was Parshuram and the third was Ram.

In Jay's village, the Ram Leela drama was frequented at night. This continued for many nights. The villagers customarily went to the nearby town to watch the Ram Leela performance, which was on a grand scale. It used to take place during the daytime and continued for ten days, before the Diwali festival. The villagers often compared the scenes and performance with their village Ram Leela.

The story of Ram showed respect for elders, affection between brothers and the sense of duty. It appealed to people of all ages. They did not necessarily follow these principles themselves or behave the way it was reflected in the drama.

When Ram and his brothers had completed their education, the king decided to declare Ram as the crown prince and the heir to the throne because he was his eldest son. The king consulted the family priest, sage Vashishtha, before making his decision public that Ram would become king after Dasharatha.

The youngest queen Kaikai, however, objected to it. She wanted her son Bharat to become the king of Ayodhya. There was nothing wrong with that. Bharat was only an hour younger to Ram and had the same education and learned the same skills. He was equally large-hearted like his brothers. He was also fond of poetry and painting and authored poems himself.

Queen Kaikai also demanded a fourteen-year exile for Ram from the Kingdom and insisted that he should spend this time in forests. Ram agreed to go to the forest for this period. He was happy to obey his stepmother. Ram's wife Sita and his younger brother Laxman also resolved to accompany him and to live in the forest, for the duration of the exile. Fourteen years banishment was chosen because at that time, there was a customary law that if some owned a land or territory for fourteen years, it would become his right of possession for ever.

King Dasharatha, however, did not like it. He attempted to persuade Queen Kaikai that "he would make Bharat Crown Prince and later he will become the king of Ayodhya". She should not impose the condition to throw out Ram from Ayodhya.

Queen Kaikai did not change her mind and insisted that Ram should spend the suggested period in the forest. Ram was an obedient son and followed the decree by his stepmother. Jay disagreed with this kind of blind obedience. The consequences were not considered. He pondered over this incident of the *Ramayana*.

The result was that as soon as Ram, Sita and Laxman left the city, king Dasharatha fell ill and died within a few days. Laxman's wife Urmila had to stay in the city, without her husband for fourteen years. What was her fault that she had to live on her own without a husband? During the last year of their exile, Sita was kidnapped by Ravan, the king of Lanka.

What was more, Prince Bharat refused to sit on the throne to rule the city state. He went to the forest to persuade Ram to return to

Ayodhya. Ram refused to come back to the Capital city, before completing his exile of fourteen years. Bharat brought Ram's wooden Chappals (khadaun) and put them on the throne as a symbol of rule by Ram. He himself moved to a village, Nandi gram, and dug a small hole and slept there on grass and leaves. He attended the state matters from there.

He considered Ram as the real ruler of Ayodhya and told the citizens that he was acting on behalf of his elder brother Ram. This also put pressure on their youngest brother Shatrughan, who was responsible for safeguarding and the security of the kingdom. He had to fight many wars during this period. That was Jay's view about Ram's exile.

In Jay's village, there were two brothers in a farmer's family. The elder one was interested in dramatics and dancing. He used to perform dance at the village Ram Leela. And in some other dramatic performances. His younger brother did not like him wearing a sari like a girl and dancing. Later he understood that dancing was an art. Not every person could perform or take part in dramatics. It was an inherited talent or was acquired through practice.

When he was studying in his village primary school, Jay noticed that there was only one boy from the scheduled caste. He was there because his house was near the school. The other parents, from poor families, and from the tribal communities, did not send their children to school. The tribal community mostly lived on the outer skirts of the village, and they thought that the school was only for villagers.

They worked on farms with the village farmers and did some domestic work as well. They were exceptionally good at making utensils with Iron for domestic use and agricultural tools like spades and other tools which were used for farming and for cutting fodder. They also made sickles which were used to cut crops. Sometimes these people were called Ironmongers.

There were no children from the sweeper (scavengers) or untouchable community in the school. Their work was not appreciated by the villagers or by the Indian society. It was a menial job. Mostly conducted by women, who carried the night soil excreta collected from cesspools, in peoples' homes. They carried it in baskets on their heads. It often dripped over their face, reaching the eyes and the nose and sometimes the mouth. It was very smelly.

The girls were asked by their mothers to carry the load on their head. They were also acquainted with the custom that they would have to do the same job, when they get married and lived with their in-laws, in another village. These people were also called untouchables.

Jay did not like this practice and often objected to its taking place in the Indian society. Once, Jay touched one of the women who was standing outside his house. His mother asked him to change his clothes and have a bath before he could enter the house. He obeyed his mother. He, however, could not do anything. It was vicious and atrocious. That was the worst side of the biosystematics, taxonomy, and exclusivity practice in the Indian society. The Indian caste system has been identified worse than the class system in other cultures and societies.

<u>3</u>

His school had only two teachers, who concentrated on teaching fourth year and fifth year classes of the primary section. The lower grades were left to work on their own, though the students could consult teachers, when needed. Jay spent two years in the village primary school. Mostly in the nursery section. In his third year at the school, he was promoted to level one, where he started to read books and study mathematics and other subjects.

After one month, a new teacher joined the school. He checked the payment book. All students were required to pay five rupees for promotion to an upper standard. The new teacher discovered that Jay's money had not been received. He asked him to bring five rupees to school the next day. Jay tried to argue with the teacher that he should not be asked to pay any money as he scored all the marks in his examination, and he reached the upper stage by his own efforts. Nonetheless, the teacher contended that Jay requested his father to pay five rupees soon.

Jay told his dad of the teacher's demand. His dad replied that "he had already paid ten rupees to the teacher who taught at the school prior to the current teacher joining." His dad worked out that five rupees were paid for the promotion of Jay's elder brother Gautam. Three rupees for his sister's progression and two rupees for Jay's upgrade, were recompensed to the schoolteachers. His father, therefore, did not give him any more money.

Even so, he did not go himself to see the teacher to clarify the details of the payment. He left it to the child to expound and face the new educator. The next day, Jay told his instructor, what his father had said. The teacher was not satisfied with the answer. Every child at the school should pay five rupees for the sake of being moved to the next standard. He was, therefore, furious, and canned Jay **once**.

Not only that he did not bring five rupees as demanded but also for answering him back. Although Jay simply relayed his father's message. The teacher expected complete obedience and that the students should follow his words. His words were his command. There was no question of any discussion or arguments. Jay was shocked and surprised.

He now worked out why the educators kept him in the Nursery Section, for two years, when he knew and learned in the first six months, all that was required to study over two years. Some students were promoted to their next level, every six months on payment of five rupees. Jay was often asked by his previous teacher to communicate and pass on his knowledge of numbers and timetable to his fellow students and to look after the group as a class captain. They appreciated and acknowledged his skills and soft manners.

After the incident at school, Jay went home for midday lunch and told his grandmother of what had taken place at the school. He was close to his grandmother who prepared breakfast for him, put cream on his face, combed his hair. She checked that he looked smart when he went to school.

His grandmother was a small lady of about five feet. She was of Sindhi origin. She used to wear lehenga (a full ankle length skirt) with a half sleave blouse as the top. (Lehenga -choli was now worn only on occasions or during ceremonies like weddings). Jay's grandmother used to put a big scarf over her shoulders. She loved her grandchildren and enjoyed cooking for them and looked after them.

She made all kinds of food, rice, lentils, vegetables, yogurt curry, chapatis, puri (puffed fried small chapatis), she made puri stuffed with potatoes and lentils. Rice pudding and semolina pudding were made for desserts. At the festival of Diwali, she used to cook food in enormous quantities to last a few days. She also gave food to water-woman, cleaner, sweeper, dhobi (washerman) and the hairdresser.

At the festival, she sent food to families in the adjoining houses and relatives who lived in the various parts of the village. Diwali is a festival of lights. Earthen lamps are lit and put on the roof terrace, outside the house and in the open courtyard. In Jay's house, they used to make a small hut with mud but would colour it, bright red mixed with other paints. Divas were also put in that hut.

A statue or a picture of Laxmi was put there. The deity Laxmi is worshipped on this day. She is considered as the Goddess of wealth, prosperity, and health to her devotees. Rice and Sugar cane crops start around this season. These are shared and distributed among the villagers. A puja (Veneration) is done of the Goddess Laxmi with sweets, Batasa and Kheel.

At Jay's grandfather's shop, a large amount of Kheel-Batasa were distributed. His dad used to bring 100 kg of Kheel and twenty kg Batasa from the town. He also used to buy sugar toys (Khilonas), which were made in the shape of small elephants and horses. Kheel is puffed rice which is made by heating rice kernels on hot temperature in sand. It could also be fried in oil.

Batasa is made by boiling sugar mixed with water till it reaches a thick consistency. It is later shaped like a coin. The makers pour these sugar coins on a clean white cloth and pick them up when they have cooled and dried.   Kheel- Batasa was distributed to many people at the shop on Diwali day. Elderly people, who could not come to the shop, Jay and his brother Gautam used to take for them at their community places called Chopals.

Children used to ask for khilonas (sugar toys). Kheel was eaten with Batasa. It would otherwise be dry. As Batasa melts in the mouth, it provides an excellent taste. Kheel is also rich in fibre, which helps in boosting digestion. It contains vitamin D and helps in easing pain. Apart from the religious element, it has health advantages.

When Jay's grandparents were head of the family, they kept at least three cows and buffaloes. There was plenty of milk in the house. Jay's grandmother used to churn yogurt and take cream out of it. The cream was then made hot and converted into ghee (purified butter).   The chhachh (butter milk) was either given to acquaintances or fed to the cows and buffaloes. It was a prolonged process but was very useful and enjoyable.

Jay came home from school, for midday lunch. He was a little upset and annoyed. He said to his grandmother, "I am not going back to that school, where I had been canned for no good reason." His grandmother did not argue with him and asked him to relax and have his lunch. When his sister was going back to school after her lunch, he asked her to bring his books and mat from the school. He used to take his own mat to sit on. Some students squatted on the dusty floor. There was no provision for mats at the school for students to sit on.

Jay left the Primary school, never went back there again. He did not see that teacher after the incident. On his refusal to go to school, his dad asked him "what would you do"? He did not want him to give up his schooling at an early age. Jay replied, "I would start to go to the bordering village school, which has been recently built." "I know many children there who used to come to our village primary". He continued his argument, "I would walk every day. It was only one mile from our village. No one has to take me there". "I am not scared of walking on my own. I will take my lunch and will return home at the end of the school hours." His dad was not satisfied but nothing was decided at that time.

People in the village liked Jay. He was known as a soft-spoken, kind, and helpful boy. Those who lived near his house or near his grandfather's shop, he called them uncle, aunty, or cousin brother according to their age and gender. The elderly ladies in the village did not like going to the shop to buy oil, jaggery, sugar, spices, vegetables, or any other item. Jay used to help them. There was a barter system. The Villagers used to bring grains. He would take their wheat or peas or any other grain and buy things for them at his grandfather's shop. They often waited at the corner of the lane. He sometimes delivered their goods to their houses.

Villagers also bought goods at the shop with money or asked for credit. Men folks asked for a bidi (Indian rolled up cigarette), that they would pay later when they come to purchase more items at the shop. Jay did not refuse a bidi, though he never received any money. They tended to forget to pay back for such a minor item. Some villagers asked for tiny amounts of mustard oil to apply to their hair. Jay did not refuse that either. He was kind-hearted, and trusted others that they would recompense him.

He was, however, reluctant to give goods on credit. He always asked his dad or grandfather whether credit could be given to a particular person who asked for it. Even though he was only nine years old and very young, he had a strong willpower, personality, and confidence. Once he decided not to attend the village primary school, he would not budge and was determined not to change his mind. Admittedly, his father refused to pay five rupees to the Primary school teacher, he wanted him to study. He did not like the idea of him going to school in another village.

Jay stayed at home or at his grandfather's shop idling away his time. He did not touch a book during this time. His eldest brother Nakul came home over the weekend from the town, where he was studying for his High School examination. Jay's brother, Nakul, was five feet six inches in height, medium built at the time and wore a half sleeve shirt and trousers. He was almost eight years older to him.

The parents informed him of what had happened in the last few days at the village school. Nakul suggested to the family that "Jay should be sent with him to study in the town where he would be admitted into First Year of Secondary School". "He was very clever and bright with a photographic memory; he could cope with the academic work".

Nakul tried to convince the parents that there would be no problem in his admission because students were being admitted without birth certificate. Many refugees had come to live in that town from Western and Central Punjab. They have school age children. They had to leave their homes because of violence, after the partition of India.

He continued, "People relinquished their belongings in the new state of Pakistan and had to depart from their villages and cities in the clothes they were wearing." Since Jay had a Punjabi surname, no one would ask for his birth certificate. He felt that the village schoolteacher might not issue a leaving certificate without payment.

Jay did not understand the partition of India, creation of the new State of Pakistan and why was there violence? But he concurred to go to town to study. Parents also consented to send him with Nakul. The admission at the Secondary School was, however, not that simple or easy as his brother Nakul had made out in the presence of their family in the village. Jay had to stay at his brother's room in the early days of his city life. While waiting for admission, he started to learn English alphabets. Indeed, he grasped the new language and could read and write small and big alphabets.

One day, he was keen to show his written work to his brother Nakul who returned from school. He was excited and said "look, Brother, I have learned to distinguish between small and big alphabets in English language". Rather than looking at the work, Nakul threw his writing book on the floor and **slapped** him, planting his fingers on his cheek. He also shouted at Jay, "why are you behaving like a child"?

He forgot that Jay was only nine years old. He had just left his parents, grandparents, other members of the family, and friends in the village. He and their parents trusted Nakul, that he would look after him and help him in achieving good education. Jay found that their trust was misplaced. Nakul behaved like an intimidating and domineering person, with his own younger brother, who had so much affection for and faith in him.

Jay was stunned and startled with Nakul's posture and approach. When they went to village at the weekend, he narrated the whole experience to his grandfather, who told Nakul not to hit Jay again, whether he studies or not. Notwithstanding, it was not for not studying or making noise that Nakul slapped Jay. It was for doing his work on time and learning a new language so soon.

After a month or so in the town, Jay received admittance at the same school, where his brother Nakul was studying. They, however, had to complete many formalities. Before admission, an English language teacher, a Hindi teacher, and the Class teacher interviewed him. For his admission, his cousin had to obtain clearance from the District Inspector of Schools' Office. Even in this effort, he (the cousin) sought support of the District Collector, who was personally known to him.

On admission, however, Jay started his regular classes. All the subjects were taught in English language. He could understand most of the subject matter but could not immediately answer questions during class discussion. It was a new language from the learning and teaching point of view. The teachers used to teach through English medium. Jay was used to speaking and listening in his mother language-Hindi.

He thought that English language would be one subject, and all other subjects would be taught through Hindi Medium. Students and teachers would communicate in the national language, which was Hindi. He also felt aloof in class at the school.

In his village primary school, he was an influential person as a class captain and taking class for the teacher. In the Secondary School, he became secluded. Still, he was trying to adjust in the unfamiliar environment. In his group, he knew only one student who came from his village. One day he did not come to school. Jay found himself estranged in a crowd of one thousand students at the school. With the result he returned to his brother's room.

He was young. There was no family member to cook breakfast for him and his brother. They did not hire a cook either. His grandfather used to give him money to buy snack at break time. On the first day of his schooling, he did really buy snack and was taking it. His brother Nakul came from the opposite direction of the school and saw him having his nosh.

Nakul questioned him, "where did you get the money from"? Jay replied, "grandpa gave it to me." He further asked, "how much money did grandpa give you"? Jay said, "Grandpa gave me four annas and I have bought snack for two pence." Nakul asked him to relinquish with the rest of three annas and two pence, and said, "you might drop and lose it". Jay complied.

In his first year of the Secondary school, Jay's grandfather gave him four annas every week, when they went home. It was for the whole week to buy eatables at the break time. But as soon as he and his brother left the village, Nakul used to ask him "whether grandpa gave him money this time as well".

"Jay always replied in affirmative." Nakul used to take the money from him, without delay. This continued throughout the academic year. Nakul used to take Jay's money but never returned it to him. He could not buy nutriments anymore. He had nothing before lunch. His body adjusted. He did not feel hungry in the morning. They never had any breakfast.

The lunch was after school hours at 1.30 pm. Jay did not tell his grandfather that Nakul takes his snack money. He developed a habit of not worrying about money. He followed the dictum that if money is lost, nothing is lost; if health is lost something is lost; if character is lost everything is lost. He thought that by losing money, he would simply go without a snack. Nakul had, however,

43

lost his character by bullying him and robbing him of his pocket money.

He found Nakul, money minded and manipulative, who showed power of a rowdy. He took advantage of Jay's pliancy. Jay and his brother Nakul used to go home to the village every Saturday and return to town on Sunday evening, in order to get ready for school, early in the morning on Monday. There was no transport from the village to the town. All the students from his village used to walk eight miles. Sometimes Jay took longer than others to reach the town.

It was especially hard during the rainy season. There were flood plains, and deep water on both sides of the river, which they had to cross. The bridge over the river was in disrepair. Jay was scared at times. He preferred to walk along the railway track, though it was a longer route, and took more time to reach the city. It was, however, safe. There was no fear of drowning.

<u>4</u>

When Jay was in the second year of his city life and secondary education, he came to the village and stayed for the whole winter break. He used to sleep at his grandfather's shop rather than at the house. One night, when he, his grandfather and Gautam were sleeping, they heard a loud noise that something fell or was thrown into the well, which was only a few yards away from the shop. Jay's grandfather opened the door. They all looked around. There was no one. They went back to sleep.

In the morning, they discovered that a woman had thrown a young baby into the well that night. The baby's body was pulled out of the well. Many villagers gathered there. The Village Panchayat Head (village Pradhan), decided to call the police because there has been a murder. The woman, who used to supply water from the well to people's home, accepted that it was she who threw the baby into the well.

She revealed to the police that a black magic priest (a cult with superstitious beliefs) told her that if she threw a young baby into the well, she would have a boy, because she already had two daughters. She was illiterate and unintelligent. She could not

45

comprehend, how by killing a baby, she could give birth to a boy. She did not tell her husband about this plan. Her husband was a farmer and had a small holding of twelve acres of agricultural land. The woman first kidnapped her sisters-in-law's baby son, who lived in the same house, suffocated him, and threw him into the well. Her husband regretted very much that his younger brother and his wife had lost their son because of his wife's ignorance and by following a superstition. When the police arrived, they arrested her and took her to the police station.

She was presented before the magistrate and remanded in custody. A case was filed against her. She was taken to the district court. The Judge sentenced her to life imprisonment. Her husband sold his agricultural land and hired lawyers, who did their best to help her, but all the evidence was against her. She had also accepted the vicious crime.

She never returned to the village. The only result was that it made her husband poor, her daughters lived mostly on their own without a mother and father who was busy because of the court case. Their mother was in prison, their father was mostly out making efforts to get her released, which did not happen. The family lost a baby boy. This farmer used to talk to Jay whenever he was in the village and asked him to write some short notes on a brown piece of paper which was taken from his grandfather's shop. The poor farmer did not bring any paper himself. His grandfather did not care about the brown paper and allowed Jay to help the farmer.

When Jay was about twelve years old and was studying in the city, he was home sick and wanted to see his parents in the village. His brother Nakul decided not to go to the village over that weekend. It was quite late in the evening. Jay started his own journey to the village. He ran eight miles, to reach home before sunset. He had to run through farmland and barren areas. He reached home before nightfall, but he got tired and became ill.

He was sick for quite a few days. A doctor came to see him in the village. He had to stay in the village for two months. He could not take his 8th Class annual examination. He had, however, achieved exceedingly high marks in his half-yearly examination. He was, therefore, promoted to the ninth standard. He, however, missed a great deal of learning, especially in Mathematics and Science.

For the High School examination, he decided to study languages and social sciences. He offered Hindi Literature, English Literature, General English, Mathematics, Civics, Indian Constitution, Economics and Economic Geography. He gave up the study of sciences. His friend Radhe was surprised that Jay was not studying Sciences. He thought that as a clever student, he wanted to become a doctor or an engineer. But he had lost interest and a great amount of learning in sciences. Moreover, his school did not have good science teachers.

He was, therefore, happy with the subjects he had decided to study. He concentrated on his studies. At High School, Jay had a few friends, but he did not visit their houses. If he needed any notes or books of them, he would wait outside their homes and return to his room with books or notes. He would do the same to return his friend's books and notes.

Their friendship was confined to school premises. Jay was in the company of his elder brother rather than with the boys of his own age group. His brother and his friends used to go for an evening walk along a canal, which was not too far from their room. They were all grown up and at least eight to ten years older to him like his brother. They used to talk in English. Jay also had conversation with them in English language.

During their walk, a passerby commented that Jay was a village boy, yet he talks in English language with his seniors. Jay had a good grasp over the foreign language and his accent was fine. It did not sound like a Hindi speaking young man who was talking in a different language. He used to talk in the natural way.

After many years, one of his older friends remarked that "you speak fluent English, despite the fact that you are a villager." Most villagers speak in their local dialect and not even in pure Hindi, what to say in a foreign language. A mature student commented once "how did the English people leave you here in India, when they left the country in 1947, after granting her independence?"

Jay smiled at the man and said that he started to learn English language at an early age in 1948. He was still in his village when the British left the country a year earlier. At that time, he was studying in the Primary school through Hindi medium.

When Jay and Nakul lived together, Nakul used to make chapatis and cooked vegetables or lentils as they thought proper. Jay used to go to buy fresh vegetables, clean the dishes and other utensils used for cooking. He also washed the floor and threw the dirt out. In the last year of Nakul's degree course, Jay took over more responsibilities and helped in making dough for chapatis.

One of Nakul's friend's brothers-in-law used to come at about 9 a.m. when food was ready to be taken. Nakul used to offer him food before he and Jay could have their meal. Jay did not like it. He said to his brother that "our father works hard to earn money for the family." "This man comes here to eat food every day. He has a job and could afford to purchase his own breakfast." But

49

Nakul argued that "if he was present at breakfast time, we could not ignore him".

This practice continued for the whole academic year. The man ate free food, and Nakul would not stop serving him, even though the man was not related in any way. He was not even his friend. He also dismissed the argument that the food was provided by their dad who worked hard for the family.

What amazed Jay most was that after many years, when Nakul had a job and his own family to be looked after, he was mostly unhappy to see his own brothers-in-law. He never offered them tea or water, what to say of food. At times he told them that he was busy. He could not see them and drove them away. Several types of demeanours with relatives and outsiders.

After about twenty years, Jay met one of his High School colleagues in Delhi. This friend came from the same village as the free loader. When Jay asked about him, his friend was unhappy to talk and told him that "the man was in prison for some financial fraud." It indicated that Nakul was not a good judge of character, but Jay noticed something fishy about that man in the early years.

Jay remembered a prediction by an astrologer about Nakul that he would get on well with outsiders but would not mix with the family members or relatives. It was proved right. Jay did not believe in these predictions, but he had to accept the reality. When he had a job and lived with Nakul, he himself faced such a truth because Nakul took all his earnings for food and lodging. Jay did not have any money left for his personal expenses and clothes or shoes.

5

In his 8th Standard at the Secondary School, Jay read a book called "Our Ancestors" (Hamare Purvaz). It was a part of his Hindi course that year. It was a collection of stories about the lives and activities of Hindu Sages and Rajas (Kings). Emphasis was laid on their sacrifices and achievements, and that they always tried to speak the truth. No one should tell a lie, even when a person could save someone's life.

Jay was impressed with such anecdotes because he had heard many tales from his dad. The narrative of Raja Harish Chandra of Ayodhya was immensely popular in India. It had been presented in many books and in many languages. In the early 20th Century, films had been made on the life of Raja Harish Chandra, who was famous for speaking the truth and giving Daan (donations). No one left his premises without receiving something or the other.

Raja Harish Chandra ruled the Kingdom of Ayodhya in the Treta Yug (some seven thousand years ago). He looked after the interests of his subjects. Everyone was happy and contented in his City State. One day Sage Vishwamitra came to his city. He was well received by the king and his ministers. Before leaving the city, the sage asked Raja to donate his Kingdom and his belongings to him. The King relinquished the throne and gave the kingdom to the sage. He was ready to leave the city, to find a job and a place to live for himself and his family. At the same time, the residents of the city also became ready to leave with their king. Rishi Vishwamitra stopped them saying that only the king had been asked to relinquish the kingdom. The public cannot leave. They would be needed to carry out the daily functions of the state.

The King and his family were not allowed to carry anything with them. They would have to leave in the clothes, they were wearing. Still the Sage said to the king that he should give him more donations. The king had nothing left. His wife, Queen Taramati offered herself for sale. Their son Rohitasva started to cry. He was not ready to live without his mother.

The man who agreed to purchase Queen Taramati, offered to buy the prince as well, and gave some more money, which was passed on to Rishi Vishwamitra. The sage demanded more donations. Raja Harish Chandra offered to sell himself. However, no one was prepared to buy the Raja. The Raja then tried to seek employment. Businesspeople were not ready to employ the king. He now started to look for any kind of job and went around in disguise.

He was offered a job by a Dom (cremation worker). He started his employment as Dom's assistant. He was instructed to charge money before allowing cremation. He did his job faithfully and passed on the earning to Dom, who paid him a basic pay which was sufficient for his living.

After a few months, Queen Taramati came to the crematorium with the body of their son Rohitasva, who had died of a snake bite. Harish Chandra asked her to pay the fee before cremation. The Queen had no money. The Raja himself had no money to pay for their son's cremation. When this argument was going on, Sage Vishwamitra appeared and said that he was only testing the king who was famous for keeping his promise and word and insisting on speaking the Truth.

Rishi (Sage) Vishwamitra contemplated that he would make Harish Chandra break his promise and lead him astray from the path of the Truth. Trustworthiness and honesty, however, could not be defeated. The king passed his test of truthfulness. Sage Vishwamitra returned the kingdom of Ayodhya to the king. He also called a doctor to remove poison from Prince Rohitasva's body. The prince became conscious and alive.

King Harish Chandra, Queen Taramati and Prince Rohitasva returned to their kingdom. The Raja had to encounter difficulties and make choices. In the end, nonetheless, he was victorious. He was still remembered as a person who faced enormous problems and obstacles, yet he did not accept defeat or succumb from the path of the truth. People should take a lesson from their lives and devotion to honesty and truthfulness.

Closer to the High School examination time, Jay and his friend revised their course and practiced mathematics together. His friend used to come to Jay's room rather than Jay going to his house. Jay continued to live in the same room on his own, where he used to live with Nakul. His brother had left the city after his graduation to look for an employment in Delhi, the capital of India.

When Jay had time, he carefully considered the character of his brother Nakul, and found him aggressive and impulsive, who behaved without forethought and without considering the consequences. In the first few weeks in the city, he slapped him on his cheek which made a red mark on his cheek. He felt that Nakul was irresponsible in his actions and manners.

In the village he displayed superficial charm and showed that he was caring, helpful and trustworthy. He often tried to make a good impression on adults, but he lacked human compassion, charity, and social concern. Anti-social conduct starts in childhood and continues in the adult life. Nakul was never remorseful for his wrongdoing.

Jay realized that Nakul would not change. He, therefore, changed himself and had nothing to do with his brother in the later years. He, however, could not break ties with him in the immediate future for social reasons. In this Nakul lost out but once he told Jay that "he was at a loss by ignoring him and working with kind and honest people." He tried to rationalize his point of view.

He had learned his lesson. It was not easy to live in the company of a dominating elder brother. He could not visit his friends at their houses or invite them to his flat. Jay had lived in the city for a few years and on his own for two years. His life had become detached. He could not co-relate with his siblings or with his friends in his village.

In the past he was close to his siblings and friends in the proximity of his house in the village. His thinking became different, as he had been influenced by the city culture. Sometimes he found himself between the two cultures, the village culture, and the city culture. People were remarkably close and caring in the villages. City life was based on individual and his\her surroundings.

Jay, nonetheless, concentrated on his studies and continued his education at school. In his 6th standard, Examination at his

Secondary school, he came First in his class. He was given a choice, either to get a scholarship or get concession in his school fee. He preferred the latter and for the next four years, he did not have to pay the school fees. It would help his dad who did not have to contribute towards his tuition charges, for the duration of his Secondary education.

He studied social sciences and languages for his High School examination. He enjoyed his course. He developed good relations with his colleagues and teachers. He was appointed class captain by the Form Tutor who sometimes asked him to look after the group of students, when he (class teacher) was not present in the room. If the peon did not turn up to collect the class register, Jay deposited it at the office.

One day, he deposited the register at the office and returned to the classroom. He did not shut the door. He sat down in his seat. The teacher questioned him, "did you find the door open, when you were entering the room"? The teacher used to keep the room door closed, because of the chilly wind and noise. Jay went back to the door and shut it. In this example, he learned a lesson that one should not change the situation, without a good reason. Before entering the room, the door was closed, he should, therefore, have left it as he found.

One of his High School friends' dads had an Ice Factory. They made Ice bricks to supply to shops in the summer, where people needed ice to cool their water. There were no freezers in those days. They also made Ice Cream. One day this friend invited a few classmates to the factory to show it. He also offered Ice-cream to all the boys. After taking ice cream, Jay and his companions paid money to the friend who accepted the payment. The students returned to their homes.

Next day, however, Jay's friend paid the money back to all of them. He explained that his dad told him that the cost was not as much as was charged by the retailers. The father also suggested that "when you invite friends to the factory; you should not take money." It should be a treat from one friend to his classmates and friends. They all accepted the refund, though they argued that it was for the ice cream they had.

Jay continued to live in the room on his own. He did not ask anyone to share it with him. He lived alone for two years. He used to cook his own food. Initially, it was difficult to make chapatis. He could cook rice, lentils and vegetables and make parathas (put ghee on the chapati while it was still on the hot plate). In course of time, however, through trial and error, he started to make chapatis. He always had enough food to eat. He never had a meal at a restaurant during his stay in the city.

Jay did not have to pay any school fee for four years, for his Secondary education. Nevertheless, to register for the High School Board Examination, he was required to remit the Examination fee of fifteen rupees. He went to see a couple of shopkeepers in the town, who did business with his dad and asked them, "if they could lend him money for his examination fee." They both declined, saying that "your dad has not authorized to lend you money."

He went to the village to obtain the examination fee. His dad was not in the village on that day. His grandfather arranged his examination fee. He sent Gautam's friend, Yusuf, with ghee (purified butter) to sell in the town market and remunerate Jay's examination fee. Jay and Yusuf walked together from the village to the town. They sold ghee at a shop. Jay managed to pay his examination fee on time. Yusuf returned to the village and told Jay's grandfather that the Examination fee had been deposited.

When his dad returned to the village, he was informed about Jay's examination fee payment. There was no cash in the house or at the shop. His grandfather had to sell ghee (purified butter). A few days later, his dad went to the town to buy commodities for the shop and saw him in his room. He gave him some money for daily expenses and asked him if he needed anything else. Jay said, "if you want to buy me something, you could purchase cloth for a shirt." His father bought cloth for a shirt and gave him money to pay to the tailor.

Jay continued to go to his village to visit his parents and other members of the family over the weekends. On a Sunday, the village Council (Panchayat) was holding a meeting to discuss how to improve the village sanitation system. Jay suggested to the villagers, that there was a need for a chairperson to conduct the meeting. Any person could present their views or address the meeting. There was also a representation of women at this meeting. A middle-aged man was elected as the chairperson to conduct the meeting. His brother Nakul was also present in the village on that day. He laughed at Jay's suggestion, for a chairperson to conduct the meeting. He thought that the simple villagers would not understand such formalities. Jay, however, wanted to introduce the same system, as existed in cities and towns and in schools and colleges. Of course, people at the meeting understood and appreciated the suggestion. They started to respect Jay, who was learning something at school and wanted to bring innovative ideas and systems to his village.

When he was in his 10th class, the school organized a mock Parliament. The Teachers and students participated in it. Some teachers became ministers and students became legislators (MPs). The MPs asked questions of ministers and sought answers on local issues. Jay played as an MP and "asked a question on road repairs and road maintenance. He also enquired about water supply in his local area." He was very much interested in civic activities.

Other students asked questions on health, housing, and the transport system. There was a proper opening of the mock Parliament, which was done by the Vice-Principal of the school. Some parents turned up to see the political drama. All who came to see the play appreciated and praised it.

Jay's grandfather's shop was the largest in the village, there was, however, no need for everyone in the family to work and stay there. In his early age Gautam used to help grandpa, especially on days when their dad went to town to purchase articles for the shop. However, when he was about eighteen years of age, he wanted to start his own business.

He started a milk dairy in the village. He employed two workers to assist him. They used to collect milk in the morning from farmers, make it hot, and separated cream from milk. They used a machine for this purpose. One of the workers used to stay at the dairy in the village, and the other used to take the separated milk to the city by train. The worker staying in the village used to convert cream into ghee, which was sold in the nearby town market.

One day the 1st worker was taking milk to the railway station on his way to the city. A police officer shouted from behind and asked him to stop. Which he did. The police officer arrived at the spot. He asked the worker to open the milk container (canister). On checking the milk with an instrument, he told him that the milk was not completely fresh, but if he paid fifty rupees, all would be good. The worker, however, did not have any money on him. Moreover, there was nothing wrong with his milk. He refused to bribe the police officer. The police officer kicked the milk canister (Container). The milk fell on the ground. The worker looked at the police officer and said that he had heard, stories of the rivers of milk flowing in ancient India, but today he had seen that the rivers of milk had started to flow again in the independent country.

What a waste of milk and loss to him and to Gautam, for whom he worked. This loss happened because the worker refused to afford fifty rupees to the police officer as a bribe. He was against the corrupt practice of bribery which was evil and should not be emboldened. He was ready to suffer a loss rather than to follow a corrupt system.

During the period, Jay stayed in the town on his own, he sometimes felt lonely. In the evening, at about 8pm, he used to go to watch and listen to recitation of the epic *Ramayana*. It was sung in a poetry form by a group of people which included the reader of poetry, his daughter, and persons on Musical instruments, harmonium, and tabla (drum). It was quite interesting, and Jay attended it two or three times a week for a few months.

During the Ramayana recitation, the speaker suggested that people with religious inclination, should go for the Ganga bath in the holy city of Haridwar or any nearby town but located on the banks of river Ganga. A city called Anoopshahr, was only about twenty miles from Jay's Village and the town, where he was studying. He was very much impressed and decided to have a holy bath after the Diwali festival.

He went to his village for the Diwali celebration and told his parents that he would like to go for the Ganga bath. His mother was not in favour of him going to the holy city, about which he knew nothing. But when he insisted that he would go. He would walk. They do not have to spend any money on this journey. His father agreed to go with him, and he would not have to travel alone. When they were going to the Ganga River, they discovered that quite a few people from their village were also travelling to the same holy city in their bullock carts. Jay and his father accompanied them. Sometimes Jay was asked to sit in the cart which he did. Though he preferred to walk with his dad. At the end of this journey, his dad said that it was a good decision, and they enjoyed the bath in the holy river Ganga and a change in the routine.

<u>6</u>

After finishing his High School examination, Jay went to visit his maternal uncles in Delhi. It was also his summer holiday. In Delhi, he used to take lunch from home to his youngest uncle, who ran a shop, which he opened early in the morning. The middle uncle used to go in the afternoon and close it at 8pm.

When Jay's High School Board examination results were declared, he was in Delhi. He told the family of his result. They were all pleased to know it. His youngest uncle took him to cinema as a treat and to celebrate the result. They watched a Hindi Movie, "**Boot Polish**," which was the story of orphan children, being looked after by an elderly man. This man treated them as his own family. He provided food and clothes to the orphan children. It was a social drama but had melodious songs. The music was superb.

Jay enjoyed the movie. He liked the songs and the story. On reaching home, they saw that his middle aunt was annoyed with his uncle. She told him that he should not have taken Jay to the movie. Cinema was not a good thing for young boys. Moreover, his father would be angry when he discovers it. Jay tried to convince his aunt that this movie would not spoil him, and he would continue with his education.

65

This was the first movie of his life, which he watched for three hours and enjoyed thoroughly. In one sense it was a part of his learning. Jay looked at the acting and dialogues, along with the making of the film. This movie was a RK Production, made by the famous Actor, Director, and Producer Raj Kapoor, who made mostly social films for entertainment but with a message.

Raj Kapoor did not act in this film. All the actors were good. Even the acting of the young children was superb. The man who was responsible to look after the orphans was an excellent and experienced actor and sang songs for them. The Children praised him through songs and called him uncle. Jay liked the story and the plot along with the music.

His parents had lived in Delhi for two years during the recession of the early 1930s. They, however, returned to the village to be with his grandparents. Jay was not born by then. His maternal grandparents and uncles continued to live in Delhi. They had their own businesses to run. They left their village for good, though they did not sell their house, and continued to visit the place. Surprisingly, Jay had an opportunity to visit his maternal grandparents' house in their village at a later stage.

Delhi was different to what Jay saw in later years. It was less crowded. Only about two million people lived in the whole city. It had tramways, which travelled very slowly. It had a conductor to issue tickets and a driver to take the tram further ahead. People could get on and get off easily on a moving tramway, without falling. It was laid at the street level. The track started from Red Fort in East Delhi, travelled through Chandni Chowk and Khari Bavly, to reach Sadar Bazar, which was the last stop. All these areas were identified as old Delhi.

The old Delhi's water was sour, which was used for washing clothes, bathing, washing the floor and washrooms. There was a well, near his uncle's house, which was very deep, but people brought water from that well. Drinking water was supplied through a huge water tank, The tanker was loaded on a big cart, drawn by bullocks. This system continued for many years. The water supply through taps and pipes started in the late 1950s.

There were cloth markets, spice market, jewellery market, book shops, hosiery market, vegetable and fruit market, dry fruit shops around that area. There were wholesale markets as well as retail shops, which served the residents. Many fruit and vegetable sellers sold their products on the pavement. They could not rent shops which were costly and unaffordable.

The profit margin was low. They brought their vegetables from the whole sale market and tried to sell their commodities on the same day. They reduced their prices in the evening to finish their goods. There was price discrimination in terms of time. Some residents of the area bought their vegetables and fruits in the evening when they returned home from work. They saved money and the family members did not have to go to the market during the daytime.

Three wheelers and Rickshaws were not popular in early 1950s. The drivers of the horse-drawn, two-wheeler tangas used to wait outside the railway station and bus stops. They would take people to their homes. As time passed, the transport system changed in Delhi. The population also started to grow in the late 1950s and 1960s. The demand for housing and transport increased during this period.

In the 1970s and 1980s, People started to own their own cars, the Metro Rail system came into existence and spread over a long area. The flyovers were built for quick movement of workers and traders. Delhi started to expand and spread in all directions, towards the east, west, north, and the south. New housing estates and townships were developed.

The Indian government created a Delhi Development Authority, for building houses and roads. Delhi also stretched outside its own boundaries and related to the bordering states of Uttar Pradesh and Haryana. A new city, NOIDA was built in Uttar Pradesh. The government also created the National Capital Region (NCR). People commuted to work from various places to Delhi and the new towns.

The National Capital Region was an urban quarter that included New Delhi, and the surrounding districts. It covered adjoining spaces in the states of Haryana, Uttar Pradesh, and Rajasthan. The major cities in NCR included Gurugram, Faridabad, Noida, Ghaziabad, Alwar and Bhiwandi. The plan to create such a Region had existed since the 1940s, but it became a reality in 1985. It covered an area of 55,083 square km and had a population of about sixty million.

Jay's village was not included in the NCR, even though many villages and towns of his district were included in this region. Gurugram, in the state of Haryana, had become a cyber city, with call centres and Information Technology offices. The Information Technology industry had flourished in this region and had provided employment to thousands of graduates from across the country.

New colleges and Universities were built. Private schools and colleges provided tuition and training to adults. The adult education classes took place in the morning and evening for accessibility for the working people, who could not attend classes in the daytime. Hindi was the main language of this region, but English, Punjabi, Bihari, and Haryanvi, were also spoken in this zone.

The NCR contributed significantly to India's economic growth. In 2021-2022, its Gross Domestic Product was 124 billion US Dollars. The Indian government had provided an environment for business and industrial development through new policies, which started in 2010. Foreign industries like Microsoft, Google, Dell, Ericsson, Motorola had set up their manufacturing bases.

Maruti Suzuki and Hero Honda manufactured cars in Gurugram which was near New Delhi. It was, nevertheless, a part of the National Capital Region (NCR). Ghaziabad, in Uttar Pradesh, had become popular for Information Technology, Oil, Gas, Textiles, and heavy Machinery.

Noida was an important sector for commerce and trade. It had emerged as the software hub of Northern India. It was one of the largest Information Technology and outsourcing focal points in the country. It had access to Delhi, by roads and Metro railway system. It had become possible to commute to Delhi from other parts of the region.

Delhi had an airport, which was not big enough to cope with the increased travelling demand. A new and big airport was, therefore, built outside Delhi, in the State of Haryana. It was known as the Indira Gandhi Airport, after the name of the Indian Prime Minister in the 1960s and 1970s. Travellers and businesspeople have used this airport to travel to other countries as well as to Indian cities like Mumbai, Chandigarh, and Kolkata.

There was a radio station in Delhi, which broadcast news and programmes for farmers, businesses, and educational institutions. Television was developed in the 1980s and 1990s. The private sector has also taken interest in providing television serials. Films in Hindi and other languages were shown on television. It was a huge industry. The biggest in the world.

In 1950s, Telephones were used only in offices. These became popular in shops in Delhi by the 1980s. People started to get them installed in their houses in later years. In the 21st Century, however, their importance had declined, as people started to own personal mobile phones and smart phones. These have become popular in every household in Delhi and throughout the country. Even the children are provided, their own smart phones. It was an excellent method of communication.

71

7

After staying for a month with his maternal uncles and aunties, Jay returned to his village. A few weeks later, he went to live in the town, where was studying. His school provided education up to High School only. He, therefore, crossed over to the nearby College in order to study for a four-year BA degree course. At the college, he studied English Literature, Hindi Literature, Political Science, Psychology, Economics and Civics.

He made a few friends there, but none-permanent. Friendship was confined to college premises as in his school days. He kept good relations with his Lecturers and fellow students. He was quite popular in his class. He had a sharp mind. One day he was sitting quietly in his Economics lesson. His lecturer assumed that Jay had not fully grasped the lecture material. He asked, "Jay, have you understood the subject matter." Jay replied "possibly."

The Lecturer further articulated "what did you understand"? He (the lecturer) would fill in the gaps, by explaining the topic and repeating the points. Jay started to explain the areas of the lecture that he had grasped. He recapitulated the entire material. The lecturer said, "that is what he has taught in the whole lesson" and pronounced that "he was proud of Jay's memory."

Jay did not have much interest in extracurricular activities and did not go to cinema to watch films. Sometimes, he played football with other students and always went for a morning walk and evening walk with his friends or the village boys. They enjoyed each other's company. He, however, lived a simple life and did not want to become a financial burden on his parents. His expenses were restrained.

During the summer holiday, he used to help his grandfather and father at the village shop. After his First-Year examination, he wanted to join the National Cadet Course (NCC) and again during the summer holidays, he wanted to do an extra course in Hindi, leading to a Diploma. There was no fee to be paid for these courses. His dad asked him whether these were parts of his degree course? Jay replied that "these were not compulsory." His dad, therefore, did not allow him to take part in these classes.

Jay continued with his studies at the college. For two years, he lived on his own. When he was in the 12th year, his younger brother Vikram joined the Secondary school. They both lived in the same room. Jay used to cook for his brother and himself. They used to bring chapati flour from the village and bought wood locally. Jay used wood as a fuel to cook. He had become accustomed to this routine by now. Though he did not enjoy it.

They kept just enough food for the week and brought flour every week from the village. They used to buy fresh vegetables at the local market. One day Jay cooked chapatis and lentils. He was waiting for his younger brother Vikram to return from school, then they would have their lunch together.

In the meantime, his dad arrived to see them. Jay asked him whether he had had his lunch or did he bring his food from the village. His dad replied that he did not bring food that day. Jay offered him his own food. Only one portion was left, which he put away for his younger brother. Jay went without food but told his dad that he had already had his lunch. There was not enough food for all of them. That remained a hidden secret.

Vikram stayed in that city and Secondary school only for two years. After that he left the town and went to live with Nakul in Delhi. Jay moved to live in another room, which he shared with his relative. They hired a cook who prepared meals twice a day for them. They both wanted to concentrate on their studies for the final degree examination. They got on well together. Overall, Jay resided in that town for over nine years. In the last two years of his degree course, he made a few good friends, who were like-minded. They used to sit on the college lawn under a tree. Gossiping and laughing. They were friendly and frank among themselves as young students tend to be. The college had male students.

There were about half a dozen female students in the college. There was no Girls Degree college in that town. The Girls College ran classes only up to Grade 12 or Intermediate level. The educated and rich families had started to send their daughters to be educated with boys at college. In the last year of his degree, a girl joined the Third Year of her degree course.

Jay was sitting with his friends under a tree, when he saw that girl. He felt attracted towards her. He told his friends that "he liked her." "He had a feeling for that girl." "He would like to know more about her and talk to her." He found out about her and became a close friend with her brother. He started to visit her house, pretending to be visiting her brother. He also lent his books to her to read and gave her his BA First year books to keep.

Her brother knew of Jay's thinking and encouraged them to become friends and more. This continued for a few months. They both started to miss each other when they did not meet. Jay, however, felt that there was no chance of them getting closer than friends. He did not want to cheat her and tried to tell her that it would be impossible for them to become lovers. She said that we should continue our friendship, or she could treat him as a friend of her brother's. she would start to treat him as a brother.

Jay frankly told her that once they had loved each other, it would not be possible to change a lover into a brother or cousin or just a social friend. Jay stopped visiting her. After completing his degree course, he left the town and never returned to live there, or to visit her, or his other friends.

In the final year of the degree course, he wanted to become a class representative for the College Union. One of his friends persuaded him not to stand for the class representative. But to stand for the position of Social Secretary of the College Union. He should work for the whole college, rather than just for his class. Jay accepted that and became a part of the College Union. They did some decent work for the welfare of the college students.

The students still walked to college. There was no transport facility to take them there. Despite making efforts, the Union could not make a provision for transport to the college. It, though organized debates, and functions, especially, the Diwali festival. Jay and his friends concentrated on their studies because they wanted to prepare themselves for their future careers.

Just before the final examination, one of Jay's colleagues was threatened by a tall Village boy who told him that he would stop him from taking his examination. Jay did not like that, but he also did not want to confront the young man. He decided to talk to other friends and concluded that they should collect their friend from his home and should not let his family know the reason, they would be walking together.

They changed their route to college. A confrontation was thus avoided. They did not report the incident to the police or the College authorities. Jay spoke to the tall boy, not to get involved in unnecessary activities, which could hamper his career. He could never work out why that student listened to his advice. Jay, being a villager had good relations with both the village boys, and the city boys, because he was soft spoken and acted like a city person. Very few students lived in the college accommodation. Jay never lived in the college students' residential halls. He lived in private accommodation and paid monthly rent of three rupees. He used to walk to college as he had done to his Secondary school. All his village boys, who were studying in the same town walked together, when they went to their village at the weekends.

They enjoyed each other's company. They hardly ever felt tired. They, however, used to stop at a couple of places to rest and relax.

There was always a good atmosphere. Everyone felt comfortable. Sometimes they carried each other's luggage, which included books, clothes, and food.

Jay had a dear friend Saran whom he considered as an elder cousin and called his mother aunty (Buaji). Although he was older, he respected Jay and introduced him to other students at the college, who were much older than him, very clever and came from rich and educated families. Two of his friends were sons of the college Principal. They were very polite and articulate.

Saran had a close friend, Harsh, who lived nearby. Jay also knew him. He had a master's degree in political science. After completing his Postgraduate degree, Harsh obtained a Lectureship in another city. He, however, resigned his position after a few months, and returned to his hometown, where Jay also lived.

In the final months of the degree course, Jay fell sick. Saran took him to Doctor's surgery and obtained medicine for him. Jay could not go to college for many days. He stayed in bed. Harsh used to come to his room and discuss political theory with him. He tried to compensate for his lectures and help him to prepare for the examinations which were only a handful weeks away. Jay was ill. He was also under the impact of medicines. He hardly understood what he was being guided, by Harsh.

As there was no close relative to look after him, his dad took him to the village, where the family members looked after him. His father called a doctor from another village, who prescribed him medicine. When Jay recovered from his illness, he returned to the college routine. He tried to catch up with his studies. There was no course work. The results were based on examination marks.

The college library had all the eighteen volumes of the Indian epic, *The Mahabharat*. Jay read the social contract in book 18th and compared it with the Social Contract Theory of modern western thinkers- Hobbes, Locke, and Rousseau. He had a comparative mind and attempted to find similarities and contrasts in the two different cultures and two different periods.

Jay also came across a letter from Subhash Chandra Bose to Jawaharlal Nehru. Bose was voted as the Congress Party President in 1937 and again in 1938. Mahatma Gandhi, however, asked him to step down from the Presidentship to make way for Maulana Abdul Kalam Azad. Gandhi appointed Azad as the new President of the Indian National Congress.

Bose was disappointed at this move. He wanted to continue as the President of the Party and put forward good policies. He, therefore, wrote a long letter to Nehru as he felt let down. He thought that he (Subhash Bose) represented the policies and views of the new generation in India, and Nehru would understand him. Jay was excited to read the letter, especially its length. It was twelve pages long. He contemplated that when he had acquired some more knowledge of the world and had accumulated many more ideas, "he himself would write such a long letter." He expressed his views to his cousin Nitin, who was also studying at the same college.

Jay continued to visit his family and friends during summer holiday. He compared the city life and the village life in India. He did not look for any drawbacks but examined the characteristics and facilities in the two locations. The city, where he lived, had roads and a railway station. It also had a big bus stop. The trains could take people to any part of the country. Sometimes people would change at bigger stations, called junctions, to continue their journey.

The buses carried passengers around the district. They also served long distance areas of fifty to one hundred miles. The city also had factories. It served as a marketplace to sell agricultural products for the villagers. Despite all such facilities, all houses did not have electricity even in the city. Jay used a kerosene lamp to study at night. His room did not have an electricity connection.

The villages did not have this kind of facility. The villagers had to walk or come by bullock carts to the railway station in contemplation of going to the other parts of the country or the state. The village people worked on farms. Some worked as builders but when there was no building work to be done, they would become farm helpers. Rich farmers employed permanent workers.

Jay, however, felt that technology would bridge the gap between cities and villages. Roads, housing improvement, water supply and electricity in houses and public places, would be good for villagers as it had been effective for city dwellers. It would lead to modernization as well as maintaining the values and culture of their ancestors.

8

There had been a move for financial empowerment of the poor villagers, and expansion of small-scale industries in villages. Women empowerment also became a policy of the Indian government. Housing improvement had been a policy of the Indian Central government. It had provided two-bedroom houses with open court yards, trees, and a garden to poor people. They used to live in huts but now they could reside in brick houses with ventilation, water supply and electricity.

There were only two or three shops in his village, though hawkers used to come to sell vegetables, every day. Once or twice a year, a utensil seller and cloth sellers and ladies bangle sellers brought their goods to his village. The Indian villages had their own characters and characteristics. Villages were distanced from each other by about one mile. In other words, the villages were only about one mile apart.

The farmers could reach their farms, work there, and return home in the evening. Their family members could bring food and water for them. These villages were mostly self-sufficient for basic needs. In the early 1950s, Jay's village was not big enough to have its own Panchayat (village council). His villagers joined hands with a nearby village to elect a Panchayat.

The Panchayat had punch (councillors) from both the villages. They used to hold meetings to consider the problems of their villages. The Panchayat's functions included cleanliness and Water-Well maintenance. There was no office for the Panchayat. The meetings were held at a Chaupal (community building in villages in North India). Within a decade, however, the population in both the villages increased to the level required for a separate Panchayat. Jay's village had its own Council from the 1960s.

There were four tehsils (treasuries) in his district. The farmers paid their land tax at the treasury. The village panchayat could collect a small amount of house tax. In his village, however, this tax was not regularly collected. The village council received a grant from the District Council to maintain wells. The roads and footpaths were not properly maintained in the 1950s.

His village, nevertheless, had a tube well which used electricity to draw water for the farms. It was outside the village. Children used to go for a bath in the pond of the tube well from where the water flow started to the farms. There was no electricity in the village, either in public places or in houses. In the summer, people used to sit under trees to get cool air. In the wintertime, they used to sit in the sunshine on the roof terrace or in the open yard of their houses. The village communities had their own baithak (lounge, drawing room or living room). The male members used to relax and get together there. Women lived and stayed inside the house. They used the outer room as a lounge and received their guests in their living room. The farmers kept their animals – cows, buffaloes, oxen close to their houses but in places surrounded by walls. It had one room for fodder and a machine to cut fodder. The machine was propelled by two men and the fodder was fed into the system by a third person.

His village had a Patwari (revenue officer). He kept records of the ownership of land and its use, like cultivable and uncultivable land or wet land. Whether the land, was used to grow fruits, flowers or vegetables or other crops, wheat, barley, millet, peas, chickpeas, and sugar cane. The Patwari also kept records of the grounds used for temples, altars, cremation grounds, rest houses, where food and water were served. When a piece of land was sold to another person, the patwari would record it in his register, and inform the transfer of ownership at the Tehsil (finance department which collected taxes. It was also known as the treasury).

In Jay's village, the Patwari was an elderly gentleman. He used his living room as an office. He did not have a desk or a table, but he had an iron chair. He used to sit and work on his bed (khat) which was his main furniture. He kept his files and register in cloth bags. Sometimes an official from the tehsil would come to visit the village and check the Patwari's register. The Patwari (Revenue Officer) was entrusted with the task of retaining a census register for tax payment and non-tax paying households. The number of inhabitants in each household, their professions and castes, incomes, and expenditure.

He also kept details about the villagers' cattle, their property and agricultural production. The taxes were paid only by those who could afford. The level of taxation depended on the family income and expenditure. In times of difficulty and crop failure, the taxes were exempted. There was no income tax on agricultural production.

There was another part-time government employee, called Chowkidar (gatekeeper or security guard), who kept a register of births and deaths. He was uneducated but he used to ask others to enter the names of the newborn in his register. Jay entered names of new births many times in his register. The Chowkidar

85

(gatekeeper or security guard) used to take this register to the police station.

The police station was about three miles from his village. They used to collect data for their area and take it to the district headquarters. The information was filtered into the State and National system. It gave the right picture of the population of the state and the country.

There were a couple of tailors in the village, and a few barbers, who used to go to their customers' houses to cut hair. The villages did not have any barber shops. Watermen and water women supplied water in kalash (metal pot) from wells to villagers' homes every day. These metal kalash (pots) were purchased from towns or from the utensil sellers, who used to come to the village, two or three times, a year. All villages did not have water pipelines, but a few people did have pipes connected to their homes in the early years of the 21st Century.

Jay's village did not have a potter. A potter from another village supplied clay pots. He used to come to the village every week. Sometimes the villagers would go to the potter's village, to acquire pots or order several pots, which were later delivered by the potter himself. He used to bring pots either in a small cart or on donkeys. He supplied all kinds of clay pots and clay cups at weddings.

86

This system had existed for thousands of years. The *Manu Smriti* (Memoirs of King Manu) stressed that the villages should be self-sufficient republics, which should produce their own food, weave their own cloth, and make their own pottery. The surplus goods should be sold to towns. In ancient times, the villages were richer than the towns.

Apart from agriculture, craft centred cottage industries flourished in villages. The unity and progress of villages was accorded through District Headquarters which administered about one thousand villages. The district officials were to maintain peace in villages and help their residents in times of difficulty and crop failure, which could have taken place due to lack of rain or heavy monsoon or draught. The same system continued throughout the Mauryan period and until the 16th Century.

<u>9</u>

The villagers provided soldiers for the emperor's army. This was the responsibility of the village head (known as the Lambardar) to liaise with the government officials in the recruitment of soldiers. This system ended when India became a Republic in 1950. Army recruitment was opened for everyone. Young people could go and take health tests and other examinations for recruitment and join the army, if selected.

Weddings were a big occasion in these localities. These took place mostly in summer season but sometimes in winter as well. Marriages could not happen within the same village in northern India. (But this rule did not apply to Southern states of India). The caste system was extraordinarily strong in villages. The boy and the girl should belong to the same caste or community.

The parents arranged marriages for their girls in another village. Agents went around in search of a match. When the date of a marriage was decided by the families, the groom's side would bring a wedding party of about thirty people to the bride's village. This party was welcomed by the girl's parents and their near and dear. Bullock carts, chariots (Rath) driven by oxen or horses, were the means of transport.

Once or twice, Jay saw that a wedding party came to his village by a bus. The village roads were not good for buses. There was always a Band to play music. Boys danced in front of the wedding procession. The party was then taken to a big hall. The villages had quite a few big halls, where marriage parties could stay for a day or two.

Food was a great attraction on this occasion. Some people attended weddings only because of food. Wheat based fried food, vegetables cooked with spices; and sweet dishes, were served to guests and relatives. During Jay's sister's wedding, his dad had seven diverse types of sweets made for the wedding guests. Pure cow ghee was used to prepare sweets and other food. The sweets were beautifully arranged in plates. The villagers were aware of this.

Jay was asked by a family, who lived near his grandfather's shop, to arrange sweets in plates for the wedding party. He did that and helped in other ways as well. When Jay was a child of ten years, he was excited to observe the village wedding parties and would wear new or shiny clothes, thinking that new clothes were worn at weddings.

At one time, his grandfather asked him, "why are you wearing new clothes"? and stated that "the wedding was not in your family." Jay replied, "I wanted to watch the procession and look good". One of his uncles lived on the other side of the village. Jay's cousin's marriage took place when he was twelve years old. The groom's father brought a disk jockey to entertain the guests and the villagers.

The jockey had Hindi Cinema songs. He asked, "Jay to select the records and songs". They were sitting in a room, and the loudspeaker was placed on a tree, so the villagers could also enjoy the music. Jay liked it very much. He felt that he was being noticed and given some importance, if not respect.

One thing Jay especially remembered was when he was asked by an adjoining house resident but very well acquainted with his family, Divesh, to attend his younger brother Vinesh's wedding party, which was going to another village. Jay sought his dad's permission and agreed to attend the wedding party.

He was invited to sit with the groom in the chariot (Rath), which he found extremely comfortable and respectful. On reaching the bride's village, the groom (Vinesh) "told the bride's villagers that Jay was his younger brother". He was thrilled with this introduction and appreciated it very much that he was not an ordinary guest but was remarkably close to the groom and his family.

The wedding party stayed in the bride's village for two days. The food was superb. He enjoyed it very much especially the hot Jalebies (curly Indian sweet). When the marriage party was returning from the bride's village, he sat with the bride and the groom in the beautifully decorated and covered chariot, which protected them all from the sun. That was the greatest fun. He enjoyed it very much. It became a reminiscence forever.

Wedding gifts, jewellery, and utensils were also procured from cities. There were stores specializing in these commodities. The shops were alongside each other and kept stocks of clothes, utensils, jewellery, spices, dry fruits, and fruits. The vegetable market was separate, where fresh vegetables were brought every day from villages and from the outskirts of the city.

The cities and towns were places for trading and transaction of goods. From these marketplaces, goods were sent to other parts of the country. The village farmers brought their surplus crops to these markets in bullock carts to sell and obtain money. They bought goods and clothes for their families there.

The villages and cities had divergent lifestyles. If someone criticized the villagers as rough people, Jay used to say that "he was also a villager and came from a village, where his family and friends still lived". In the later part of the 20th Century, some villagers started to move to live in cities and towns in search of employment and education for their children. The children attended Secondary schools, colleges, and Universities in cities, which were not available in villages.

They were still in contact with their villages, where they had agricultural land and grew crops. They used to work on farms. Now they hired workers to look after the crops. They provided employment to landless workers in the villages. Some of them leased their land to other villagers and received part of the crop or money.

Jay recalled, a farmer who lived near his grandfather's shop. He had three sons. He and his wife had asthma. They both died in their fifties. Their eldest son was in his early twenties. For a brief period, he joined the Indian army. After his parents' death, he returned to the village and started to work on the farms. A few years later he got married and had a son within a year.

His brothers looked fine, though the middle one, Jeet had speech problem and could not speak properly. Most people could understand what he was communicating. He was healthy, polite, and behaved normally but was mentally disabled. He was helpful to Jay's brother Gautam and did some heavy work for him, especially in cutting fodder for the cows and buffaloes and lifting heavy bags.

Like his brothers, Jeet had a share in the family agricultural land. In one sense he had inherited a small piece of farmland. But he could not work on it. His elder brother was responsible for growing crops and paying bills. Jeet was provided food and clothes. He, however, used to spend a great deal of time at Jay's grandfather's shop. Just sitting there and helping anyone who needed to carry things from the shop to other places.

When Jeet's brother had a son, his attitude changed. He started to pay full attention to his offspring and forgot the welfare of his brothers. He also felt that his brothers would receive their share of the agricultural land. He started to discriminate against them and did not provide food on time. Sometimes, he shouted at them.

Because of the neglect, and starvation, the youngest brother who was only eight years old, died within months. No one in the village noticed what was happening to the boys. A few months later, Jeet also looked pale and weak. He was not provided food on time. He did not beg, steal, or ask for anything. Sometimes, he used to eat raw food on the farms, especially at night when he was very hungry.

93

He would fill his stomach with green peas, barley, corn, sugar cane or any other edible food. One night he was found dead on a farm, because of cold and hunger. When Jay discovered of his death, he cried and felt that he could not do anything for Jeet, whom he liked because he understood his problems.

Jeet was only fourteen years old, well-built, and always looked good. Jay thought about the conduct of his brother. What kind of man was he, who could not look after his younger brothers? They had a right to land, and their share of crops grown on those farms. Jay felt that there should have been a system in the village, where physically or mentally handicapped children or people with problems, could obtain some assistance and justice in society.

<u>10</u>

After his final examination, Jay returned to his village. Apart from providing education to their children, Indian parents felt responsible for their marriage. Arranged marriages were common in the 1950s. Jay's parents also thought that Jay had now completed his graduation, and a few families had approached them to wed their daughter in the family.

Jay was not against parents' arranging his marriage. He, however, expressed the view that he wanted to get a job and start to earn some money before getting married. His mother said to him that "he does not have to take his wife with him, immediately after marriage. She could stay with the family in the village."

Despite Jay's opposition, his parents agreed with a family that they could arrange their daughter's marriage with him. "His father said that he has given his word to the girl's father." Jay respected his dad and knew that he (father) had always supported him since childhood. Even in his decision to leave the village at the age of nine and not to attend the primary school.

Marriage was a social and religious occasion. Social in the sense that it brought the two individuals and two families closer. After the wedding, the girl tends to live with the boy's family. The boy was also integrated as a member of the girl's family. It was a religious event because many rituals and events took place at this juncture.

After the introduction of the young couple and their families, engagement was the main event, when a date for marriage was finalized. The date could be within weeks, months or more than a year. A Shagun (gift) was provided to the boy, by the girl's family. It was considered auspicious and a blessing. Often sweets, dry fruits, fruits, and an envelope with money were accoutred to the would-be groom.

The other functions were to take place during the wedding week. These included, the Haldi (Turmeric is applied to boy's and girl's body by their relatives and family members), the Mehdi (Hina) and the Sangeet (Music), were held by the families in accordance with their convenience. Both the families celebrated these moments.

When the marriage party arrives at the bride's house, the groom and bride place garland on each other's neck. The members of the marriage party are also garlanded. It is a welcoming symbol. This custom was started by Maharaja Dushyant of Hastinapur more than five thousand years ago. He also started the ring ceremony, when he wed Shakuntala who lived in her father, Rishi Vishwaamitra's ashram (education campus).

Jay's marriage took place during the same summer season, when he finished his college education in the city. He had never met or seen his future wife. A group of relatives and village people went to the bride's village by train and bus. The ceremony was performed according to the ancient Hindu social and religious tradition with hymns and seven rounds around the fire.

It was called Saat-Phere (seven circumambulations). It could be translated as a nuptial rite. There was no registration or legal document. The only witnesses were the relatives of both families present at the ceremony. The question, Jay asked himself, what was the significance of Saat-Phere. (seven rounds) around the fire?

What was the substance and meaning of this process? Fire had been considered sacred in Hinduism and Zoroastrianism. This had existed for thousands of years and had been explained in the *Manu-Smriti* (Memoirs of Maharaja Manu) and the *Saam Ved,* which dealt with the social customs.

Each phera (circumambulation) round the fire symbolized a commitment by the couple. This was an oath or determination of seven acts in married life. It was a representation of commitment by the bride and the groom. They did not normally pronounce it, but the priest explained and spoke these pledges on behalf of the marrying couple.

First, Phera was for food and nourishment. The couple walk together praying to the deities to provide food. It was a promise that a married couple would work together in order to provide food for the family. The **Second,** Phera was a covenant to grow mentally, physically, and spiritually fit to enjoy their lives together. The third Phera indicated a promise to earn an honest living. So, they could live comfortably as a family. The **Fourth,** Phera was to maintain a strong family relationship and to share happiness with parents and other members of the family. The **Fifth Phera** was a bond to make their children healthy and courageous. It was for their character building as well. The **Sixth**, -Phera was for a long and peaceful life in the community. The **Seventh,** -Phera was for living a life of love, compassion, friendship, and mutual trust. These seven Pheras made the marriage eternal, happy and sociable. This social custom was also considered as a religious ceremony. It had persisted in the Indian communities for a long time.

At this occurrence, Jay did not invite his friends from the college days, though his dad asked him to countenance a few friends. He told his dad that "he left the college and the town. He did not want to carry any baggage from the old times. He did not believe in having permanent friends". The marriage party came back to his village with the new bride, who was looked after by his family. He did not have an opportunity to see her or to speak to her. A few days later, the new bride's brothers took her to their parents' house. Jay stayed in his village and started to examine the progress of the villages. The rural development in India was slow. While urbanization started and continued since the 1950s, villages remained underdeveloped. The Indian villagers depended on agriculture and related jobs. Most villagers were land holders but there were some landless labourers.

There had been some efforts to provide land to these workers through the Bhoodan Movement (Donate land). The large landowners were asked to dispense five acres of land to landless people, who could cultivate their own crops as well as to continue to work for others. It would increase their income and make their life secure.

Still the problem has not been solved, and villagers continue to flock to cities in the hope that city life would be better than their life in the village and they would have better food and enjoy other amenities in the city. Jay saw such a situation in the case of a landless farmer's family who lived in the north-east of his village.

99

The farmer himself worked for large farm owners. His wife worked as a cook and domestic cleaner at the feudal lord's house. Because of lack of health services and lack of dental hygiene, they both lost some teeth and looked more than their age. They had three sons. None of them went to study outside the village. All of them had only the Primary education. But all three boys were smart. The eldest son Paras started to work on daily wages. Sometimes he could not find work.

Due to heavy rains, their house fell. There was also malaria and dengue in the village. The farmer and his wife died in this pandemic. There was not much work available in the village. The boys decided to try their luck in a big city like Delhi. They had enough money for the train fare and expenses for a few days. They were under the impression that the city people were rich, and they lived a comfortable life.

They left the village and walked to the railway station which was three miles away. When they were on their way to the local station, they dreamt of eating food of their own choice in the big city. The eldest of them, Paras said that when he finds a job, he will have Puri (fried small chapatis) with mixed curry of pealed potatoes and peeled tomatoes. Semolina pudding for dessert.

The middle one Chetan said that he would be happy with parathas and cauliflower and potato vegetable. It should have green coriander on top of it. He would have boondi and yogurt raita with his food which would be satisfying. (Boondies are fried tiny balls made with gram flour).

The youngest Chirag, who was only fourteen years of age, said that "I would like to have the same food as mother used to make in the village. I would have mixed green saag (Puree) which should contain mustard green leaves, Fenugreek, green chickpeas leaves and spinach". "Mother used to make all that and serve with chapatis. I would like to have butter milk (Chhachh), which should have dry mint, a little salt and black pepper in it".

Conversing with each other and expressing themselves about their choice of food, they reached the local railway station. The eldest brother Paras who had money, bought tickets for Delhi. The train was crowded. They entered a compartment which had seats available. They sat down alongside each other. The train reached Delhi junction in three hours. Many trains arrived at this big station from various parts of the country.

They came out of the station. Paras and Chetan (the eldest and the middle boys) were together. The youngest boy Chirag was pushed in the crowd and got separated from his brothers. Paras, the eldest of brothers said to Chetan that we have lost Chirag. We should not try to find him. He would not get a job because of his age and will be a burden on us. If we cannot see him around, so be it.

They both moved on and did not look for their youngest brother who was alone in the big city. They reached Shakur Basti, a shanti town where they stayed overnight. A family from another village provided them a room where they placed their clothes and other possessions. Next morning they both set out in search of a job. After a while they decided to buy a big basket made of straw (called Jhallie) and reached Sadar Bazar.

They were hired to carry shopping by households. Old Delhi's lanes were small. Raksha could not go there. Jhalliewalas (basket carrier) used to take the shopping to people's houses. Shopkeepers also hired Paras and Chetan to bring goods from their warehouses. They liked working for the shopkeepers rather than carrying goods for the shoppers.

They became attached to some businesspeople who were close to each other. It became their permanent work. They did not have to wait for individual shoppers to be asked to take their shopping to different houses. The businesspeople felt that the workers would bring goods from warehouses. Paras and Chetan were sure they would have employment, though it was on daily wages and not permanent. Often the goods were brought in bales which were wrapped in jute cloth sheeting and had iron bands around them.

The shopkeepers kept their goods in warehouses because their shops were small, and they could not keep many things there. As the stocks were sold to customers, they used to acquire from their warehouses. If a shopkeeper did not have enough work, he used to ask his neighbouring businessperson to use the services of Paras and Chetan. For the brothers, there was something or the other to do every day. They were earning some money. But their income was just enough to pay rent, buy food and other essentials.

Initially they slept on the floor in a room. After two weeks, they bought two folding beds. They used to fold the beds to make space to cook food. They continued to work in Sadar bazar and lived in the Shanti town, Shakur Basti. They forgot about their youngest brother and did not remember him at all.

When he was separated from his brothers at Delhi railway station, on the first day in the city, Chirag looked for them all around but could not find the duo. He continued to walk straight. Sometimes turning back or looking sideways for his elder brothers. He reached Fatehpuri cloth market, which was a wholesale market for cotton and woollen cloths. He was tired and stopped outside a shop. The owner of that shop was an elderly gentleman in his late fifties. He saw this tired and frustrated boy. He offered him a place to sit down and water to drink.

He asked him whether he was lost or was new to Delhi. Chirag told the businessman that he came to Delhi from village with his two brothers. Because of the crowd outside the railway station, he was pushed and became separated from them. He looked everywhere but could not find them. "I do not know anyone in this big city. We came to start our new lives." "I do not have any money. All the money was with my eldest brother Paras."

The shopkeeper was a kind man who guided Chirag to a nearby Dharamshala (Inn) where he could stay overnight, free of charge. He also gave him some money for food. Chirag said that he could not take any money from him. The shop keeper asked him to clean the outer part of the shop. This money will be a payment for his work. He also helped the shopkeeper to arrange the cloth bundles on the shelves.

He then accepted the money for his help. It was just enough to buy him food, water, and a cup of tea. The shopkeeper asked him to come back to his shop, if he does not find his brothers. Next morning, Chirag went around markets in the vicinity, but he could not see his brothers anywhere.

Chirag then went back to the shopkeeper who told him that he could not offer him a job, though he needed a helper to show the cloth to customers. He was still underage, for employment. He, however, said "you could bring lunch from my house and help the lady of the house with some domestic work, for which you would be provided food and a room to live." "I will find you a room at a convenient place." "We will also provide you pocket money."

Chirag accepted the offer. He used to bring lunch for the shopkeeper from his house and wait at the shop when the shop owner had his lunch. He observed the trade and the dealings with customers. He started to learn basic accounting. He knew reading and writing. He had done numbers, division, and multiplication at his primary school.

He could work out the cost of cloth by multiplying the length by price per meter. He also picked up English words and could recognize the address on bales of cloth. This continued for three years. Chirag had learned the art of cloth business. He also saved some of his pocket money.

When he was seventeen years of age, he started to help the shopkeeper and sit on his own at the shop when the owner had to go out. He could look after the shop. Open in the morning and close in the evening, if needed. He gained experience and earned the trust of the businessman. He sometimes dealt with customers and their purchases without help from the owner. Chirag was a soft spoken and polite young man. The customers and other shopkeepers were impressed with him.

At the age of twenty, he ran a retail business. He would report everything to the shop owner. He had gained respect along with trust. The shopkeeper helped him in finding his own place to live, which was a two-bedroom flat at Fatehpuri in old Delhi. An elderly lady used to cook his food. He was a contented and happy young man. His body and face changed because of age compared to the time when he arrived from the village.

One day, he was walking through the Chandni-Chowk market. He saw both his brothers on the pavement. They were going to some place. They stopped at a public water tap to drink water. He recognized them but they could not recognize him because his face had changed in six years from the age of fourteen to over twenty years now. They had not seen each other for that period. He asked them who they were and which village they came from.

He did not tell anything about himself. Neither did they question him. He asked whether they would like to come to his house on a Sunday. When they agreed, he asked them to meet him at the corner of Fatehpuri market at 12 noon, next Sunday. Paras and

Chetan turned up at the appointed time. Chirag took them to his flat. He gave them water to wash their hands. He served them food of their choice, which they had discussed on their way from the village to the local railway station, more than six years earlier.

Their food was served on the dining table. Paras and Chetan were asked to sit in chairs. He himself sat down with his food on a mat on the floor. Paras and Chetan were surprised to see the situation. The elder one Paras asked him. "Sir why are you sitting on the floor, when you have offered us, ordinary workers, to sit in chairs and our food laid on a big table". Chirag said to them "please have your lunch, I will explain everything when we sit down in the sitting room".

After finishing their meal, they all sat down on a sofa. He looked at the elder one and said "your name is Paras. The younger of the two is Chetan. You belong to a village near a railway station". When you walked from the village to the railways station, you talked about having food of your choices in Delhi." This was the food you decided to have." "Puris and Potatoes mixed with tomato curry for the eldest." "Cauliflower -potatoes vegetable was served with parathas for Chetan." "The village type chapatis with mixed saag puree with butter milk was provided for Chirag."

They both questioned again, "but how did you know about our conversation, on the way from village to the railway station". Chirag said, "if only three people knew about your personal choices, both of you have lived together for more than six years, it should be obvious that the third person is your youngest brother Chirag". "I am Chirag, brothers."

Paras and Chetan felt ashamed for their action and thought that the youngest would be a burden on them. He would not be able to obtain an employment. They noticed that he had made substantial progress and had become a businessman on his own right by working hard and honestly. The older brothers were still daily wage earners and carried straw baskets. They could not face him and left his flat. They never met again because they had different ways of thinking and actions. Their standards of living had changed. Now they were living in separate locations. One had a middle-class job as a shopkeeper. The other two were lower working class, living in a shanti town.

11

Jay was aware that in India, agriculture depended on Monsoon rains, but wells and canals had existed for many years. In the 1950s, tube wells started to be built to provide water for agricultural land. The governments, both Central and State, had implemented the rural development policies. The Agriculture and Rural Development department coordinated the policies.

They investigated the food grain prices, sales and purchase of surplus commodities. The government furnished the Minimum Support Price (MSP). It also implemented Crop Insurance, Irrigation facilities, and Life Insurance for farmers. Still there was enormous poverty in villages because of lack of job opportunities. He thought about the village life and questioned how could the life of villagers be improved, and poverty eradicated? He discussed with some government officials, academics and villagers and felt that non-farm employment should be created in these communities. There should be basic industries like handicrafts, dairy products, and food processing industries. There was a need to improve transportation system and village infrastructure.

The main objective of rural development was to encourage people to continue to live in villages, rather than to move to live in cities which had their own problems of overcrowding and congestion. If the quality of life in these communes could be improved and villagers' economic welfare considered, with housing improvement, transportation, and electricity supply.

There was a need for skills development, setting up of banks for financial services. Citizens always needed health services. There had been a desire to provide these services to villagers. Young people, when they were students, thought that if they became medical professionals, they would serve their people in the villages.

However, after gaining their qualifications, they either forget their commitment or their circumstances changed. They did not return to serve their people. In the later part of the 20th Century, the government made it compulsory for young doctors to serve in villages for three years. It aimed to provide health and social services in rural areas.

They were appointed to the village clinics but there was no method to check whether a doctor was present at the clinic. Often the doctors lived in cities and towns. They did not attend their clinics in villages but continued to receive salaries. They did their medical practice from their homes in cities and earned extra money. They also looked down upon the villagers and were not ready to help them or attend them sympathetically.

The same principle applied to Engineers and good and qualified teachers. The qualified engineers were not building roads and bridges in rural areas. They did not even turn up to supervise the work and preferred to live in cities and dealt only with paperwork. Qualified teachers were reluctant to teach in villages and argued that they did not have the same facilities as in cities, especially access to libraries.

Often the villagers themselves decided that their children should stay away from villages. They should work and live in cities. They should make progress there to earn more money than they would be able to receive in villages, This, however, has led to stagnation in villages. Some people lacked service instinct and did not think for the welfare of others. For them, the individual uplift was more important than public and social advancement.

Jay believed that educated people tend to be comparatively more efficient than uneducated folks. They could grasp the situation and make future plans, change their habits, and avoid hazardous path. They could become more adaptable socially and productive economically. Those who work with professionals and educated

111

personnel contribute to increase their efficiency and learn necessary skills.

It did not happen in Indian villages because not may professionals lived in these areas. The villagers were, therefore, stuck in traditions and superstitions as their ancestors had lived for hundreds of years. Jay argued that education could become a vehicle for modernization and could generate skilled workers, administrators, managers, technicians, and entrepreneurs.

It could augment the horizon of adults and provide an opportunity to understand their environment. Education provided self-knowledge and self-awareness, which were the essential ingredients for social and economic uplift and professional mobility.

The villagers had developed an inferiority complex. When they see a city person, they automatically think that they were better off, better qualified, and better knowledgeable. If the educated people interacted with villagers, communicated with them, lived in the same vicinity, they would understand each other better. They could also discuss ways and methods to improve life in villages.

There was a need to improve health and social services, build roads and provide transport facilities, better education, and sports facilities for the young. The villagers could also learn about the government policies for village uplift and how a strategy could benefit the villagers. If only the uneducated populace continued to live in villages, they would not progress or modernize or be aware of the environment around them.

Jay maintained that as Science and Technology progressed, education would become a condition for national survival. The uneducated community was fast becoming an economic liability and unproductive. By being educated, did not mean that everyone should be an engineer or have a degree. He contended that there was a need for practical and mass education.

Any effort to concentrate on elitist education could be counterproductive and might not benefit everyone in society. A pompous education could produce an economic class, with built-in limits on the enlargement of purchasing power of the masses, with a clear-cut hierarchy of economic strength with a dangerous antagonism between diverse groups in the community.

Despite Jay's argument for mass education, which was essential to change the society, he also maintained that higher education could not be ignored. Both quality and quantity were important for the progress of villages and the country. It could be identified as the workforce pluralism. All kinds of functions could be conducted in villages as well as in cities.

113

It was, therefore, essential to produce educated people at all levels, with all kinds of qualifications, skills, and training. Jay sustained that a nation which was unable to develop its human resources, would be unable to develop much else. In the villages, practical education could be imparted. It would develop an adequate reserve of talent which was needed to accelerate economic development and social progress.

The Central government of India and the State governments, investigated the problems in villages, examined the causes of poverty, and general life of residents there. Brick roads were laid in these localities. General conditions started to improve. There was less pollution in villages compared to cities and towns. Jay liked this improvement in the lives of the people.

He also contended that it was not possible to provide jobs to everyone in small scale cottage industries. He, therefore, felt that modern industries could be set up in villages. Capital investment, which came to cities, could be diverted to rural areas. With improved road- transportation for carrying raw material and manufactured goods, it was possible to develop industries in these places and locations.

The workers from nearby villages could travel to work in factories and return home in the evening. They could continue to live with their families and have a social life. It was, however, not happening. Industries were not being brought to villages. Village people continued to move to live in cities in order to escape poverty and find employment.

Unemployment and lack of income was the cause of poverty, which led to idleness and superstitions. When villagers borrowed money, they had to pay high interest rates to sahukars (money landers). There were not many banks in villages. A mobile bank would have been of immense help, but there was the question of safety and security. The mobile van with money could be robbed.

Poverty in India as whole but more particularly in villages, increased because of imperialism in the 18th and 19th Centuries. Wealth was drained. The imperialists collected taxes of the landlords, who extracted rents of the tenants. The money was taken out of the country. No money was spent on amenities for the villagers.

It was, however, true that the villagers knew each other. They met one and all every day. They work for the welfare of their families and the welfare of their neighbours. Social and economic equality was to be found, where people were closer to one another. It was possible to leave the village, but many people found this move from villages to cities extremely hard to sustain.

It created slums in big cities because of the shortages of housing. There was no provision by the state governments and the local authorities to provide houses to these new immigrants. They lived in self-made huts of bamboo and tarpaulin which could be blown away in rain and storms. There have been examples of lost lives and material in rainy season.

In cities, the only work these villagers could find was in retail trade or as domestic servants. The women worked as house cleaners. The Middle class in Indian cities, think of themselves as new aristocrats. They keep servants and cleaners as a symbol of their status. They also hire tutors for their children to assist them with their homework. These tutors were, however, paid low wages. The city dwellers were socially and economically exploiting the villagers.

Some shop shopkeepers, however, paid a reasonable salary to their workers, who were skilled and educated. They still did not secure a work or attain a salary suited to their qualifications. Quite a few people could not find permanent and regular jobs. They tend to assemble at specific places in various parts of the city. The residents who need their work done, could find them from 8 am onwards.

These were skilled and unskilled manual workers. Carpenters, brick layers, plasterers, and painters. They carried their tools with them. Unskilled workers were hired to clean houses when required. Often, they agree, the level of payment in advance. Some workers continue to wait to be picked up for work. A few of them do not get any job and wait the whole day.

Builders and sweet vendors also hire such temporary workers. They work as Raksha pullers or carry shopping to residents' houses. They work as delivery people. Despite obstacles, not many people return to their villages. They hope for better conditions and stay in city slums, thinking that the conditions would improve.

They attempt to understand the city people as their contact increases. The city residents also recognize their skills, as they notice and observe them more regularly. The city schools were better equipped than the village schools. These new workers start to send their children to schools. It gives them aspiration that their children's lives would be better than theirs.

<u>12</u>

In this sense, mobility from villages to cities was beneficial. It had led to interaction of people from different communities and backgrounds who meet each other. They exchange views and witness systems which would have been impossible in villages. There was an opportunity for conversation between the newcomers from villages and the city people.

This expectation for future betterment retains them in cities. They think that their suffering will lead to an improvement in the conditions for their children's future. If the infrastructure, roads, railways, education, health, and social services could be improved in villages, they would not have to leave their homes and be compelled to live in the city slums.

Jay himself left his village and did not return to live there permanently, though he continued to visit his family and friends as long as they stayed there. The quality and the quantity of education increased in the later part of the 20th Century and early years of the 21st Century. The backward communities, Scheduled castes, and scheduled tribes, OBCs, were being accoutred free education which would lift them socially.

Special assistance had been arrayed to girls and young women, in the form of payment for books, school uniform and bicycles to travel to other villages to attend school and college. Sixty percent of all young people under the age of eighteen, in India had gained some kind of education. In the Southern State of Kerala, the education level was 100%.

Yet, there had not been much progress in social change. The reservation of places in education and employment had not helped upward mobility. The attitude and bearing of people ought to change. Some people think that they were superior to others and could control them. Such people, nevertheless, reflect their inferiority complex, because superiority does not lie in controlling others, but in controlling their own emotions.

A superiority complex was a deportment which suggested that one person was better than the others. It was an exaggerated opinion of oneself. These groups, however, hide their low esteem or a sense of inferiority. It was a mechanism of a feeling of inadequacy. Their boastful claims were not backed by reality. They were unwilling to pay attention to others' views. The superiority complex was different from genuine confidence, which was the result of having real skills, success, or talent in a specific area of competence. The superiority complex was a false confidence with little or low achievement.

After thirty years since leaving his village, Jay visited the place to see the current situation and found that things were moving forward. Changes were taking place. Indian villages were no more stagnated self-contained republics in the old sense. Social and economic mobility was visible. Though lower classes and lower castes were gaining less access, they were, nevertheless, making progress.

Some farmers and professionals from his village built their houses or second homes in the nearby city. Their main purpose was to acquire higher education for their children. Secondary schools and colleges were still uncommon in villages. There were hardly any girls' colleges and technical colleges around his village. The city colleges had good libraries, computer laboratories and science laboratories. These facilities encouraged farmers to educate their children in cities.

Landowners, who had agricultural land in the village, but had started to live in cities, continued to visit their ancestral places. Sometimes they stayed in the village for days and saw the activities for themselves. It was mostly done when the crop was ripe for harvesting. They could then decide how much farm products were to be sold. It has been noticed that in the 21st Century, agriculture productivity had increased because of application of technology and developed infrastructure.

There was a gradual shift towards modernization. Less workers were needed to work on farms. The tractors were being used for all farming functions. Trucks and tractors were also used to carry crops for sales in the city markets. Tractors were efficiently used for ploughing the farms, tilling, and harrowing. Seed sowing and harvesting was conducted with machinery.

Animals like bullocks were not used for farming any more. Farmers had become rich. There was also a saving in the labour cost. Farmers with small holdings owned small tractors, which were either manufactured in the country or were imported from China. They were affordable. The government also provided loans to farmers.

Jay was told that farming has become a profitable enterprise. He, however, found that his village farmers did not grow sugar cane anymore. They continued to grow wheat, peas, barley, corn, mustard, and chickpeas. Vegetable farming was carried out in his village. He was acquainted that two or three crops were grown, and the farmers were busy, full year-round.

In the past, farmers grew only one or two crops in a year. They used to sit idly by or make ropes with jute. Now their incomes had gone up as the number of crops had increased. He found them happy and contented. While in the village, Jay recalled a story of cheating and over confidence of crocodile and a monkey.

"A crocodile lived with his wife in water off the island country, Sri Lanka. His wife was a meat eater. She said to her husband that she had never consumed a monkey's meat. "If you could obtain a monkey from across the sea in southern India, I would like to taste its heart." "I have been told that monkey's heart was very delicious".

The crocodile swam through the sea and reached the southern coast of India. He saw a monkey sitting on a tree, close to the sea water. The crocodile became friendly with him. In the Indian cultural tradition, the monkey looked after him, fed him properly. One day the crocodile said to the monkey "you have shown me love and respect." "I must return your hospitality." "Will you come with me to Sri Lanka?"

The monkey agreed to accompany him but said, "I cannot swim in water." The crocodile said, "you could sit on my back; I will take you through the water". They both left the Indian shores. When they reached about twenty miles down the sea, the crocodile stated,

122

"my wife would be pleased to see you. She always wanted to eat a monkey's heart."

The monkey replied "dear friend, you should have told me that at the start of the journey. I have left my heart on the tree. Without the heart, I would be no good to your wife." "You should take me back to India in order to collect my heart." The crocodile turned back and brought the monkey to the Indian coastal region.

The monkey jumped off the crocodile's back and climbed up the tree. The crocodile asked him "to collect his heart and come down, we got to keep going to Sri Lanka." The monkey said to the crocodile, "you fool, you are not a friend. You wanted to kill me and feed my heart to your wife." Go away and get lost.

Jay discerned that the moral of this story teaches us to consider our own protection and welfare. "Those who want to take away something of you and deprive you of your belongings, harm you physically, could not be your friends." Beware of such friends because they were hidden enemies. They could and would be dangerous and detrimental to a person's welfare and safety.

A selected number of people think that they were cleverer than others. They could, therefore, coerce them or exploit their gentleness. It was vital to understand and analyse the character and aptitude of such individuals. They should not be allowed to profit from other people's innocence or deprive them of their possessions.

13

Temporarily, Jay moved to live in Delhi in order to search for a job and to decide his next step. What was he going to do and what kind of career he would undertake after completing his degree course? There were no careers' advisers at his college or in Delhi. He looked around and thought that he was disposed to become a teacher, and teaching would be a profession for him.

Since he had studied Hindi Literature and English literature at the degree level, he decided to become a language teacher. He made applications to teachers' training colleges and attended an interview in a city in West Uttar Pradesh, close to Delhi. There were more applicants than the places for trainee teachers to be admitted at that college. Jay was not offered a place immediately. He therefore looked to other locations.

At Dhamipur, in the Punjab, there were still vacancies and interviews were taking place on the spot. Jay went to that city, which was about eighty miles from Delhi. He was accepted. He deposited the tuition fee but could not decide whether he would live in the college hostel or rent a private room. The course was to begin in September.

In the meantime, he continued to help his brother Gautam, who had started a shop in New Delhi, where Jay was staying with his eldest brother Nakul. At the end of August, Jay went to his village, where his parents lived. He collected his clothes and bedding and some money for expenses and the fees to be paid in the future months.

He told his mother that Nakul paid the initial deposit. This money should be paid back to him. She told him that Nakul had already collected his money, and you should not feel obliged to him. Jay's dad also expressed the view that he would meet all the expenses of his children's education. He did not want anyone in the family to oblige them financially.

Jay left for Dhamipur, a couple of days before the course was to start. He saw that there were quite a few students from his old degree college in Uttar Pradesh. He decided to live in the student's hostel and shared a double room with one of his old colleagues. They knew each other well but were not necessarily close friends. Jay paid the hostel fee in advance and a deposit. He also paid for his meals. The hostel had incredibly good facilities for students dining. The food was always good and nourishing.

The hostel warden lived next to Jay's room. He also taught Educational Philosophy on the Teachers' training course. He was six feet tall, kind and intelligent man. The other Lecturers were also knowledgeable. Since the city of Dhamipur was in the Punjab state, every student had to study Punjabi language at basic level. Surprisingly, the Punjabi language lecturer was from Uttar Pradesh, a Hindi speaking state.

In 1972, Punjab was further divided, and a new state of Haryana was carved out with the eastern districts. The Punjab was divided in 1947, when the Western Punjab with its Capital Lahore, was given to Pakistan. In 1972, Dhamipur became a part of the new state of Haryana. During Jay's period of training, however, it was in the Punjab state with Chandigarh as its Capital city. Chandigarh remained a joint capital for both the states, Punjab, and Haryana.

Apart from the subjects like Educational Philosophy, Educational Psychology, Teaching Methods, and languages, the practical teaching, or teaching practice, was carried out in local schools. Jay did his teaching practice at a High School, where he taught English and Hindi for one term (about 13 weeks). He wanted to teach both the subjects, Hindi and English, simultaneously.

Dhamipur city had a degree college, a Textile Engineering College, along with the teacher's training college. There was a diversity of students at the training college. It had 120 male students and eighty female students. They came from across the country. The students were from Uttar Pradesh, Punjab, Delhi,

Rajasthan, and Madhya Pradesh. One came from the southern state of Kerala and two were from West Bengal.

The students were of all age groups. Young students of 20 years and 21 years, who had just graduated. Experienced teachers of thirty years or even forty years of age, who wanted to gain training to enhance their careers to become headteachers or to move towards administration. The same principle applied to female students. Most of them were young graduates. Some had experience of working in other professions but wanted to become teachers at a later age. One female student was almost fifty years old. There were college lecturers with master's degree but wanted to add teachers' training to their qualifications.

Jay got on well with his roommate. They were getting training in different subjects. While Jay was acquiring training to become a language teacher, his colleague wanted to become a Geography and Mathematics teacher. Jay always respected mature students and was close to them. They looked at him as a younger brother.

Once Jay fell sick, he was taken to a doctors' surgery by a mature colleague. There were no Rikshaws in those days. His friend took him on his back. There was no medical facility at the students' hostel. There was a canteen at the college premises. Jay did not drink much tea in those days. He used to go to the city market with friends to have street food. They all liked Soft pakoras and sweets. There was a good library at the degree college. The trainee students could borrow books at that library, which was nearby and associated with the training college. A rich businessman built both the colleges. Some lecturers taught at both the places. The objective of the training college was to serve the state, the nation, and the world community. Some of the colleagues from the teachers training went to teach abroad including Jay, who moved to the United Kingdom, after teaching in Rajasthan and Delhi for a few years. The teachers were prepared for a multicultural society, in a rapidly changing world.

The aim of the college was to prepare active, confident, self-disciplined, skilful, and socially sensitive teachers. The college Principal laid emphasis on morality. The female and male students attended the same class. There were female lecturers as well as male lecturers. One male student and a female student, however, became close to each other. They wanted to be recognized as boyfriend and girlfriend in the Western cultural fashion.

It was not acceptable in the Indian society in 1950s. The couple, however, resented it. The girl became pregnant. The college Principal felt that they had broken the code of morality. He expelled both of them. They went on strike and sat at front of the college gate. But the Principal did not change his decision. Surprisingly, the trainee students did not come out in their support. They did not want to be involved in a social change or social activities. The couple had to leave their training and the college.

During the Christmas holiday, the college organized two educational tours. One group went north in the Punjab state and the other went to Maharashtra, a holiday resort. It looked like a part of the training, teaching, organizing methods and how to deal with students and their problems, when they were outside the city. Jay could not go on either of these educational tours. It was expensive for him. He did not want to spend his parents' money except on essentials like food, rent and college fees.

Dhamipur city was famous for temples. It had 300 temples. It had been suggested that the city received its name from goddess Gauri Dhami, Lord Shiva's wife. Jay visited some of these temples with his colleagues. There was a seven hundred feet high hill, close to the city. Some students from his college went on a day trip to that hill. They climbed to the top, which was easy, but descending was scary. The hill was a part of the Aravalli Mountain.

Jay recalled an experience when he went to attend his degree convocation at his previous college in Uttar Pradesh. He thought that while he was near his village, he should visit his family overnight. His father questioned "why he travelled from Punjab to Uttar Pradesh. It would cost five rupees from Delhi to the training college and then from Delhi to Village and going back." He thought that it was an unnecessary expenditure. A waste of money and time.

The college authorities would have sent his degree certificate by post. A villager spoke in support of Jay. He told his dad that "convocation was an essential part of education." Moreover, Jay would be able to shake hands with the principal, awarding the degree certificates and "he would be able to take a photograph in gown and hood, with the certificate in his hands," which would be remembered for ever.

Jay walked on foot from his village to his old degree college. He took part in the degree ceremony and saw his old colleagues. One of his dear friends said to him that he had told his mother that Jay would have dinner with his family and would stay at his house overnight. Jay thanked him for his thoughts and kindness but told him that he would stay with Nitin who was still living in the same room where he used to live in his final year of the degree course.

He would be able to see his other friends and buaji (aunty) there and leave the city, next morning. It was convenient for him to travel from that locality. The railway station was closer to Nitin's place. Next morning, he left for Dhamipur as planned. He did not stop to visit his relatives in Delhi.

One of his old school friends was studying at the Engineering college, in Dhamipur for the Textile Engineering degree. They had known each other since the age of eleven, when they both were in High School. They were friends in the early years. Jay had visited his house and knew his dad, who was a well-built man. He was manager of a big factory in the town.

For the High School examination, however, Jay decided to study social sciences, whereas his friend chose Natural Sciences. They were, nevertheless, in touch with each other. When his friend came to see him at the hostel, Jay was very pleased and paid a return visit to him before finishing his training. They both enjoyed each other's company and recalled the earlier years at High School.

Jay did not watch any movies during his studies for the degree. It was not until he started his teachers' training that he went to watch a Hindi film with his colleagues and friends. The movie was called **"MadhuMati"**; which was a remake of a French Film. It became immensely popular and had eight hit songs. The story revolved around a mistaken identity. The heroin of the film was kidnapped and killed by a feudal lord. Unaware of his girlfriend's death, the hero went around searching for her.

He saw a similar face at a railway station and mistook her for his fiancé, whom he so dearly loved and was to get married. But the lady at the station was with her husband. The hero wanted her to come back to him. He questioned her, where had she been? He had been looking for her everywhere. The lady said that she was not his fiancé. She was happily married and introduced her husband to the hero of the film.

The other film Jay watched during his training period was "**Phaagoon**". It had the same heroin as in **MadhuMati** (Vyjanthimala). It also had excellent music and beautiful songs. It was about the Spring Season. Both the hero and the heroin sang songs in the fields full of flowers and ripe crops. Most Hindi Movies were musical, had songs and dances. All sorts of movies were made in India. Hero based, Heroin based, and Events based. The story was developed according to circumstances. Many Actors worked in different films at the same time.

After completing his training, Jay returned to Delhi, where he did some part time teaching. Initially it was time consuming to go by train to old Delhi to teach for a couple of hours. The remuneration was small, but he had no choice. It was difficult to find a full-time

K. C. Arora

teaching job at that time. The schools in Delhi and Uttar Pradesh had started the teaching session in July, when Jay's training finished at the end of August.

<u>14</u>

He tried to find a job but with no success. His brother Nakul advised him to start to teach private tuition by helping students with their homework. He started to teach for a few hours each day. He had to go to different houses and teach different subjects at all levels, where he did not use his knowledge and skills, he had acquired in the training or at the degree level.

The first tuition he started, was near the shopping Centre, Chandni Chowk. It was close to old Delhi Railway station. Jay travelled to this place by train from home. Even though the old Delhi station was the next stop and about three miles from where he lived with Nakul. He bought a monthly rail ticket to travel for convenience, and it was cheaper than buying a ticket every day. At the end of the training, Jay received his deposit money back from the training college. He used this money for his expenses in the early months of living in Delhi.

For his first tuition, he was required to teach four boys in a businessperson's family. The boys had different demands because they were of different age groups and in different classes. He used to spend more than two hours, helping them with their homework in English, Mathematics, Science and Social Studies. He did not receive his fee monthly. After three months, he asked for payment for teaching two hours a day. The children's father paid him ninety rupees for ninety days. One rupee per day.

Jay argued that he was teaching his four sons with different demands. He had to travel to their house, which took time. The businessman asked him to continue to teach and he will consider increasing the remuneration, from the next month. Jay, however, wanted to know his monthly payment, without delay.

When the businessman did not tell him, the new rate of fee, Jay told him that he would not continue to teach four boys at the rate of one rupee per day. He stopped teaching them. Though he taught for another week in the fourth month. He was not paid for those days. Jay paid these ninety rupees to Nakul for his food and lodging.

After giving up tuition at that place, he started to teach at another house, about five minutes' walking distance from Chandni chowk. This house was inside a narrow lane in old Delhi. He tutored a daughter of another businessman who was a garment manufacturer. He sold readymade clothes at his own shop which he owned at the main market. He employed quite a few workers, at the clothing manufacturing factory as well as at the shop, selling readymade garments.

They also had another employee, who helped with the domestic work. This family had a grown-up married son and two daughters. The son helped his father at the family business. Among the daughters, the elder was reading for her high school examination. She needed help with her English, Hindi and Mathematics, which Jay could provide. He taught her for the whole academic year. They paid him forty rupees a month for teaching for one hour a day, which was more than he received for teaching four boys at the other place. This payment was prompt on time. Jay did not have to ask to pay him the money.

The younger girl sometimes needed assistance with her homework. The elder one would not let her receive any help, suggesting that Jay was her tutor. He attempted to argue that he would teach her for the full hour, and would help the younger one, in his own time, which he sometimes did. It was, however, difficult for the elder girl to concentrate on her studies. She used to drift in her thoughts. She was a sixteen-year-old adolescent and was only four years younger than Jay. She was, however, mature for her age.

She would kick at Jay's feet under the table. She would sometimes write a note, and it put in the book, "I love you." Jay was a good

137

teacher and tried to discipline her and asked her to pay attention towards her studies. He even showed his anger at her manners. The girl's mother and sister-in-law were always present in the room during the teaching hour. Once or twice, they also noticed her attitude and warned her to be serious during studies and to be orderly and practical about the subjects.

The other tuition, he taught was, to an English medium student in Khari- Bavly, about ten minutes' walking distance from the girl's house. He had to travel from one house to another in the scorching heat of old Delhi. They were a nice family and the boy, who was eleven years old, was very disciplined. He was well mannered and intelligent. Still, he needed help with his school homework.

Some parents provided tuition to their children for prestige reasons and to show to their friends and relatives that a teacher comes to their house to tutor their child. Jay was paid forty rupees a month for this tuition. It was the same as the other tuition he taught. Jay never had to wait or ask for a remittance. The boy's father used to pay at the end of the month. If the last day of the month fell on Sunday, he would pay the amount on Friday or Saturday.

Jay continued tutoring these young students until the end of their examinations in April. He used to pass on his tuition money to his brother Nakul, for his food and lodging. He did not want to be identified with the stigma of a free loader. He kept only five rupees to buy a monthly rail ticket. He did not eat out or buy any tea or water. He did not buy any shoes or clothes during this period. He sometimes felt hungry, but he lived with it. Nakul never said that he does not have to pay all his earnings.

In the month of May, he did not have any work in Delhi. He decided to go to his village for the summer period. There he helped his grandfather at the shop and used to take food for Gautam, every day by bicycle. He travelled four miles to reach the town, where Gautam was supervising the construction of a house and two shops on the land, which their dad bought a few months earlier.

Jay biked back four miles to reach the village before sunset. He jaunted eight miles a day in the burning heat of May and June, just to take food for his brother Gautam, who could have asked someone to cook for him in that town where he was to start a new life and was to run a shop. He should have developed close association with people around the area and should have become acquainted with them. Jay did not rest or stay in the village for a single day.

<u>15</u>

He, however, had to find a full-time teaching job. He, therefore, returned to Delhi and made applications. He found a typing school nearby and asked the owner to type applications for him. He sent many applications to schools in Delhi state, Western Uttar Pradesh, and Rajasthan.

After about three weeks, he received a telegram asking him to join a school in Somanpur, in Rajasthan. First, he was surprised that he had been appointed without an interview. Later he discovered that the school did not want to waste energy and money by calling candidates for interview. They could judge the ability of a teacher based on the candidates' application. One of their managers had a degree in Philosophy and Psychology. He could judge people, based on their writing style and writing skills.

Jay was delighted to have a full-time teaching job. He could now use his qualifications and knowledge. His brother Nakul tried to persuade him not go to Rajasthan but to stay in Delhi. He argued that he (Jay) could earn the same amount of money through private tuition. On this, Jay did not agree with Nakul. It was different from having a teaching career.

He was excited for being appointed a full-time teacher. He also realized that he earned money during the previous year, through private tuition but paid the entire sum to Nakul. He did not have any cash or funds with him for expenses. A few years later, he discovered that Nakul wanted him to stay in Delhi, so he could continue to pay all his tuition money to him, which he would not receive from Rajasthan.

Jay went to his village and asked his mother to lend him some money. He told her that he will receive his salary at the end of the month. He will have to pay for a room rent and food, and of course for the rail ticket to Somanpur. He also collected some clothes and his quilt and bedsheets. He returned to Delhi the next day. His dad came to see him off at the local railway station. He reached Delhi in the afternoon.

The same night, he started his train journey to Somanpur, one hundred- and twenty-miles South-West of New Delhi. and reached the city next morning. At Somanpur railway station, he hired a horse drawn tanga (which were the only means of transport at that time) and went straight to the school hostel. He asked to see the warden. He was given a room where he left his luggage.

A teacher took him to school and introduced him to the headmaster, who further introduced him to other teachers and office staff. The headmaster gave him his teaching timetable and took him to his first lesson, which was a Hindi subject of Tenth standard. Jay grew up to face the class fully prepared and that the teacher should know what he was going to say and teach.

He had not seen the subject syllabus and the topic to be taught on that day. He was not fully prepared to talk to students on the topic to be taught. When the headmaster left the room, he smiled at students and introduced himself as a trained graduate teacher. In that lesson, he was required to teach Hindi medieval poetry of Kabir Das. He leaned on the table, as if he were sitting on it and asked the students to talk about themselves, and what they have learned so far in the subject?

Half the lesson time was over in this conversation. He then started to talk about Hindi Cinema and a film based on the life of the poet, whom they were studying. The Title of the film was "Dhool Ka Phool" (Flower of the Dust), released in 1959, only a year earlier and Jay had watched it. It had famous Hindi Actors, Rajendra Kumar, Mala Sinha, Nanda, Ashok Kumar, Manmohan Krishna and Mehmood.

In the story of the film, a young man falls in love with an orphaned young woman, but he married another woman at his father's behest. The orphaned woman discovered that she was pregnant.

142

After a few months' time, she gave birth to a baby boy. She took the baby to the house of her old boyfriend who told her that their relationship was a mistake. She was asked to leave the house, which she did without any argument.

The young lady used to live with her uncle On the discovery of her pregnancy, she was thrown out of the house. She had no place to live. She. therefore, abandoned the baby in a forest. The baby was found by a passerby, who took him to his house and eventually adopted him. When the boy started schooling, other children teased and taunted him, saying that he was illegitimate.

The child left the school and became a petty thief. He was caught by the police and was presented at the Magistrate's court. His mother turned up at the hearing. The hero of the film (Rajendra Kumar) was the Presiding Magistrate, who was also the child's biological father. He recognized the boy's mother, who was his college girlfriend. He admitted his fault and wanted the child to come and live with him.

The film had the classic song sung by his adopted father. "Tu Hindu Banega, Na Musalmaan Banega, Insaan Ki Aulaad hei Insaan Banega." It could be translated "that you would be brought up as a human being, because you are a child of human beings. You would neither be a Hindu or nor a Muslim". Even though the

143

child was born to Hindu parents, he was brought up by a Muslim guardian.

Jay related this story with the life of the poet he was supposed to teach. He gave a good impression to students and told them that they could treat him as their friend and discuss any matters with him. Some of the students were only three or four years younger to him and older than his own youngest brother. At the School, he adjusted himself very quickly and was a popular teacher.

From the next day, Jay started to prepare his lesson and teaching plan. He was always well prepared to face the class in both his subjects- Hindi, and English. He also became acquainted with other colleagues, who taught different subjects at the school. They were all friendly and, in their twenties, except for the Headmaster and the Humanities teacher, who had crossed thirty years in age.

After a few weeks, he was asked to become the "Teacher Editor of the School Magazine." One of the language teachers objected to it. Being senior to Jay, he himself wanted to be the Chief Editor. "The authorities were, however, advised by some experienced teachers, who had worked with the other language teacher, that this new teacher was the only one who could edit the school Magazine successfully." The other teacher may not deliver it.

The school Magazine was to be published in April, just before the Summer-holiday. Jay felt that April was still seven months away. There should be a hand-written magazine (HAST LIKHIT PATRIKA) produced on Mahatma Gandhi's birthday, 2nd October. The magazine would be prepared by students, in their own handwritten work and all the articles would be based on Gandhiji's life and work.

He encouraged students, to author articles for the magazine. He wrote an editorial, which recognized the importance of creative writing and producing new literature. It would also encourage students to think and frame their ideas and present them in an essay form. He added, "A man's experience and thoughts lead to the creation of literature which mirrors the society."

He stressed that the work could be in the form of poetry, story, essay, or a historical account. This Handwritten Magazine was a collection of views of students. They had offered their homage, respect and feelings through poems and articles, "on the life of this great man, Mohan Das Karam Chand Gandhi", commonly known as Mahatma Gandhi.

Jay continued, "Though there was enormous literature on the life and activities of the Mahatma, the young students at the school, had added to the existing literature." He praised his students, when he wrote, "their work was greatly appreciated, because of their originality and expression and perceptions." He advised the students that "they should continue to write their observations and experiences."

"The creation of literature ends the struggle and leads to cooperation, understanding and a prosperous life. It creates a consciousness to work for social uplift, progress, and welfare." Jay also thanked the students for their efforts and cooperation in producing the Handwritten Magazine.

Jay himself authored an article on Gandhi's concept of Ahimsa (non-violence) in education. "In this age of science and technology, Gandhi believed in non-violence (Ahimsa) and practiced it. In one sense he was more compelling and potent than the conquerors and creators of empires. It was his spiritual power which won the hearts of the people around the world."

Jay developed this theme in greater detail, which the readers found interesting and useful. He asserted that "it was rare in history that an empire was ended through negotiations and an Act of Parliament, rather than through defeating and killing the imperialist administrators and their army." It was, nevertheless, only the political freedom.

146

For Gandhi, it was essential "to accomplish economic and social reforms." He (Gandhi) wanted the "Indians to remain away from the European influence and to develop and spread an Indian education system of their own." Gandhi advanced the view that the study of "Asian culture was equally vital, as was the learning of western sciences." He maintained, "The vast treasure of Sanskrit, Arabic, Persian, Pali, and Tamil should be rediscovered." The idea was not only to feed on or to repeat the ancient cultures but "to build a new culture based on the traditions of the past and to enrich it with the experiences of the later times." "For Gandhi, vocational and practical education was paramount for economic progress. He expressed the view that Ahimsa (non-violence) removed the psychological dark points of envy, jealousy and ill-will." He believed in building a humanity which was important for a country, a nation, and the world. He sustained that people should attempt to adjust themselves in accordance with their circumstances.

After completing the magazine, with articles and poems, it was bound in red colour, and presented to the headmaster on 2nd October, Gandhi's birth anniversary celebration at the school. The head of school liked the magazine, so much, that he circulated it to the teaching staff, and the management, who were surprised to see the originality and the standard of articles. They could not believe that the new teacher was fresh from training college and was not an experienced educator.

Later the magazine was placed in the school library for students to see. Apart from editing the school magazine, Jay helped students in organizing the Students Union activities. He was also the Senior President of the School Cultural Association. With the help of students, he staged a drama in which he also sought help from his ex-students, who had left the school but respected him and stayed connected with him.

Jay was also asked to organize the half-yearly and annual examinations. In April, the High School Board examinations were held. His school was the Examination Centre for four schools. Apart from his School, students and teachers came from three other close- by institutions. He had to organize invigilation duties. He was fair in providing duties equally to all teachers because it was a paid job. The teachers would receive money for their commitment during invigilation.

The security and safety were the responsibility of the headmaster, who kept the examination papers locked in a metal cupboard. The envelopes containing examination papers were opened in the presence of teachers, just before the examination time. After the examination, the scripts were sent to the Examining Board, through railway parcel system on the same day. All teachers took their duties seriously and there was no obstacle of any kind. A couple of times, Jay himself accompanied the examination scripts to the local railway station.

Teachers from other schools became close to Jay's colleagues and they used to discuss about the school curriculum, atmosphere in their schools, the administration, and attitude of their management and the headmaster. Jay became friendly with the language teacher at another school. They had similarities in subject teaching. They both came from Uttar Pradesh, though from different regions. They used to have conversations every day.

When the examinations were over, the teachers and students at other schools were to leave for their towns and cities. Jay's friend asked him to continue their friendship. They exchanged their addresses. After two weeks of their departure from Somanpur, the other teacher wrote a letter to Jay reminding him of their decision to continue their fraternity and to maintain correspondence.

Jay read the letter a couple of times. He was extremely impressed. It had emotional content and sometimes complaints that Jay would forget in course of time, just as the sand slips from the hand. Jay replied to him stating that their companionship was not temporary.

It should continue for as long as possible. His letter, however, was more rational than emotional. It took the shape of a poem, in which he expressed his views about continuing their affinity:

"I have countless perceptions and conceptions,

Which cannot be converted into words.

Vast number of people live in this world,

They, all do not become friends.

Compassion, consideration and warmth grow,

Among those who have similar viewpoints and beliefs.

It is the law of nature to meet and to part,

They, however, leave an impression on their minds.

Memories always persist in their hearts,

Even though they are not constantly together.

If they are distanced, why worry,

There is a hope to get together again.

To meet and to get separated is imperative.

It is not my intention to become hard-hearted,

In the desert state of Rajasthan.

Temper teaches us to remain happy and elated.

I do not like the practices of the world,

Where adoration and attachment are taken away.

If allegiance and endearment are not perpetual,

There could not be forbearing, love and understanding."

It would be right to suggest that 'love is not love,

if it alters, when alteration its finds."

In real circumstances, however, it was not possible to continue their bond for long. They faced different circumstances, had their own commitments. They taught at two separate locations. They never met again.

16

Reena's father wanted her to get married into a large joint family. He found Jay's family with the characteristics, he was looking for. Jay had elder brothers, younger brothers, sisters, parents and grandfather. Reena's father could not visualise the problem that could be encountered by his daughter in a joint family, in a faraway village, where she had no acquaintances. Jay's mother never approved her from the day she put her foot in the village. She did not let anyone know of her perspectives and thoughts.

In the months and years, she made sure that Jay did not meet his wife, Reena. It was not that the young woman lived with her parents all the year round. Indeed, his mother Nanda used to send his younger brother Vikram to bring her to the village, to live with her and other members of the family.

At Diwali time and during summer holiday, however, she was sent back to her parental home. Jay used to come to his village only during these periods. Reena used to live at Jay's parental house in his absence. Nanda continued to exploit Reena, as long as she lived with her. Other members of the family could not do anything. It was not easy to question the female head of the family.

Men folk did not know how Reena and other daughters-in-law were treated within the four walls of the house. A joint family did not work for everyone and all the time. It could create social and psychological conundrum. People should attempt to analyse their interests carefully and logically.

They should not undermine others. Jay felt that they should show respect to each other and not impose their will and philosophy. The same principle applied to nations, which was vitally important for co-existence and survival. They should seek cooperation rather than conflict, reconciliation and not to impose their cravings and whims on others.

Jay and his wife Reena, nevertheless, could not work out the reason for this arrangement. One could only imagine, what a young married woman would feel to live with her husband's family in his absence. They both were in their early twenties. Jay had a job and sent his earnings to his parents.

His wife looked after her in-laws and did the domestic work, cooking, cleaning, grinding flour every day. Sometimes she was mistreated, as if she were a burden on the family. She had no one to talk to about her feelings, and what did she want? Whether she was happy there or not, whether she wanted to live there or not?

153

Still, she did not moan, because she had no support. No one physically assaulted her, but mental agony was there. Someone told the head of the house that a few houses away, Atul's mother beats her daughter-in-law with a stick or slaps her by hand. No reason was provided for this behaviour or for telling the family all that.

On a winter night, Reena (Jay's wife) fell sick and was suffering from high fever. She wanted to stay in bed for a little longer and not to get up at the normal time of 4 am. Rather than giving her medicine or calling a doctor, Jay's mother Nanda asked her to get up at that hour, and to start grinding flour. Reena begged the mother-in-law to let her rest for a few more hours in bed and she would do the housework during the daytime.

Nanda did not care for such a pleading and ordered her to leave the bed instantly and to begin to grind flour. She said, "there was a lot of work to be done during the daytime." "Moreover, when you start to work, your fever will go away." What was Reena's position in the family? Was she a daughter-in-law in the house, wife of an educated teacher or a slave?

The innocent soul had no choice and without the brace or backing of anyone, she started to grind flour. She worked all day- cooking, cleaning, washing clothes. Reena spent all her time in the service of her in-laws, who were happy because they had hot meals to eat and washed clothes wear.

She was shunted from her father's home to her in-law's village every few months. Although she was a married woman and was treated like one, no relative or member of her family attempted to find out, her wishes and thoughts or her happiness. She attempted to tell her father of the conduct of her mother-in-law, Nanda. He brushed aside and "asked her, to sustain hardship for a bright future with her husband."

Jay's parents never considered sending her to live with him. They wanted her to work for the family and serve them. They were the parents and parents-in- law, who needed to be looked after. At the same time, they were receiving money from Jay. What kind of social and psychological impact did Reena have? It was difficult to visualize. There was enormous discrimination in their dealings. Some members of the family thought that she was not needed there, except when she brought dowry from her parent's house and worked hard for the family. That was the dilemma in a joint family. The female head of family dominated and controlled everything and everyone. New and young members of the family simply obeyed her and did, what they were asked to do. They had no say in family affairs.

155

"In a country where goddess Durga, Laxmi, Radha, Sita, Parvati and Gayatri were worshipped, how could a young woman be treated in such a manner"? Reena's problems, her health and her welfare were ignored. She was not the only daughter-in-law in the family who had suffered hardship and harsh treatment by Nanda.

There were two elder daughters-in-law, who faced similar fates and behaviour. For years, they were grinding flour, cleaning the dishes, washing clothes, and did the cooking. All under the control of Nanda. They tolerated it, at that time, but never forgot the conduct of their mother-in-law.

In the years to come, when they set up their own families, they did not invite her to their houses and did not visit her in the village except at the times of wedding of the younger daughter and the boys. The fourth daughter-in-law was surprised when she experienced the same approach as the elder ones. When she went to her parents' house, she told her father about Nanda's mode towards her.

The young lady's father wrote a long letter to Jay's dad, criticizing him and reminding him of the old days of his life in Delhi in 1930s, during the recession. Jay's dad could not understand why his daughter-in-law's father had written such a bitter letter. He was not aware of the manipulation of his daughters-in-law in the house. He used to go there only to eat food. He did not interfere in the domestic affairs and left everything to Nanda as female head of the family.

It was difficult to suggest whether Nanda changed her habits. This daughter-in-law also moved out of the house and started to live in a separate place in the same village and later moved to live in Delhi with her husband and children. The youngest daughter-in-law, however, always lived with Nanda. Jay's youngest brother inherited all the properties and the wealth. His wife, however, showed no special respect for Nanda. During the last years of her life, she felt as if she was a responsibility and obstruction to her youngest son and daughter-in-law. They never took her to doctors when she was sick.

They did not provide enough nourishing food and gave her only sufficient food to survive. Her milk, vegetables and fruits were stopped. Even after thirty or forty years, the elder daughters-in-law did not forget how they were treated in the village. She was not visited by them or invited to their houses, even at the time of festivals like Diwali and Holi or Navratri celebrations.

Jay felt pity at this situation and offered that she should come to live with him. His wife Reena promptly stopped him from doing so. She was very frank and told him that even in her old age, she would make their lives miserable. He was not aware of the modus operandi that Reena sustained in the village because he was never informed of the happenings in the past. Nanda continued to live with the youngest son until she died at the age of eighty-seven.

Going back to the early years in Jay's life, it was not until the summertime, four years after their marriage, that Jay met his wife and spent a whole month with her in the village. Jay wanted to get married at the age of twenty-three anyway. He, therefore, did not think of the past years, or how his wife lived in his absence? She did not tell him anything about the last four years or the dealings and the treatment by other members of his family.

At the end of the summer holiday, he returned to his school to teach. He was very busy with his schoolwork, preparing teaching plan, reading, and writing. In October of the same year, a war broke out between India and China. Commonly known as the Sino-India war of 1962. His father was a little concerned about the war's effect on Jay, who told him that the war was taking place in North-East India in the Himalayas. He lived in West Central India in Rajasthan. There would be no impact of the war on him personally. There were many soldiers, in the India army, from Jay's village. One of his village soldiers, Rohan was sent to fight in the 1962 war against China. Jay knew him well. His house was only six doors away from his parental home. Rohan was reported missing, but he never returned to the village. After a few months, he was assumed dead. Rohan was 6ft. 2inches tall, well built, polite and ever smiling. He was always ready to help others, when required.

He was a High School graduate, but he was very smart and clever. He was an athlete and passed the entry examination and health test to join the Indian army. He had two brothers. The elder brother worked on the farms. He was educated only up to Primary education. He did not leave the village to obtain any further education. Rohan's younger brother left the village after his Primary schooling but returned home after completing his High School education and started to work on the farms with his eldest brother.

The death of Soldier Rohan was a great loss to the family, the village, and to the nation. Many young men joined the army in the past from Jay's village, but he had never heard of any casualty. The Indian government sent a sewing machine to Rohan's widow. She could start an independent life by earning her living by stitching clothes for the villagers. She lived a lonely life and never married again. She continued to live in the same house with her in-laws. Her brother-in-law always gave her share of the crops and met any other requirement she asked for.

159

The question Jay asked, "why did China attack the Indian Borders, when the politicians of both countries were talking"? Several reasons could be considered to seek an answer. China had been an aggressor nation since the Communist takeover in 1949. It occupied Tibet in 1950, when the world's attention was drawn towards the Korean crisis.

Another view was that China wanted to disrupt the Indian economic development and defence preparedness before India became powerful to be taken on. It wanted a disruption in India, which could lead to the fall of her democracy and the Nehru government. It thought that the Indian people would accept Communism. China made fun of India's non-aligned policy. The Chinese domestic reasons might have compelled her to seek diversion.

In 1962, the Superpowers (the United States of America and the Soviet Union) were engaged in finding a solution to the Cuban crisis and the world attention was centred on that issue. China took advantage of the situation and attacked India. By controlling Indian land area, it built the Sinkiang-Tibet Road, through Aksai-Chin area of the Ladakh province of India. The Chinese had consolidated their position in Ladakh, and the Indians could do nothing to stop them.

160

The result of the 1962, India-China war, was that Prime minister Nehru lost faith in human nature. He trusted Zou-Enlai and treated him as a friend. Yet, the Chinese broke their promise and commitment to solve all disputes by peaceful negotiations. They should have respected the Indian sovereignty, not attacked it. In the past, China had recognized the Indian borders.

<u>17</u>

After the Indo-China War, Nehru's health deteriorated, and he died within 18 months of the Chinses aggression. The other changes also took place. General K.S. Thimayya resigned his post and was replaced by General Jadu Nath Chaudhry (JN Chaudhry). One of Jay's colleagues and friend commented that with the appointment of General Chaudhry and Défense Minister YB Chavan, the Chinese stopped fighting and withdrew from some of the Indian territory.

He saw some kind of similarity in the word "C." He commented that Ram killed Ravan the king of Lanka, and Krishna killed Kans, the king of Mathura. With Choudhry and Chavan on the helm, the Chinese stopped their encroachment, though they did not totally withdraw from the areas occupied in the short war of October-November 1962.

With the defeat of India in 1962, there was great uproar in the Indian Parliament. The Défense minister was asked to resign, which he did. But Jay asked a question to himself and others, could one person be held responsible for the national debacle? Of course, as an in charge of the Department of defence, the Minister had the responsibility for the implementation and success of the departmental policies.

The national security, however, was the responsibility of the whole Cabinet, the Parliament, and the country. The finance minister did not allocate enough resources to the defence department. No new equipment was purchased from abroad and arms production in the country started only after 1957. The Research and Development (R&D), Hindustan Aeronautics Limited (HAL) were also established in mid-1950s.

After the defeat in 1962, the Indian government appealed to public to donate money, gold, and other valuables for the national security fund. Finances were raised in schools and colleges, offices, shops, and other organizations. Jay's school made a collection. Teaching staff donated one week's salary; students brought money according to their affordability.

His school organized a function which was attended by the Chief Minister of the State and the Defence Minister of India. The headmaster handed a cheque, for the value of collection, to the Indian Defence Minister. It was very much appreciated.

India's defeat at the hands of the Chinese was mocked by Zulfikar Ali Bhutto, of Pakistan. He said that India was finished, and she had no future. He started to make preparation to attack India on her western borders to grab the Indian state of Jammu and Kashmir. He persuaded the Pakistani President Ayub Khan to take on India. He expressed the view that India was a weak nation at that time.

Indeed, Pakistan attacked India's western borders, but her army was defeated within ten days. India controlled a large part of that country and surrounded the City of Lahore in west Punjab. The army was waiting for orders to enter the city. The people of Lahore were fed-up with the army rule in Pakistan. They were waiting with garlands to welcome the Indian army as liberators.

The foreign intervention and India's own policy of non-occupation of any country, however, stopped the soldiers from entering Lahore. The soldiers stayed within the Indian borders and returned to their barracks. The Soviet Union organized a meeting between India and Pakistan at Tashkent in Central Asia. India returned all the Pakistani territory that her army had occupied during the short war. The Indian Prime Minister, Lal Bahadur Shastri died in sleep in Tashkent. The reason for his death remained a mystery.

However, in 1967, India and China fought again in Chola and Nathula- Pass, at the height of 16,000 feet near Sikkim. It was argued that aggression was an aggression, and it got to be vacated. India won this war. It restored a parity between the two Asian countries and revived India's pride. The two countries lived peacefully for over fifty years. Certain skirmishes started again in 2020-2021. A great deal of dialogue and meetings had taken place between the two armies and their foreign office officials.

Jay's villagers had joined the army, three generations up, and perhaps before then. He always liked talking to elderly people. He did not necessarily ask them questions. They themselves revealed to him and told stories of the times gone by.

He recalled when an elderly neighbour conceded that when he was in the army, he was given a letter to post. There was no post office in the nearby vicinity. He, therefore, ran 18 miles to post the letter. He did not stop at any place. He was a little tired at the end. But now after so many years, remembering that episode, he laughed at his action. Of course, he returned to his army base, the same day. He travelled thirty-six miles on foot in one day.

There was another gentleman, whom Jay called grand uncle, though he was not related to him. This gentleman retired from the army even before Jay was born. He was, however, provided a pension for his army service. It was four Rupees (equal to one dollar) a month in those days. His sons used to take him, in a bullock cart, to the city, to collect his pension. He did not necessarily need this money, but it was his right. He felt proud that

165

he was in the Indian army and was receiving a pension in his old age.

Over two million Indian soldiers participated in the Second World War. They were in Singapore, Burma (now Myanmar), and Malaya (Malaysia) in the East, and France, Italy, Egypt, and other European countries in the West. They fought in many war theatres. One soldier from his village was in the United Kingdon, defending the London Airport.

200,000 Indian soldiers lost their lives between 1939 and 1945. They were of all ranks. From Jay's village, however, there were only sergeants, lieutenants, and soldiers. In the 1950s and 1960s, many young men from his village joined the army. Due to domestic reasons, some returned to the village, after a few years' service. Others made careers in the forces.

One Youngman whose family lived near Jay's granddad's shop, joined the Indian Navy. He progressed through the ranks and retired as a naval officer. He then joined the merchant navy to earn money. He was paid more in the merchant navy than in the Indian Navy. On full retirement, he did not return to the village for permanent residence but built a big house in the nearby city and started to live there with his children and grandchildren.

In the later part of the 20th Century, a man reached the rank of Lieutenant General. When he retired, he decided to live in the city, because of the amenities. He, however, continued to visit the village, where he had ancestral agricultural land. He employed personnel to work on his farms. He also kept a supervisor to look after the farms and the workers. The supervisor reported to him regularly.

18

The Indian army was not the only attraction for Jay's villagers. People were interested in education. In the later part of the 20th Century, they sent their children to study in cities, for the High School examination, Intermediate level and some completed their degree. There was an elderly teacher, who retired as Primary School headmaster, and another was still employed as a headteacher. They were both of his dad's generation. Many of Jay's generation became teachers.

They taught in Primary schools and Secondary Schools. They, however, had to complete teacher's training before being appointed as teachers. To teach at a Primary School, they did their Junior School Teaching Certificate (JTC) and for High School teaching, they had to do Bachelor of Teaching (BT) or Bachelor of Education (B Ed) degree.

None of them taught in their own village. They used to teach in other villages and in the nearby towns. At one stage Jay's brother Nakul was offered a teaching job as soon as he passed his Intermediate examination. But he did not want to become a teacher. There were quite a few friends of Jay's, who were teachers. One of his cousins taught only for a year. After that he joined the Indian Railways.

Another cousin, however, remained a teacher all his active life. His eldest cousin's son also remained a teacher all his life. He moved to live in the city, where he graduated. They all found teaching, very rewarding because they provided education in a developing country and lifted people from ignorance.

There were young men who preferred to work in the Indian Railways. It was a satisfying profession for them. They did all kinds of jobs, including Engine driver, Ticket collector, station master, accountants, and administrators. They had to pass an entry examination to join the Indian Railways. The Indian railway system started in the 19th Century to move raw material and manufactured goods to ports, for exports. Railways took goods to other cities in the country in order to sell to shopkeepers and to consumers.

The Railways also led to industrialization in India. Machinery had been introduced in the country which possessed iron-ore to make iron and steel. Industrial development in India started in the late 19th Century but it was slow because of imperialist administration. The railways, however, transported manufactured goods from factories and brought raw materials for use in those places.

One thing Jay noticed in the nearby district of Delhi. A small railways gauge track was laid near the villages and farms to transport sugar cane to mills to manufacture sugar. The speed of the railway train was so slow that people could get on and get off easily, and it would continue to travel. Apart from carrying raw materials and goods, the trains were also used for travelling but Jay never sat on these trains. He enjoyed watching them move slowly. After 1950, emphasis was laid on comfort for passengers. Modernization continued throughout the 20th Century, from the use of coal to electrification. In recent years, large cities have developed their own Metro-system for local people. The first Metro was built in Kolkata (Calcutta) in 1984. Delhi built its Metro in 2002, Mumbai (Bombay) in 2014 and Chennai (Madras) in 2015.

The process was continuing in Lucknow, Bengaluru, and other cities for furtherance for the residents in big cities. Despite all these conveniences, one of Jay's villagers never travelled by train. He hardly ever went far from the village. If he went to town, he travelled in his bullock cart or walked on foot.

One of Jay's cousins joined the civil service and became an administrator in the Ministry of Finance. He spent all his working life there and retired at the age of 60 years. But he never went back to live permanently in the village. Though he used to visit his relatives and friends in the village. Another person held an administrative job in the Central Ministry Urban Development. He spent all his working life in the department and retired as a higher-grade administrator and received a pension.

His wife asserted that her husband's pension increased every six months. She was exaggerating the claim, to show their vanity, that they were above others in the vicinity. Their standard of living did not reflect anything special. They had lived in the same house since they moved to live as young people. Some people did not tell the whole truth. This family was one of those boasting few.

There were two men from his village in the police force. One of them was the son of the retired Headmaster and another was a friend of Nakul's. Jay took interest in both and whenever they were in the village, he used to talk to them in some detail about their job and professional satisfaction. They both joined the rank of police Sub-inspector because they had acquired the educational qualifications and passed the Provincial Police Service examination.

The modern police system in India started in the 1780s. Before that the village Zamindar (Landlord) was responsible for the security of the village. The Nawabs and Maharajas were the Judges of

171

Higher Courts. One of the sub-inspectors from his village was later promoted to the rank of Inspector of police.

The Inspector oversaw a police station in urban areas. In rural areas in India, an Inspector of police managed a circle which comprised two or more police stations. He was also known as the Circle Inspector of police. Constables, head constable, an assistant sub-Inspector, and a Sub-Inspector, worked under his supervision. A Sub-Inspector could run a police station and assisted the Police Inspector.

They dealt with both the civil and criminal complaints. After investigation, they were required to refer the matter to the courts and to provide protection to witnesses. There had, however, been complaints by the public that the Police did not register complaints of the poor people. It could be true but there were social welfare organizations to assist such people.

A complaint could be lodged to higher authorities, against the lower grade officers, or the matter could be referred to courts. The court or the higher police officer could conduct an enquiry. The police officers could be suspended or discharged from the service, The Police Superintendent himself could visit a police station, especially when a complaint had been lodged against it. The redresses were available.

172

The law enforcement in India was the State matter. The Central Ministry of Home Affairs was responsible for internal and external security of the nation. There were two types of services, the Indian Police Service (IPS) and the State Police Service (SPS). The Police Sub-Inspector came under the State Police Service. He was normally in charge of a police station. He could file a charge-sheet in Court and was usually the first investigating officer.

The officers under him could not file a charge-sheet in Court. They investigate the case and submit a report to him. They also work as Station House Officers (SHOs). Most Sub-Inspectors were directly recruited into the police service. They had better qualifications than the lower rank officers. The SSC (Staff Selection Commission) was responsible for recruiting eligible candidates at national level.

In exceptional circumstances and with experience, some assistant sub-inspectors and constables could be promoted to the post of Inspectors. There had been examples of such promotions. But Jay's villagers entered as a Sub-Inspector through examination. One of them became an inspector because of his hard work, experience, and efficiency. Jay's villagers served in many police stations and in many states. They spent time in Uttar Pradesh, Madhya Pradesh, Rajasthan, and Maharashtra.

173

Before retiring, one of them was posted in Uttar Pradesh, where he was immensely popular and was respected for his fairness. He used to talk to Jay whenever they both were in the village at the same time. He suggested to Jay that he should study for a master's degree after graduation and also take a law degree. He should practice as a lawyer in a Court and later become a politician. Jay, nevertheless, decided to become a teacher instead.

India was an agricultural nation but due to pressure of population on land and lack of opportunities in villages, people started to move out of the villages to cities in search of employment. This mobility introduced social and economic challenges among the village people, including Jay's villagers. A substantial number of residents moved to cities and started new types of jobs.

From Jay's village a family moved to live in Mumbai to work in textile factories. Delhi also had textile industry. Many people from his village worked there. They were in Cotton textiles. They used to make several types of cloth from a variety of cotton. Some of the Indian cotton was not of high quality. The Indian Textile industrialists imported high quality cotton from Egypt. Indian cotton cloth had been famous in the world from the ancient times. Modern cotton mills in India started in 1830, when the first mill was built in Surat (Gujarat). Mills had, however, existed in the

Middle Ages and in ancient times. In the Mauryan times (300 BC), five hundred workers were employed in a factory. Muslin was used to make clothes for the gentry. A muslin cloth was displayed at the Great London Exhibition in 1857, which weighed three ounces and two penny weight. It was ten yards in length and one yard in width. It could pass through a small ring.

<u>19</u>

Apart from thinking about his village and the villagers, Jay continued to teach at Somanpur. The High School Board results, for the previous summer examinations, were exceptionally good at his school. It was, therefore, awarded a prize to visit historical places in India. The Indian Railways provided tickets for fifteen students and two teachers.

The students insisted that Jay accompanied them on this educational tour, which was to last twenty days. The teachers and students would have to give up their Diwali holiday. Before starting the tour, Jay went to visit his parents in the village. He told his dad about the educational tour to central India. His dad expressed a desire to come with him to these beautiful cities and tourist attractions.

Jay told him that he would not enjoy the company of young students. Moreover, a teacher's dad to come with students would not look nice. It could put restrictions on their movement. Jay's dad agreed with this argument. They thought it would be a clever idea to go on an excursion as a family at a later stage.

Jay and his school team commenced their educational expedition during autumn season. They visited tourist places at New Delhi, Agra, Jhansi, (in **Uttar Pradesh**); Gwalior, Bhopal, Indore, Ujjain; (in **Madhya Pradesh**)" and Chittorgarh, Udaipur and Jaipur (in **Rajasthan**). They Transited through four states of India. They used to travel at night by train and visit tourist sites during the day. There was no problem for anyone. They all enjoyed the getaway and returned home safely.

Jay authored a report on this educational tour, which provided information about the places. The features and characteristics of cities and the reason for these cities to have become famous tourist attractions. Jay noticed that all his students were city dwellers and there was no representation from the village pupils. The city life perhaps did not provide full contentment.

They wanted to see different things, or the city people were used to getting out to other places as their parents and grandparents had gone in search of "employment" or for business, in different parts of the country. A substantial number of businesses, in large cities like Mumbai (Bombay), Calcutta (Kolkata) and Delhi, were owned and run by people from Rajasthan.

After leaving Somanpur, Jay and his school group reached **DELHI.** Apart from being the National capital of India, it was a

177

business Centre and a tourist attraction. Connaught Place was built in the 1930s. Chandni Chowk was almost three hundred years old. It was a market for Silver (Chandi in Hindi) jewellery and was therefore known as Chandni Chowk. The famous Red-fort, Kutubmeenar (it was also known as Ashok's Pillar), the Lotus temple, and the Zoo were main attractions. Jay's students visited all these places. They found food in Old Delhi very tasty and enjoyable.

They did not stay there for long and left the same night by train for **AGRA**. Since they reached Agra at midnight and had not booked rooms at a hotel, they squatted at the station, which was not liked by the railway station staff. In AGRA, they visited the Taj Mahal, which was bult by Emperor Shah Jahan in memory of his wife Mumtaj. This building was constructed with white marble. It was considered as a symbol of love.

A tourist guide told the story and significance of the Taj to students. They also asked their inquisitive questions and did shopping of models of the Taj. They visited the Agra Redfort, which had some similarities with the Delhi Redfort. Jay, his colleague, and students did not stay there for a long time. The same evening, they took a train to the other place on their itinerary.

They had scarcely completed fifty miles journey from Agra, when the train stopped. They peeped through the window of the railway compartment and saw a large station with blazing lights and beautiful decoration, casting spells all around. It was the dead of night. The nature was dozing, though it was not in sound sleep. The wind was stirring the trees and plants, producing a whispering sound. The chattering of birds was altogether mute.

The moon was shedding its light. The beauty of nature provided a feeling of ecstasy. The entire platform was full of hues and cries of hawkers, who were selling their provisions to passengers. There were tea stalls in the middle of the platform. The school group decided to walk along the platform. Four students stayed in the compartment with their luggage. Many of them had tea but some young students preferred to have cold drinks.

While walking along the platform, Jay noticed that a young girl, of about twelve years, was sobbing and crying. Her red dress and physical features showed that she belonged to a middle-class family. On an enquiry, it was discovered that an old woman had kidnapped her from a village, and she had sold the girl to two persons for substantial money. The old woman disappeared. There was no trace of her.

The young girl did not know where she was. She continued to sob and cry. She insisted that she wanted to go home. It reflected her distress. Her cheeks and dress became damp with tears. The two men who bought her, did not allow the girl to go to her house. There were none of her acquaintances who could have shown any sympathy or could have obtained her release from the clutches of human traffickers.

A crowd gathered. A couple of people suggested for informing and calling the police. When the police arrived, they took the girl under their care. They asked her questions about her parents, the name of the village, and other details. The kidnapper woman and the men who paid for her, vanished, on seeing the police officers. One of the police was a woman constable. The girl was now in safe hands. It was time for Jay's train to leave the station. All students entered the compartment and sat down in their seats. Jay noticed that the old woman and the men who wanted to take the girl with them, also entered the same compartment. He wanted to do something but there was no way to inform the police about them. He found himself without resources. The train took speed and soon left the station. He simply uttered "What a cruel world?"

In course of time, they reached **JHANSI**, a city in Uttar Pradesh. This city had wide roads. This area was also known as

Bundelkhand. Jhansi Fort, the Rani Mahal, and the Museum were popular visiting places. The Museum had Pre-Modern Indian Artwork from the 4th Century B.C. This city was famous for the bravery and chivalry of the Rani of Jhansi (the queen) who fought the imperialist British in 1857. Her husband had died of illness and there was no heir to the throne. She took the reins of administration under her control. When the British attempted to annex her kingdom, she preferred to give them a fight rather than to surrender the city state.

From Jhansi, the school group travelled to **GWALIAR**, where they visited a huge fort and the Laskar Palace, which belonged to the Maharaja of Gwalior. The carpets at Laskar Palace were very thick. Jay had never seen such thick carpets at any other place. Apart from these buildings, the Maharaja built a four hundred room house. Jay was surprised to see such a huge building and questioned why did he need such a big house? He did not have a large family.

He could have built a school for the people of the city or built houses for the poor. It could have accommodated a small town, if not a city. The Maharaja was a rich man. He started a shipping company, which provided employment to the public.

181

INDORE, a beautiful city in Madhya Pradesh, was the next visiting place. It was suggested that this was the cleanest city in India and had won awards for that. The Magistrate of the city had taken responsibility for this purpose. Jay's school party enjoyed their visit. They went around to see the tourist attractions.

The city of Indore was famous for cotton handloom industry. The students visited and watched carefully how weavers wove cloth. Street food was also famous there. The students and teachers enjoyed the food. The other tourist attractions were the markets and palaces. This City had famous temples.

The Khajrana Ganesh Mandir, Annapurna Temple, the Gamatgiri Jain Temple, Kanch Madir made with glass pieces, and Bada Ganpati Mandir, were very popular. Saraf Bazar (Jewellery market) and the Raj Wada Palace, were also visited by the students and teachers. Raj Wada Palace belonged to the Maharaja of Indore, who ruled the city state before the state was amalgamated with the Union of India in 1948.

UJJAIN was the next place to visit. This was a city in Madhya Pradesh, near Indore. It was a holy city. One of the twelve Shiva temples was located there. It has been suggested that some five thousand years ago, Lord Krishna (the author of *the Bhagavat Geeta*) studied there, under the supervision of Rishi Sandeepan.

Maharaja Vikramaditya was a famous king of Ujjain. When he set on the throne on the first day of Navratri, he started the Hindu calendar with Vikram Samvat, which was 57 years ahead of the Christian era or AD. For example, the year 2025 AD would be 2082 Vikram Samvat, which was followed as their calendar year by the religious minded Hindus.

Sanskrit poet Kalidas was born in this city. He wrote his famous plays and poetry. Shakuntalam, Meghdoot, and Raghuvansh, were just a few books. This city was built on Kshipra River, which was considered as a holy river like the Ganga. Ujjain was, however, famous for its temples. People flock to visit those temples. Mahakaleshwar temple, Bada Ganesh temple, Mahadev temple and Gopal temple were of great architectural beauty and excellence.

KHAJURAHO, another vising place in Chhatarpur district of Madhya Pradesh, was Jay's school group's next stop. It was not a city anymore. It had been deserted and destroyed over a period. It looked like a big village. It, however, had a collection of temples built over two hundred years from the 9th Century to the 11th Century by the Chandolas, who were the main rulers in the medieval time in Central India.

It was not only the political capital of the Chandola kings, but it was also a cultural and religious city, for the people of that region. When a king built a temple, his son would build larger and more temples in number. Altogether they built eighty-five temples, many of them were destroyed by the Muslim invaders. Only twenty-five temples survived, which are now world heritage, under UNESCO. The Khajuraho temples were also famous for their sculpture.

This place was now recognized as the "Museum of temples." These were tourist- attractions. No one prays in these temples and there were no priests. Only Museum staff looked after them. The temples had Hindu and Jain statues of various deities. King Yashovarman built the Lakshmana temple and Vishwanath temple. King Vidyadhar built the Mahadev temple.

The other temples they visited were the Brahma temple, Vamana temple, Parsvanatha temple, Parvati temple, Duladeo temple, Adinatha temple and Santhinatha Jain temple. There were no big shops there. It had very few places for tourists to stay.

From Khajuraho, the school party left for **BHOPAL**. This city was originally known as Bhojpal, after the name of Raja Bhoj who was born in Ujjain, in 980 AD. He came from Parmar dynasty. His

184

father was Sindhu Raj. Bhoj was very intelligent and learned the Vedas and Puranas by the age of seven.

He himself wrote eighty-four books and was recognized as a scholar king. He was a great mathematician, also wrote books on Astronomy, Astrology and Medicine. He provided patronage for Art, Literature and knowledge which left a lasting impact on culture and intellectual culture. His father died when Bhoj was quite young. His uncle Manju took over the reins of the Kingdom. It was thought that Bhoj would Become king after finishing his education.

Manju became greedy and wanted his own son to become king after him. He plotted to kill Prince Bhojpal and sent him to Orisa to be killed by assassins. They told the prince that they had been hired by his uncle Manju. to kill him. He did not object to their plan but wrote a short poem in Sanskrit, to be given to his uncle,

"Mandhata ch Mahipate, Krit Yugalankar Bhuto Gateh, Shanturyan Mahodhado, Viranchetah. Kwasha Dasha Shantkey. Anye Chapi Yudhiristram Prabharatayo, Yata diva Bhoopatsya, Nake Naapi, sang gatva Vasumati, Manjusaya tuam Yashashawti." It could be translated into English that "there had been great and famous people like Mandhata in ancient times and Yudhistir in

185

Dvapara age, but this earth did not go with them when they died. Oh Manju, will this earth request to take it with you, when you die? The assassins were so impressed after reading this poem and felt that all worldly things were ephemeral and for worldly use only. They decided not to kill Bhoj. They were asked to bring the head of Bhoj. They did really take somebody else's head and presented it to king Manju. They also gave him the poem written by Bhojpal. Manju realized his mistake and started to cry and felt disgusted at his decision.

When the assassins realized that Manju had understood his mistake, and was repenting, they presented Prince Bhoj at the gathering. Bhoj was crowned king when he was fifteen years old. He ruled from 1010 AD until 1055 AD. He built a new city Bhojpal not far from Ujjain. He continued his patronage for education and culture and built many temples including the Saraswati temple.

Jay's school Students have read a great deal about Raja Bhoj, his devotion to Hindutva, defending the Hindu religion and his commitment to culture and education. In the eleventh Century, Islamic invasion had started in different parts of India. Raja Bhoj helped in defending the state of Kota in Rajasthan and restored the Hindu Raja by defeating the Muslim invaders.

In Bhopal the students went to see the mosque which was the biggest mosque in India. Thay also visited temples and other famous places. They noticed that there were remnants of Hindu temple in the mosque, especially the pillars. They were curious and wanted to know more about the changes.

A guide who had good knowledge of the cultural changes and destruction of temples by the Muslim invaders, told them that the Great Mosque of Bhopal was built on top of the Saraswati Temple which was built by Raja Bhoj. It was known as Bhojshala. It was a college in the district of Dhar, an area of Bhopal.

The invaders destroyed the existing Hindu culture and architecture in central India. They established their own culture except for music which they adopted and improved. There was a common use of Dholak (horizontal drum) to mix with sound in songs. They divided the Dholak into two parts and created Tablas (vertical drums) which could also played by both hands at the same time as was carried out in the case of a Dholak.

Bhojshala was now a part of Kamal Maulana Masjid. The pillars and the prayer hall ceilings were built from the material of the Bhojshala temple. The mosque also contains engraved stone stabs with valuable compositions. The Bhojshala or Saraswati temple was converted into a Mosque in 1305 AD by Alauddin Khilji. The

187

inscriptions in Sanskrit show that it was a temple. Khilji also killed one thousand two hundred Hindu scholars and converted the campus into a Dargah.

In 1902, George Curzon, when he was the Governor-General of India, sent the Vaagdevi's idol to the London Museum. In the precinct, there was also a large Havan Kund. The Architecture Survey of India (ASI) discovered inscriptions and statues of Hindu deities. The guide explained to students that it was a disputed place like the Ram Temple in Ayodhya, Shiva temple in Banaras and Krishna Janam Bhumi temple in Mathura. These premises of Hindu temples were converted into Mosques.

Bhopal was now the capital city of Madhya Pradesh. It had the Upper Lake and the Lower Lake, Van-Vihar National Park, which was the home of tigers, lions, and Leopards. Raja Bhoj was a devotee of Lord Shiva, but he built temples of many other deities. The other attractions were the Birla Mandir, Vidyagiri Cave temples, Gauhar Mahal, Regional Science Centre, Kewa Dam and Fish Aquarium, Sanchi Stupas and Moti Masjid. The Bhimbetka caves, Laxmi Narain temple, Birla Museum. Bhojpur temple was built by Raja Bhoj in the 11th Century. Gohar Mahal, Rani Kamlapati palace was built in 1722 by other rulers.

188

Bhopal had been a scene for film making in 1960, for a Bollywood Hindi movie, Naya Dor (New Times). A guide told the whole story. Jay and some students had an opportunity to sit in the same horse drawn Tanga, which was used in the movie, the Naya Dor (New Times).

CHITTORGARH in Rajasthan was the next city, Jay and his students visited. It was an old city built in circa 7th Century. The Fort was on a hill. It was the capital of Mewar, a part of Rajasthan now. This was spread over seven hundred acres of land. There was no other fort or palace like this in India or abroad. The school party enjoyed this place. A special arrangement had to be made for lunch, because there was no restaurant in the fort. It turned out to be tasty food and everyone enjoyed it and their visit to the fort.

The tourist attractions were Kalika Mata temple, Rani Kumbh palace, Meera temple, Rani Padmini palace, Ran Singh palace. Sita Mata wildlife sanctuary was also in the fort. Tulya Bhawani temple reflected the tradition and culture of Rajasthan State. It was also of a great architectural beauty.

Chittorgarh was famous for its history and past glory. Famous Maharajas ruled this city state. They were great warriors and fought wars against the invaders, especially the Mughals in the Middle Ages. The Ranas moved their capital to a new city, which

189

they built near the old one. White marble was used to construct the whole area. It was, therefore, known as the White Marble city of Udaipur.

In 1559, Maharaja Udai Singh founded the city of **UDAIPUR**. It was set around the artificial lakes. The City Palace, overlooking lake Pichola, was a complex of eleven palaces, courtyards, and gardens. This Palace was in the middle of Lake Pichola. The sight of the palace and the lake was extremely inquisitive. The Lake Palace was like an island. Fatah Sagar lake was connected to lake Pichola by a canal.

The other famous buildings were the Jag Mandir palace, Monsoon palace, Ahar Museum, which had a collection of earthen pottery. A metal figure of Buddha was also visible in the palace. Jagdish temple was dedicated to Lord Vishnu. Sahastra Bahu temple was also dedicated to Lord Vishnu. There was a Wax Museum within the vicinity. A Jain temple was located on the foothills of the Aravalli Mountain, 22 km from Udaipur. The palace was a three storied building.

Before returning to Somanpur, the group also visited **JAIPUR,** the capital of Rajasthan state. It had the Hawa mahal (the air palace) which was quite large, the town square with Johri Bazar (Jewellery market) and Bapu Bazar. Some students bought a few items from these markets. The food was good. But the party did not stay there for long, though they went to see the Amber palace, which was on a hill. It had a famous restaurant. Some students wanted to have an elephant ride. The tourist authorities had suspended such a ride as there had been an incident when an angry elephant killed a passerby.

It was, however, a wonderful experience of educational value to visit so many places in the company of a colleague and students from the school. All cities had their distinctive attributes and exclusivity. Some were quite old. Some had grown over the years. But none of them was a new modern town. These were all historical places. One thing was common in all of them. They had temples, Hindu temples, Buddhist temples and Jain Temples and of course there were mosques and Churches.

The whole educational tour lasted twenty days. Jay, his colleague, with students returned to the school city. After a few days, Jay submitted his report about the tour to the headmaster, who read and circulated it among the Parents-Teachers Association. There was a discussion among the students and at the Students' Union meeting.

<u>20</u>

The students who could not go on the Indian Railway supported tour to various places, were excited and wanted to go on a day trip, if not for a longer period. It was decided that all students and staff should go to Khetri, where the world's largest copper mines were being developed. There were other places to visit in the nearby vicinity, but Khetri was the nearest tourist attraction of educational significance.

This tour was to take place in the new year, a few months before the examinations. It would be a good change for students. They would feel fresh. The Journey was to commence by bus on a fixed day. The school group could leave early in the morning. The main aim of this tour was to get acquainted with the geological conditions of the place and to visit the world-famous copper mines. The students have read a great deal about the beauty of nature, the mountains, lakes, and the mines. When they learnt that they would witness all these things, their hearts leapt with joy. There was a great uproar about it. The journey took place by bus, on a Monday at 9.30 am. They went in search of the natural phenomenon, not through books but by viewing and seeing, with their own eyes.

The bus left early in the morning from the school premises and took speed. Outside the city, students and staff saw the beauty of nature. The trees and plants were scattering excellence and grace. The yellow mustard fields looked like streams of melted gold. There were small hills alongside the road, which was an amazing sight to watch. The mounds of sand on one side and hard stoned hill on the other side, looked gorgeous.

When the bus reached near the copper mines, the students burst in joy and laughter, expressing their happiness at the change of scenery. There were mud houses and millet plants near the mines. But these were no less attractive than the houses made with bricks and cement. The bus travelled along a hazardous route of hills and valleys.

The school bus stopped near the face of the mines, in a large courtyard surrounded by hills on all sides. The workers' quarters and the engineer's Office were nearby. The engineer provided a guide, who led the school party into the mines. The guide was holding a lamp to enter the dark and deep mines.

The students and teachers felt the heat, which was suffocating, because of lack of oxygen. Still the miners were digging and cracking the stones in such dangerous situations. That was the only way raw copper could be brought out of the mines and converted into refined copper in furnaces by melting and separating copper from the dust.

Jay thanked the miners for their hard work and the guide for taking his school group into the mines. When they came out of the mine, they all breathed fresh air. The guide suggested to the group that the Khetri mines, were the largest copper mines in the world. The work started in 1960, and it continued for many more years.

For Jay and his students, it was an experience. Everyone expressed sympathy for the mine workers including the guide and the engineer who lived in those conditions outside a village. About nine miles from the town of Khetri, there was the Ajit Sagar Bandh (dyke). There was a huge hill on one side and dense forest all around. A beautiful Shiva temple was on the Ajit Sagar Bandh, and a rest house for travellers to relax. The garden and the groves were attractive and provided fresh air.

The market inside the town was quite good. Students and teachers made their purchases and had their lunch there. The party then visited the Fort which was on a hill. There was no smooth road or path to climb. The students had to be careful in walking on the rough rocks because there were ditches on both sides of the footpath. The castle was in a dilapidated state, but the beautiful

194

sculpture survived. The paintings on the walls and ceilings showed the Rajasthani Art.

The castle was looked after by a caretaker who allowed Jay and his group to see the Sheesh Mahal and other apartments. The Mahal was made with glass, marble, and other materials. The artists had done an excellent job. Beautiful pictures were hung of the King holding the court proceedings. The fort was surrounded by a high wall to stop invaders entering the castle. Like many other parts of India, this city had been invaded in the Middle Ages. Safety and security arrangements had been made to stop attacks and invasions. There after the school group went to see the Amar Kund (pool), which was their last stop of this trip. The Amar Kund was situated at a short distance from the fort. The route was hazardous with a narrow footpath. Sometimes the view was frightening because of the deep valleys on one side and hills on the other side. There was a waterfall. Its water fell into a pond. It had been stated that there was always water in the pond, because of its continuous flow. It was a secluded place, but excellent and graceful with natural phenomenon.

After visiting all these places, everyone started to ascend, and they reached the plain ground. There was a saying that "it was on the mountains that the sounding cataract haunts like a passion and the gloomy wood was an unforgettable sight." After refreshment, students and teachers sat down in the bus and returned to Somanpur. It was a good adventure and a learning of great informative value and enrichment.

<u>21</u>

Jay could not go to his village for almost six months. After the summer months, his wife went from his parents' village to stay with her family. A few months later, she discovered that she was pregnant. In these circumstances, she was to return to her in-laws, where birth of the child would take place. Her parents did not inform Jay. Neither did his own parents let him know. His mother, nevertheless, sent his younger brother Vikram to bring back Reena, to the village.

Reena arrived at the family home, two months prior to the child's birth. When the time of the delivery came, it was just after midnight. There were only three people in the house, Jay's wife Reena, his mother Nanda, and a midwife. "It is a girl." The midwife pronounced." "She is very tiny and looks weak." "Nanda asked the midwife to take the baby girl to the fields, outside the village and discard her there," "Animals would eat her."

The mid-wife said, "but madam, she is breathing." "I know, she has not cried yet." Nanda said. "Put a barley seed in her mouth." "She would suffocate and stop breathing." There was no barley seed in the house. The midwife replied, "I cannot commit a sin and a crime by throwing away or suffocating a breathing and alive child." She refused to obey the instructions of Nanda. Thus, the baby survived. Otherwise, she would not have lived to see the world and the society.

(N.B. No wedding party came to a village in Central India, for twenty-five years, because baby girls were killed by the villagers at birth. In the desert state of Rajasthan, the villagers buried a baby girl in the sand immediately after her birth. After five hours of birth of the newborn, her parents decided to see the face of their baby. They went to the same spot and found that the baby was still alive. They brought her back home. Later she became an excellent dancer of world standard).

The next day, however, the male members of Jay's family, were informed of the child's birth. They were pleased to hear that Jay's wife Reena had given birth to a child. Jay's dad said that "This birth should be celebrated because the family has not had a new baby for almost a decade". He distributed sweets among his friends and relatives in the village.

He informed Reena's parents and other relatives about the newborn. Jay's elder brother Gautam wrote to him that he has become a father of a baby girl. Jay was delighted to know that. He, however, did not disclose it to his colleagues or celebrate the new birth. Jay sent his savings to his parents in the same month when the child was born. Vikram suggested to their mother that the child was lucky. "We have received money, (a symbol of Goddess Laxmi) albeit from Jay."

Nanda told him, "Lucky or not, take the money to your youngest sister's in-laws" and "ask them to buy a new sewing machine, which they do not have." "This would be a gift from us to them, for the birth of a child in our family."

During the summer holiday, Jay went to visit his family. When he reached home, he found the baby on the bare floor. Reena was cleaning dishes and the cooking ware. She herself was sitting on the floor. Jay's mother was standing in the room. She did not care to pick up the baby or to put her in a cot or on a mat. Jay picked up his daughter and held her in his arms. Jay's mother Nanda was surprised to see that. She slowly muttered that "She was expecting Jay to scold his wife Reena and would ask her to throw the baby away." Reena did not react.

Later Reena expressed to Jay that "he should take her and the baby with him to his school town." There was no complaint or expression of how they had been treated in his absence. She had faced some behaviour, which was worse than in jail or with a slave. It was quite common in Indian villages that mothers with newborn babies were provided milk and other nourishing food. So that the new mother could breast feed the child, who would not be able to digest cow milk or any other food.

Jay's mother did not do that. She provided Reena, butter milk (Chhachh), in a small cup, with a small piece of jaggery. It did not produce any milk because it was cream less and had no nutrition. There was no provision for any other food supplement for her. Nanda wanted the baby to die of starvation and lack of nourishment. The baby did not like her mother's milk, because it was sour. Consequently, she used to cry with hunger.

An elderly village lady suggested to Nanda that Reena should not be provided butter milk. It was bad and harmful for both the new baby and the mother. Jay's mother did not accept that. "She said that she was doing the right thing by supplying a piece of jaggery every day with butter milk, (Chhachh)." "She was not going to buy cow milk and spend money on her daughter-in-law and her baby."

Nanda did not realize that the baby was her granddaughter. Jay's father, however, did not like the baby crying all the time. He was not aware of the reason and could not even imagine that the child was not being properly fed and was being starved. He took the child to Doctor's surgery every week. The doctor could not diagnose the reason for the child crying.

At the end of summer holiday, Jay took his wife and daughter with him to his school town Somanpur. There his wife and daughter were taken to the local hospital, which was recently built. New and young doctors were appointed along with the experienced staff. At that hospital, a young doctor examined the baby and tested Reena's breast milk. He discovered that the breast milk was sour and that was the reason, the baby would not suck her mother's milk.

The Doctor did not prescribe any medicine, but Reena was advised to change her food habits. She and the baby both changed their nutriment. Reena started to drink cow milk and ate sustenance food, including green vegetables and fruits. Their lives improved and they both became normal. The child stopped crying and did not see the doctor again for a long time. They were a happy family. Reena made new friends in the town. Children from the nearby house used to come to play with the baby. Since Jay was a teacher, he had lots of books at home. His baby daughter started to look at the books and play with them. Always holding a small book in her hand. Jay returned to his routine. Nothing fascinating happened in the next few months.

There were no places of cultural importance in that town, where Jay could take his family to visit. Even the shops were small and there was no shopping Centre there. It had no parks or museum either. The family mostly stayed at home or visited friends, and friends visited them.

His school and the adjacent college organized a cinema show and screened Hindi films, in the college hall, every week. Jay used to take his family to watch films made in the 1950s and early 1960s. They liked several of them which were immensely popular in the country. Some films were popular in South Asia, the Soviet Union, the Caribbeans, the Middle East, Eastern Europe, China, Türkiye, and Afghanistan.

After watching many Hindi films, Jay became curious and wanted to find out about the Indian film industry. It was an industry because many people worked in it, actors, directors, make up people, assistants, script writers, dialogue writers, song writers and singers, music composers, music directors, marketing personnel and in many other related fields like dress makers and jewellery suppliers. He discovered that the Indian Film industry was as old as any other film producing countries in the world.

In India, the first film was made in 1898. The early films were silent films. In 1912, Dadasaheb Torne made the Marathi film

202

"Shree Pundalik". In 1913, Dadasaheb Palkhe produced "Raja Harish Chandra" in Marathi and Hindi. He was considered the pioneer of the Indian Cinema. These films were produced in Mumbai (Bombay). Initially, women did not work in films. Men used to play the role of women, and they wore the women's clothes. These were all silent movies.

Talkies came in 1930. Films started to be made in many Indian languages including Hindi, Bangla, Marathi, Tamil, Telugu, Malayalam, Kannada, and Punjabi. Mumbai (Bombay) became the Centre for Hindi films. In later years this was to become Bollywood and the movies were called Bollywood Films. Half of all the films were, however, made in the South, especially in Madras (now Chennai) and Hyderabad.

The Indian Film Industry was recognized as the Second largest in the world, after the Hollywood. The Indian film industry progressed through the 1960s and 1970s. By 1986, it produced 833 films annually. India became the largest producer of films in the world. In 1996, there were six hundred million viewers, and 3.6 billion tickets were sold around the world.

Emphasis was also laid on music and dance. Regional and local songs and folk dances were represented through the films. Later international influence emerged on music. The western dances were seen in Hindi movies. Various locations were sought to make films. In India, the principal areas were Manali, Shimla, Sri Nagar, Darjeeling, Kodai Kanal, and Amritsar. Udaipur, Jaipur, Jodhpur, Jaisalmer, Delhi, Goa, Puducherry (Pondicherry), and Kerala were also preferred sites.

Some producers looked for foreign locations. Scotland and London were selected in the United Kingdom. Switzerland and Hungary were popular in Europe, depending on the need of the time.

There were numerous heroes and heroines from time to time. Some liked playing romantic roles, others liked and were suited for tragedies, while some others became popular for comedies and comic parts. There were countless actors over the course of a period, who were appreciated and liked by the public. One actor could play double, the role of siblings. Some functioned as father as well as a son in the same movie. There were thousands of good actors. The Indian Film Industry employed 2 million people in different roles at the beginning of the 21st Century.

The Indian government established a Films Division in 1946 and produced two hundred short documentaries on rural and urban life of people. These documentaries were released in eighteen languages. The central government of India also took interest in Films and provided the required facilities. It also subjected foreign exchange to purchase instruments and to send actors for training abroad.

The films represented the Indian culture. In the 21st Century, another feature emerged in Bollywood. It expanded and became popular with the ownership of television by families. Apart from big screens, small screens entertained and overwhelmed people. These programmes had their own actors.

They were half hourly dramas based on social customs and prevailing social circumstances. These were also known as family dramas. Family problems and changing of settings were considered and acted upon, reflecting the drawbacks, superstitions, and conflict in families.

The family structure has not changed due to economic and financial constraints. The domination by the elders has continued. Young people and their aspirations were not being taken into consideration. As crime has increased and has become known, various initiatives had been taken on the ongoing criminal activities. These included the Police and Detective application and looking for forensic expertise. There were programmes related to police action on criminal elements.

Once Jay's school organized a play performed by students. Jay took his family to see the play. His school was a boys' school. In the play, however, there was a role for a girl. Not many boys could play the role of a girl. The Secretary of the School Cultural Association performed that role. For costume, Jay sought the help of some of his ex-students, who arranged clothes from their own houses by borrowing from their female family members.

The rehearsal for the play, was mostly conducted by the headmaster, who was interested in dramatics. The students asked a local man to perform the Bharatnatyam dance. He did a superb job but continued to perform for longer than the allocated time. The story of the play revolved around a boy and a girl, who liked each other but society would not allow them to live together or get married as they came from different communities. The girl's brother advised the boy to take his sister away and move to live in another city.

Some comedy scenes were added, which boosted the entertainment. The acting by the participants was superb. The audience liked and appreciated it. The acting of the Hero was so good, people started to suggest that he should join the Indian film industry in Mumbai (Bombay). Jay kept an eye on all the activities. He himself gave a commentary and explained the theme of the play. A professional artist was hired to help with the decoration of the stage.

In Somanpur, there were quite a few old buildings, which were beautiful and had Rajasthani paintings on the walls and artistic designs on ceilings. Rich families lived in these big houses which were owned by businesspeople who had their businesses in large cities like Delhi, Mumbai (Bombay), and Calcutta. Jay and his family, however, continued to live in a small flat in a peaceful locality. The land lady was exceedingly kind and looked after Jay's family. Her grandchildren used to come to play with his daughter. The land lady often provided yogurt to his family. She never charged any money for that.

<u>22</u>

After about seven months since Jay and his family came from the village, his younger brother Vikram came to visit them. He was surprised to see the way Jay, Reena and their baby daughter lived in a quiet environment, with good friends and good people in proximity. There was a happy encompassment in the house. They cooked the right but simple vegetarian food. They ate clean nourishing meals. Jay bought fresh cow milk every day from the next-door resident who kept cows and sold milk.

Vikram expressed the view that he had visited other brothers, and he himself lived with parents in the village, "he has not witnessed such a satisfaction as at Jay's place". He (Jay) has earned respect at the school because of his hard work and social attainment. His colleagues and students admired him for his contribution to school life and the school community.

During his stay with Jay, his younger brother Vikram stated that Nakul's friend, "Naresh had been granted a work visa by the British government. He was planning to go to the United Kingdom in April of that year." Jay was not acquainted with Naresh. He had heard that he (Naresh) was not a clever man. He was a cunning person, who smiled from outside. It was difficult to know him and assess his personality. The standpoint Jay had heard about him was not particularly impressive.

He had a job with Jay's brother at an office in New Delhi. But he also worked in other places during duty hours. He used to ask people for money, even though he would have some in his own pocket. He would offer it to other people, even when they did not ask for it. He would ask his colleagues to lend him money. Sometimes he put his hand in their pocket and took money out and lent it to his other friends or colleagues. He never imparted his own money to anyone at any time. Still, he behaved like a helpful and caring person.

Anyway, what interested Jay, was the method Naresh received his visa? Did he have any special qualifications or a sponsorship from the United Kingdom? Vikram told him that his employment voucher was for migration from India to Britain. No conditions were attached. This aroused a curiosity in him. He thought that one day he would like to go abroad, possibly to Britain, because he knew English language which could facilitate him to adjust in a new country.

In the short run, however, Jay wanted to move to live and teach in Delhi. An opportunity became available within a month, when a

209

temporary teacher's vacancy emerged at Nitin's school in old Delhi. A permanent teacher had taken three months' leave to prepare for and take his examination. It was a temporary position for three months.

There would, however, be three new teachers' vacancies in the next academic year. The school was expanding its student numbers and classes. With Jay's experience of teaching at that school, he would certainly be made permanent. He, however, would not be paid for the summer holiday. Jay considered the position very carefully. There were advantages and disadvantages in this change.

He would have to give up his permanent teaching job in Somanpur, and would not be paid, when school closes for the summer holiday. He had no time to give three months' notice to his current school. He would, therefore, have to pay three months' salary to the school in Somanpur. It was impossible to take a decision without more information. He decided to go to Delhi to discuss the details with the school authorities, and members of the family there.

In Delhi, he taught for a whole week at that school. The school authorities offered him a temporary position as a teacher. Over the weekend, he returned to his old school in Rajasthan. He discussed it with his wife Reena who expressed no opinion. She was expecting their second child.

Jay felt that there would be relatives in Delhi, to look after her in her pregnancy and at the time of childbirth. Though his landlady attempted to persuade them, not move to a new place at that time. She would look after Reena, like her own daughter. She had done so in the past when another teacher lived in the flat a few years earlier and they had a new child. Jay, however, decided to grasp this opportunity to teach in Delhi.

Without giving three months' notice (required by his school), he left Somanpur. Of course, he went to see the headmaster and other colleagues and returned the library books. He paid all the bills in advance and decided to pay three months' salary in place of notice, required by the school. He did really ask his headmaster whether he could take three months' leave without pay, to try out at a Delhi school. He refused to help.

Jay packed his belongings and left for Delhi with his family. Temporarily, they stayed with his brother Nakul. Jay started to go to the new school by train. The journey was time-consuming. The trains were always packed and crowded. He, however, had no choice but to travel by train. His wife and daughter stayed at Nakul's house. Reena had to do the domestic work at his place.

Even though she was to give birth to a child in a few days' time. She had no time to relax and rest.

After six weeks, Naresh was to depart for London in the United Kingdom. He resigned from his job and was looking for someone to take over his private tuition, which he provided to students who attended English medium schools. He helped them with their homework. Naresh felt that only Jay could teach through English medium, among all the people he knew.

He asked Nakul, if Jay would be interested in taking over his work in providing private tuition to these students. Jay went to visit the children at their houses and started to assist them with their homework. He discovered that Naresh did not properly support the children. They feared his tall stature. They often kept quiet, even in their own homes. Naresh was not a trained or qualified teacher. He worked in an office and had no knowledge of child psychology or child behaviour and how to be accessible to children.

Nevertheless, Jay started to teach them because he needed money at that time. He was not to be paid any salary by the school for summertime. In one sense he lost three months summer pay and had to pay back three months' salary to his old school. He managed

The Quest to Succeed

to do all that without any help from the family. He paid in full for his family's residence and food, to Nakul.

Jay was busy during the summer period. He not only took over Naresh's private teaching, but he also agreed to do two more hours of tuition in other locations. He used to travel from one site to another area in the summer heat of old Delhi. He continued to work hard, despite the hot and scorching weather.

During the summer period, he sent his wife and children to live with Reena's parents in the village, about fifty miles north of Delhi. The village climate was comparatively cool because of the nearness of the Himalaya Mountain ranges. Her parents and brothers were delighted to have them in their house. They looked after them without any payment. The village environment was also good for their children, with an open courtyard and cool breeze. They avoided the hot temperature of Delhi.

Jay continued to live with Nakul and paid all his earnings to him rather than just for his food and lodge. He felt that no one should question him that he lived with his elder brother, without proper payment. Moreover, he did not know how much he should pay. It was for Nakul to work out the expenses for one person. He should not have taken all his emolument, which Jay realized for the expenses of his family.

At that time, he was living on his own as a single person at Nakul's house. Nakul as a gluttonous man, was glad to take money from anyone, whether he deserved it or not. After the summer break, when the school opened for the new session, Jay was evaluated by the school authorities and was offered a permanent position.

His teaching experience and work at the school facilitated his appointment. On receiving full-time employment at the school in Delhi, he gave up part of the private teaching and kept only three hours of tutoring in three different houses. He still needed the money in order to start a life in Delhi, the capital city of India.

During the vacation, though, he felt lonely. He did not visit his family at his in-laws, or his own parents in the village. In the autumn, he first went to see his mother and father. In the third week of the month, during the school break, he went to his in-laws' village and brought his family back to Delhi. After staying for a few more days with Nakul, he rented a flat, in the nearby locality and started to live a family life with his wife and two children.

When they moved to the new place in North-East-Delhi, Jay did not have much money left in his pocket because he used to pay all his proceeds to Nakul. It was middle of the month. The rent was forty rupees (about three British pounds) a month. He had only

214

twenty rupees with him, which he paid as a deposit to the landlady who accepted it.

She allowed him and his family to move into the flat. Reena gave him money, with which he bought basic food supplies for a few days. Jay did not have a bed or any other furniture. They all slept on the floor. Residents in the house noticed that the young children were sleeping on the bare floor. They gave Reena a small bed for the children to sleep on.

A few days later, Jay received his salary and paid full rent to the landlady for the whole month and one month's deposit, which was customary in Delhi at that time. He bought food supplies and a bed. Jay could not work out why Nakul was taking all his money, even though his income was more than his salary in Rajasthan, where he lived with his wife and daughter and met all the expenses and had money left with him at the end of the month.

Later Jay discovered that there was another family in the same situation, where a younger brother lived with his elder brother who was, however, charging only ten rupees for the room and fifteen rupees for food of his younger brother. Twenty-five rupees in total. Jay was paying ten times of that, because of his ignorance and Nakul's rapacity, greed, and acquisitiveness. Still, Nakul told a neighbour that Jay was very stubborn, who took his own decisions without consulting him. He wanted Jay to continue to provide his earnings to him and did not realize that Jay had his family's expenses to meet.

In the summer period when Jay's family was at Reena's parental house, he was receiving all his money. Indeed, when Jay rented his own flat, Nakul sent a relative to borrow money of Jay's. This relative returned the money to Nakul who did not pay back to Jay. Such a greedy and money minded person could not be found everywhere.

Jay noticed that Nakul had some criminal elements in his character. He bullied him when he was only a nine-year-old child and took his snack money of him. He behaved like an extortionist. He took all his earnings and did not leave any rupees for clothes or shoes or to meet an urgent demand and finally he attempted to grab Jay's house, when they both were grown up and had become granddads. He remained fabulist and prevaricator to the end. He fabricated stories about attempted burglary and breaking in at Jay's house. Often argued that he had achieved a great deal. He does not deserve it or need the materialistic possessions even when these were necessaries and essentials for daily consumption.

Naresh migrated to the United Kingdom in the spring. After a few months, he wrote to his friend Nakul that he liked the new country where he slept on money. Even though he was working as an unskilled labourer and earned only about ten pounds a week in London. He adhered to showing off and exaggeration. His expenses were meagre. His family was still living in India with his wife's brother.

He attempted to encourage Nakul to migrate to England. Nakul was not interested in leaving India or his family, even for a short period. Moreover, immigrants had to face all kinds of problems. He was not a person who could face conundrums and work hard. He had sustained a comfortable living even when he had to lie to parents or cheat his siblings.

A few months later but before the end of his first year in England, Naresh wrote to Nakul that he should ask Jay whether he would like to move to live in Britain because there was a demand for teachers in London and other parts of the country. He argued that Jay would get a visa, because at that time, the United Kingdom government was issuing Visas to Graduate professionals. Nakul spoke about Naresh's letter to Jay who did not pay any attention to this proposition. He was trying to settle down in his new teaching job in Delhi.

When the persuasion came repeatedly, he felt that there was no harm in making an application for a visa to the British High

Commission in New Delhi. There was no fee for the visa application. The education certificates and teaching experience certificates were to be put forward with the immigration form. Jay had a letter from his old school that he had more than three years teaching experience. He, therefore, put forward his migration application forms personally at the British High Commission in New Delhi.

Of course, Nakul went with him to ensure that he did not back down or throw away the forms. Jay did not hope that he would get a visa. Secondly, he could decide later whether he should go to England. He would have a choice to live in Delhi or move to live in the United Kingdom. Within six weeks, however, Jay received a letter from the British High Commission that his visa application had been successful. The letter stated that "the work visa for which you applied has been acquired at the Commission. Please bring your passport to collect it."

For many days, Jay did not tell anyone that he had received a letter regarding a visa to go abroad. The only people who saw the letter were his wife and his brother Nakul, who used to come to his house to eat food because his family had gone out of Delhi, to stay with his wife's relatives during the summer holiday. Nakul did not pay

218

a penny for the food he received three times a day for twenty-one days. Jay always paid for his food whenever he stayed with him.

Nevertheless, Jay had to tell his relatives in Delhi and the village, and colleagues at the school that he had received a visa to migrate to Britain, but no decision had yet been concluded. His mother was not happy with this news. On hearing that Jay was planning to leave the country, she came to Delhi from the village and angrily told Jay that "he should make proper arrangements for his wife and children. He should not leave them as burden on her and the family."

Jay never wanted to put strain on anybody or make his wife and young children financial or social responsibility for others. Only a few months earlier, someone had rightly said, that "Jay was the most misunderstood person around." He had paid back all the money to his parents, that they spent on his education including expenses on his Teacher's Training.

He was not going to make his young family any trouble for them. He had really expected such a reaction from his family, especially his mother. He had made enough savings for his family for the next three months to live in Delhi, and then he would send money from London. If he did not like the new place, he would return to Delhi and look after them in India.

After careful consideration, he decided to relocate to Britain in order to obtain some experience of a European country and the society. He knew a few people who had gone to live in England. Jay asked a relative to help him in obtaining a passport because in 1960s, the Indian government did not issue passport easily. Several guarantees were required and someone with an asset of ten thousand rupees should stand a security. None of Jay's relatives were rich enough to stand a guarantor for ten thousand rupees.

Jay asked a distant relative to enquire if his employer would stand a paper surety. No money was to be deposited at a bank. Jay's relative introduced him to his rich boss who agreed to help him. Jay's sojourn then started. He used to visit this rich man every day, during the summer months. When Jay visited him at his house, he suggested that he would go to the land registry one day.

He used to tell stories that he himself wanted to go to London in 1950s. He, however, laid a condition on Jay for the guarantee. "On reaching London, he (Jay) would send him a new ford car". Finally, the day arrived when they were ready and willing to proceed to the Land Registry, where they acquired an ownership certificate. He (the relative's employer) was, nonetheless, furious to see the document.

The Ownership Certificate showed that he was insolvent for up to ten thousand rupees only. This was the only condition for a warranter. He was a very rich man and owned many properties in north-east Delhi and thought that his abundance and affluence would be reflected in the certificate. On receiving his signature as an underwriter and a copy of the ownership certificate from the Registry, Jay submitted his passport application form to the Indian authorities.

He received his passport by post within a fortnight. Jay's relatives were still not keen with his decision to go abroad. They continued to ask him questions, "how would you pay for your flight"? "Who would look after your little family in your absence"? Jay and his family were living in a small flat which they rented a year earlier, when he was employed as a full-time permanent teacher in Delhi. He was not obliged to answer any of these questions. He made his own arrangement for the family.

In the autumn, he decided to fly to a country, distant across the seas, of which he knew little except the language. He could not visualize at that time, what was in store in England for him, because he did not have a relative or friend there. "It was a leap in the dark, also a quest to succeed". It was a repetition of the same circumstances, when he left his village school as a child or when

221

he resigned from his school in Rajasthan, without considering the repercussions of his decision and without proper planning.

He had taken many chances without forbearing the ramification of his actions. He had, however, discussed with his father-in-law, who offered to look after Reena and the children for three months. There was a marriage in his family as his youngest daughter was getting married soon. This had been a useful and helpful arrangement for Jay's young family.

23

Jay had been interested to go abroad for a long time. He thought of it, when he was fourteen years old and was studying at the Secondary school. One day his class colleague and friend Shafique took him to his house, where his father asked Jay, "what was he going to do after completing his education"? At the tender age of fourteen, he had not considered or decided his future.

As a villager, he did not think of his distant future. Then he (the friends' father) said, that Shafique would go the United States to study Law and would settle down there, because in India there would be less opportunities for Muslims. Jay did not conjecture all that, but it created a curiosity in his mind that it would be good to study in an advanced country.

When the real time arrived for Jay to go to the United Kingdom, he felt that it was unpremeditated. "He borrowed two thousand rupees for his air ticket and flew to London in the autumn, leaving his gentle wife and innocent children on their own to face their problems, as he was to struggle and solve his enigma in a strange land".

His children were noticeably young. They did not know what was happening around them. His wife suggested that they should all go together but Jay could not borrow more money. He had given his four years savings to his parents and to his brother Nakul. He thought that he paid all his savings to others, when he himself could not borrow fifteen rupees for his High School Examination fee, only a few years earlier. Who would lend him five thousand rupees for his family to fly out to the United Kingdom?

On reaching London, however, he was to stay with Naresh. Nakul had discussed for this arrangement. Jay had read one of Naresh's letters to Nakul. He reached the conclusion that Naresh was not his type of a person because he had unusual ways of thinking. He expressed his views to Nitin. Initially, however, he was prepared to stay with Naresh in London.

When he left for England, Jay's family remained at the same flat in Delhi, where they were living with him. His brother Gautam did not like the idea of them living on their own, when they had an extended family. They were, therefore, moved to Nakul's place which was nearby. Reena, however, had no desire to stay there. This was an erroneous decision and inequitable action. If Gautam took them to his house, people would have understood it, but to leave Jay's family at Nakul's place, where they did not want to live, could not be accepted.

Reena did not speak to Gautam because he was Jay's elder brother. She observed a purdah (veil). She did not oppose Gautam and left the flat with him. The Children were too young and had not yet started to speak. After, ten days of staying at Nakul's house, Reena and children went to live with her parents in the village, where he had a big house and Reena herself grew up there.

In London, Naresh came to receive Jay at the Heathrow airport. He said that he was delighted to see him as a friend's brother. "I would treat you as my own younger brother here". "I must tell you that there was not many Hindi speaking people in London". "I am pleased to see you". He continued, that most of the Indians, "who live in the United Kingdom, were either Punjabi speaking or Gujrati speaking."

"Many Punjabi soldiers were in the British Indian army during the imperialist rule". "They fought for Britain during the Second World War. They were encouraged to emigrate to Britain." A few old British soldiers went to Punjab to recruit them. He stressed that "there was a shortage of factory workers" at that time. The British soldiers knew that Indians were faithful and extremely hard working.

Naresh showed his knowledge and stressed that "the Gujrati Indians came from East Africa, where they were shop keepers, businessman and government employees, working for the colonial administration there." "They were given British passports and British citizenship in order to ensure the supply of labour for Britain". It was the British government policy.

However, when the British passport holder Indians came to Britain, the British people resented them. Still the Indians from East Africa were allowed to settle in different cities in Britain. They used their experience and expertise to adjust in the new country. "They opened retail shops in England." "At one stage they owned sixty percent of retail trade in the United Kingdom and also became small post office owners." "They worked hard and long hours." "The entire family helped at the shop, which opened from 6am to 10pm".

Naresh asked Jay to stay with him as he had free accommodation himself. He, nevertheless, told him that no one helped anybody in London. He would have to find his own way including a job. Jay knew nothing about the British way of life or the British system. Naresh said to him that he should look for a job in a factory. He maintained that "although you have been a visa as a teacher, no one would like you to teach their children in Britain." "Your qualifications have helped you to obtain a work visa, but the British want you to work in a factory."

Jay could not make out, why was he talking like that on his first day in London? In his letters to Nakul, he had expressed the view that he was happy and earning a lot of money. He had an excellent job and so on. Next morning on Saturday, Naresh introduced him to a couple of his friends who came to visit him. He asked them to convince Jay that he would not get a teaching job in England.

He had been given a visa to work in a factory. One of his friends tried to suggest to Naresh that Jay looked smart, and he would get a job in an office, if not as a teacher straight away. Naresh was not ready to accept that and insisted on his views.

Jay set out in search of a job on Monday morning. After three enquiries he was offered a job and was asked, by the Manager of the company, to get a National Insurance Card from the government office. He gave him the office address, where Jay went with his passport and work visa. He was given the National Insurance Card without delay.

Jay started to earn his living the next day or within four days (including the weekend) of his landing in London. On the second Saturday of Jay's life in London, Naresh took him to the market to do shopping. Jay wanted to pay for bread and other essentials. He had three pounds in his pocket which he brought from India.

Naresh, nonetheless, insisted that he should pay for television rental which was thirty shillings (one pound and fifty pence) and said, that "you should watch television programmes and News." Jay paid the money for Naresh's television rent. He, however, moved out of his house within the next few days and did not watch any programmes on his television at his house.

Jay could not see Nitin before leaving Delhi to fly out to London. He, therefore, wrote a letter to him and explained the situation and how he decided to emigrate to Britain. After reading Bose's letter to Nehru at his degree college, he wanted to write a long letter to Nitin. From London he wrote, "it is long, since I promised to narrate my experiences and observations in detail."

"There had, however, been very few occasions in my life, which have left a permanent impact on my mind." "Certainly, my coming to England brought changes in my living. The roots of this go back to January of the previous year, when I was fast asleep at my flat in Somanpur, Rajasthan. I heard a knock at the door at 4 am. This woke me up. I opened the door and was astonished to see my younger brother Vikram standing there with a colleague of mine."

"While I was pleased with his presence, I was also surprised to see him there at that hour. This was unexpected and I had not been informed about his plan to visit us." "We all went to sleep but started to talk in the morning. During our conversation, it emerged that an acquaintance, in New Delhi, was going to England in April." "He had been granted a work visa by the British government". "I became curious and thought that if I had an opportunity, I would like to go abroad one day." Nitin did not reply promptly.

Jay did not receive any letter from India for quite a few days. He was trying to adapt in London. He did not know the date, when his wife and children went to live with Reena's parents. Naresh heard of this situation. He did not like it. He said to Jay that "you should know the where-about and welfare of your family." "Your brother should have informed you, when they left Delhi."

Naresh himself wrote to Nakul, who was his friend that "he (Nakul) was mature enough and clever enough to write that Jay's family had gone to stay with their maternal grandparents". Nonetheless, Reena and the children went to her father's village to attend a family wedding. It was customary in India that family members (even married) used to stay in the family house. They could arrive earlier than needed and would stay much longer, even when the wedding ceremony was over. It was not out of the ordinary.

Naresh, however, wanted to interfere in Jay's family affairs and showed that he was a caring and a family man himself. Nakul did not like anyone questioning him. He did not reply to Naresh's letter. He wrote to Jay that "he had prompted Naresh to write to him. If he was so concerned and worried about his children, why did he go to London"?

Jay could not comprehend, why Nakul was so upset on a simple questioning by his own friend. He himself had encouraged him to emigrate to Britain. He did not want to get involved in any argument and let the matter slip. He did not care about his brother's views and behaviour. This became his nature, not to spend time on other people's thoughts and reactions.

Moreover, Naresh wanted his friend Nakul to migrate to Britain, but it was Jay who took a chance to relocate himself to a new Country. Naresh was surprised that Jay had received a visa, because he did not expect him to apply, what to say of receiving it. He said to Jay that he was simply "teasing you and thought that you were a lazy man and would not try to immigrate to Britain, where Indians had to work hard, and they were discriminated, because of the British Empire in India". Some British people carried the imperialist tag and looked down upon Indians.

After moving out of Naresh's place to another part of London, Jay continued to visit him. One day, they both were sitting near a fireplace in the front room of his house. He (Naresh) revealed that "when you arrived in London, and stayed with him, you were in deep sleep after day's hard work." "I wanted to suffocate you with a pillow and throw you into a furnace to which he had access."

Naresh's workplace used coal for central heating which was done through a furnace. He could easily have disposed-of Jay's body. He, however, realized that Jay had already informed his family in India, that he had reached London safely, and was received at the Heathrow, airport by Naresh. He further told Jay that "if there was an enquiry from your family, they would have questioned him about you, especially when they would not receive any letters from you."

Jay could not believe what he had just heard. Only a few days earlier, on his arrival at the Heathrow airport, Naresh told him that he was glad to see him as a Hindi speaking person who were scarce in London. While Jay feared Naresh, that he could lose his sense at any time, he calmly said, "you are not criminal minded, so you

231

could not have committed a murder." He ignored the entire conversation.

He was, however, careful in the future. Jay did not ask Naresh, for any explanation, "why did he think so and why did he want to murder me"? I have a young family to look after and had just moved to live in a new country", on his urging and persistence. Jay forgot the entire episode.

It was not until about twenty-five years later that he recalled the incident and told a dear friend Puneet, who was a Senior Lecturer in Law at the University, where they both taught. They were having tea in the canteen, sitting near a window. Jay disclosed of the murder plot by Naresh. Puneet said, "why did he want to do that"? "He would like to talk to this man Naresh and ask him why did he think of killing Jay"? It was not possible for Puneet to ask anything of Naresh because he had moved out of London.

When he became bored of eating bread and potatoes, Jay bought a hot plat (tawa) to make chapatis and other utensils needed. Naresh discovered of Jay's purchases and questioned him "why did you spend money on such things?" He did not realize that Jay spent his own money on the items he needed to make food.

In the new year, Jay started an external degree course of the University of London. After a couple of months, he registered at the University Senate House and paid a registration fee. He was already attending evening classes at a local college. For examination, however, the students were required to register at the Senate House. Otherwise, they would not be able to take their examinations.

Naresh did not like that either. He wanted Jay to attend college only to tell his relatives in India that he was studying. He should not take any examination or obtain a qualification. He should not spend money on registration or on books. He asked Jay to borrow books of the library. There was no need to purchase books. Libraries were incredibly good in London. Every Borough had many libraries in their boundaries.

The money that Jay earned should be given to him, when Naresh had no role in his life. He simply stayed with him for a few days, on his arrival in London. He paid for his television rental. Naresh wanted to control him, his activities, and his life. He wanted to dominate Jay by remaining in close touch, long distance, or remotely. Once Naresh's wife told Jay that they know all about him. He watched, Germany V England soccer game at a neighbour's place. Jay did not have a television in those days.

Naresh used to find fault and criticize every decision of Jay's. Even regarding his job, writing letters to friends and family. "Why did you write so quickly"? "Why did you call him brother when he was not related to you"? He wanted to become Jay's elder brother, consultant, and advisor. Sometimes he called him, 'immature,' 'unable to take right decisions at the right time'. On the contrary, Jay found Naresh playing – "big brother, psycho, brute, bossy and bully."

Yet, Naresh continued to ask Jay for money. Whenever they went out on a bus or by train, Jay paid his fare, but he also expected him to pay bus fare for his friends, if they were accompanying them. Jay did not like that. He refused to comply. Naresh once said, "you should learn something." What was that something? He did not explain but expected Jay to spend money on him and his friends.

Once Jay enquired of Naresh, whether he would help him financially in his need at some stage. He refused and said that he did not have any cash available in his bank or at home. Yet, a few months later he again asked Jay to lend him a lot of money.

Jay discussed about such "money asking" with his colleagues and friends at his office, who warned him that there were people who exploited innocent man, for their advantages but would not help in other's requirement. "An experienced man, Param Sigh told him to be careful and not to lend your money to any-one". He said,

"You would not be able do anything and possibly lose time and money and might be put under an emotional pressure."

Jay decided not to lend any more money in the future to Naresh who, however, could not comprehend that he should not ask for finance. We all earn to pay our bills and meet our family expenditure or save for unforeseen circumstances. Whenever, Jay visited Naresh, he continued to ask for funds and often said that "your family would not be able to join you without a house." "You cannot buy a house." "You should, therefore, lend me all your savings, I would buy a house, where you could live in a room on nominal rent."

Naresh's demand for cash looked like a stuck gramophone sound, which repeated the same tune. Whenever Jay met him, he spoke the same words in the same tone and same stature. Naresh's wife did really suggest that rather than asking Jay to lend him his savings, he should help him so that his family could join him from India.

Naresh shouted at his wife and scolded her, "what would we gain by helping him." "He is a fool and would give us money as he has done in the past." Naresh continued to tell his wife that "we would have properties in this country without investing our resources."

235

Jay did really lend Naresh money three times during his first eight months, since arriving in London.

Jay did not like being asked for money on every stopover. He discontinued to visit Naresh. He really moved to live in another part of London but near an underground station, so he could travel to his office by tube. Naresh constantly phoned him. Whenever Jay picked up the phone, Naresh's first words would be, "are you still alive"? This annoyed him. What was he trying to do? "Why did he behave like that"? He could not work out, except that he was not a normal social being.

Despite Jay's non-interest in Naresh, he arrived at Jay's place on a Saturday morning and asked him to accompany him to see one of his friends whom Jay also knew. He said to him that "you have also been invited for lunch by this friend." Jay had commitment on that day. Still, he followed him to his friend's house. Naresh's friend did not give an impression, that Jay had been invited by them for lunch. Although this friend of Naresh's smiled, which was not very welcoming. He could not grasp why did Naresh lie to him?

They had simple vegetarian Indian lunch. After lunch, everyone sat down. Naresh asked Jay "to give all his savings to his friend on his guarantee." Jay replied wow, "that was an expensive lunch." "To give all the savings for two chapatis." Naresh's friend said, "you do not have to pay anything." He was thinking of a payment for a friendly lunch at his house. Jay replied that "he was not going to do anything like that any way."

He, nonetheless, understood, what Naresh was up to. But his friend could not comprehend, Naresh's thinking. Jay was not surprized but felt that this man would never apprehend a basic refusal. He had very feeble I.Q. (intelligence quotient"). Naresh still tried to argue that it was in his (Jay's) interest to lend money to his friend. When Jay realized, Naresh's bad manners, he retorted to him, "what is your guarantee"? "You do not have a property. You live in a Council house. You cannot put that house as a guarantee." "You do not have any fixed deposit account at a bank, otherwise you would not have asked me for money"?

Naresh's vanity was scorched, when Jay refused to lend finances to his friend and questioned him about his vulnerability to stand as a guarantor. Jay believed that the simple words of an ordinary employee with an earning of seventeen pounds a week were not sufficient for a four hundred pounds loan in the 1960s.

Naresh thought that "he had a persuasive power and would be able to convince Jay that it was for his good that he should give all his savings to his friend." Furthermore, he also believed that Jay

237

would not refuse to lend money in the presence of a friend and his wife. There were only four people in that room at that time.

With Naresh's vanity hurt, he decided to break all connections with Jay and maintained that if he could not be of help to him and to his friends for funds, he (Jay) was of no use to him. He was, therefore, not worthy of a friendship. His friendship was based on selfish interests for financial position. Jay questioned him about his earning situation as he wanted to become a surety for his friend.

Jay had other priorities. He bluntly refused to give his money to anyone. He conceived the idea that if his family could not come to the United Kingdom, he would return to India. However, if his family joined him in London, he would use his savings to finance a deposit in order to purchase a house or a flat. His own family's welfare was paramount to him.

<u>24</u>

Naresh, nonetheless, continued to argue and attempted to convince Jay that he would not be able to buy a house in London. "You would not be able to obtain a mortgage because you have not lived in the UK, long enough to qualify for a house loan." "If you returned to India, you would not obtain a job because of high unemployment." He had all the negativities.

Jay decided not to argue with him because he would not discern or grasp, what was he trying to communicate? Within a few days of this episode, Jay discovered that Nakul had not told him that his wife and children had received their Passport from the Indian government, four and a half months earlier. He had provided this information to his friend Naresh, who did not apprise Jay about their passport."

Jay found it a strange way of communication, because Nakul did not illuminate of the receipt of his wife's passport, whereas he communicated to his friend who kept the message secret and still attempted to obtain money for his friend in London. Nakul wanted Jay to send some more money as if his family was a hostage. Jay had already sent enough money for their air fare and necessary purchases.

Naresh wanted money from Jay, so he could coerce him, and force him to continue to live as a single person in England. His wife and children would be living in India. A divided family. Jay, nevertheless, worked out the conspiracy "by a person, who could never think positive or for the welfare of others". He had, however, been talking to experienced and clever people, who had advised him to be careful about parting with the resources.

He, therefore, could not be easily persuaded or convinced that all was in his favour, whatever Nakul and Naresh were plotting. In a sense information about Jay's family's passport was edited and scrutinized by keeping him in dark and to exploit the situation. Nakul failed to inform Jay, when he was the first person to be reported to, because it affected him and his wife and children.

Naresh did not tell him. Even though Nakul had written to him. Nakul continued to behave as if it did not matter, and it was not of any significance. Later Naresh laughed about this incident and "said to Jay that he was aware of his family's passport, as soon as it was delivered at Nakul's home in New Delhi, where Jay's wife with children was living at that time."

Nakul did not write a separate letter to Jay, perhaps to save money on postage. The same thing happened when his family came to London, many months after their passport had been received from the Indian government. Nakul informed Naresh, as soon as their flight was booked, that Jay's family was coming to London.

Jay was not informed of the day or time; they would arrive at the London Airport. He, however, sent him a telegram a day before their arrival. Nakul charged ten rupees for the telegram but Jay's thousands of rupees were not considered and never returned to him. Jay found Nakul money minded, mentally sick, and morally bankrupt.

Naresh also attempted to create a friction between Jay and his brother Nakul. He tried to persuade, "Jay to give an ultimatum to his brother that his family should be sent to the United Kingdom by a certain date." At the same time, he wrote to Nakul that "he should not send Jay's family to join him." If his family arrived in England, he would not help him (Nakul) financially in the future.

Jay was very forgiving and did not take any action against any of them. He found "Naresh an Angel of Darkness" and "an Apostle of Doom." On Jay's refusal to help his friend at his house in Southeast London, he felt humiliated and insulted.

241

His wife told Reena that "Jay had insulted him in front of his friend. He should retract." Jay had done nothing wrong. There was no question of any apologies. Jay looked at this episode and compared with the story of a monkey and the crocodile. Naresh was smooth when he told him that he (Jay) had also been invited by his friend for lunch.

After lunch, however, he asked Jay to give all his savings to his friend. In this example Naresh behaved just as the crocodile had behaved in the story. But Jay was cautious. He refused to part with his money to anyone. It was his money, and he had plans to use it for his family, when they arrive in the United Kingdom.

Nakul had his own plans. He encouraged Jay to emigrate to England but asked him to send his earnings to him. What socked Jay was that when his family received their passport in November, he did not inform him that his wife and children were ready to come to Britain. He wrote to his friend Naresh about it, who did not inform Jay. Naresh also wanted Jay to continue to send his money to Nakul.

He revealed that "the whole purpose of you being encouraged to come to London, was that he and his friend Nakul would continue to take money of you". He questioned, Jay "when you were in India, why did you send your earning to your parents." "You should have forwarded that money to Nakul who had many children. Your money would have convenience him in bringing up his youngsters."

Jay started to examine Naresh's character and personality again. He attempted to make a psychological analysis of his behaviour. He was not a rich man, yet pretended to be rich and would readily offer financial assistant to his friends and colleagues. He, however, never transmitted his own money to any one at any time.

He was exploitative and Machiavellian. He wanted to exhibit that he could control and direct others by intimidating them into submission. Jay perceived that Naresh might have a personality disorder, which could have been caused by an identity crisis.

He was an Indian man living in Britain, where he had faced prejudice and discrimination. He, however, thought that he was an Italian rather than an Indian man. He could also be antisocial, because such people behave impulsively without forethought and without considering the consequences. They are often remorseful not for their wrongful act but for not achieving success with their plan.

Antisocial people tend to be easily irritated and respond to even a minor frustration. They could come across as self-assured and self-confident. They often create a good impression on a new contact, only to take advantage of their recently developed friendship. Jay observed that these characteristics existed in Naresh who wanted to impress others of his greatness and power.

He thought that he had a strong personality and could influence people surrounding him. He, however, had double personality with narcissistic disorder. It was not easy to deal with such a person because "they tend to fantasize to behave normally". "The narcissistic personality disorder has a pattern of self-centred and arrogant thinking. They lack empathy and consideration for other people. They make excessive demand for admiration. They tend to be manipulative and patronizing".

Jay did not let Naresh know about his opinion of him and continued to treat him as his brother's friend. Even though he had no regard for him. Naresh did really ask Jay to praise him in front of his friends who lived in the same house where he lived. They knew him personally. Jay did not acclaim or applause him as he desired. Naresh expected regular approbation and admiration from others.

In Jay's opinion, he lived in an illusion of paradise. "He was conscious of his self'-esteem and self-respect which was fragile". Jay found "Naresh a control freak who wanted to treat him as a satellite, who should orbit around him, listen to him and function

244

as directed by him". He (Jay) should not take his own decisions or do anything by himself.

Jay thought that he (Naresh) lacked insight into the feelings and needs of other people. "Such a person daydreams about prosperity, victory, influence, and admiration". He also exhibited a feeling of entitlement. "Such people believe that they should receive special privilege and respect, without doing anything positive or constructive. A sense of superiority pervades in them."

"They perceive their success more than that of the persons, who worked to attain it. They go into an episode of humiliation, if others ignore them or criticize them. A sense of arrogance pervades in such folks". Naresh forgot that he himself undervalued the work and accomplishments of others. He was a manual worker. Many of his other acquaintances were in middle-class white-collar jobs.

Jay endured that Naresh's personality might be the result of his cultural background. He came from a village farming family, who could not adjust in an advanced industrialized society in Britain. He did not realize that he was a new immigrant and should have observed the socio-economic environment of his adopted country. He should have attempted to visualize and consider the new situations, rather than carrying the old baggage. If he had changed his habits, he could have become accultured in the new nation.

Naresh, however, used to hide his feelings of envy and jealousy. He used to get angry over the success of others, especially when they had good jobs or bought their own house in England.

In course of time, Jay forgot all about Naresh, but realized that once he had spoken to Puneet about him and his actions, he should reveal it to his wife Reena. On hearing the story, Reena said, "rightly, we broke all connections with that criminal minded man. We should not waste our time and energy on such a person, because it would be good to leave them and not to fight with such people."

Nakul was partly responsible for creating a misunderstanding, about Jay, in Naresh's mind. The former had told the latter that Jay did not care about money, though he worked hard to earn it. When Jay lived in Delhi, he paid all his salary and tuition fee to Nakul. He also easily parted with his pocket money of four annas weekly, as a child, when he initially went to study at Secondary School, in the city, near his village.

They both, however, did not realize that Jay had a strong dynamism and walked out of his village primary school at the age of nine. Never saw the school or the teacher again. Once he left Nakul's house, in order to live in a rented accommodation, he never lived or stayed with him again. Though Nakul insisted that he and his family should move back with him before departing to London.

Jay did not believe in clashes or hurting others. He wanted to comfort people and put them at ease. Some people were, however, determined to ignore all advice and sensitivity. They felt that they were right when their welfare was contrary to their belief. Jay was not a rich man, yet he never displayed his poverty or made an exhibition of his problems. He did not show-off either. Still people expected him to support them financially and in many other ways. Naresh was not the only person, who had asked Jay for money, whenever he visited him. His friend Nahar had similar habits. He did not ask for money directly; Naresh borrowed money for him of Jay. It was Naresh's habit to promise assistance to his friends just to show off. Nahar would, however, insist that Jay went out with him and pay his bus fare. Often, he requested him to purchase an ice-cream for him.

Another individual who took advantage of Jay's simplicity was Prashant. He requested him to accompany him to the Registry to file a divorce petition. Jay had never seen his wife, yet he went along with him to the Registry, for moral support. A few months later, Prashant approached him again, and said that he wanted to get married to his ex-wife and "could he come to the Registry"?

247

Jay saw something fishy in it. He refused to oblige. He even did not give Prashant, his new address, when they moved to live in a new locality. He did not want to see him again.

25

Jay had his own problems to solve. He and his family did really face problems, in those early years. When his wife returned from her parent's home to New Delhi, Nakul's family made it difficult for them to live peacefully. Reena had to do all the domestic work including cooking and cleaning for that family. She did not have much time for her own children, for whom she was fully responsible in the absence of her husband.

There was no place where she could rest. Nakul's wife, on the other hand, thought that they were a burden on her and her family. Reena bought her own food supplies and paid a rent. She was not allowed to live in a separate flat. In the summer season they used sleep in the open courtyard of the house. There was not much space in the rooms and there was no electric fan.

One night it started to rain. They needed to come into the room. Nakul's wife, however, shut the door and left them outside in the rain. They had to spend the night standing under a balcony in order to protect them-selves from the rainfall. Yet they got drenched. When Jay found out about that incident, he concluded that it was the worst period of their lives.

He started to consider Nakul and his wife's behaviour in this episode. Why did she act the way she did? Nakul's wife was illiterate. She still lived with primitive instincts of sex and hunger. Nakul did not take her out on holiday or for shopping with him. She had not seen the real world of those days.

They never went to Chandni Chowk, Khari Bavly, or Connaught Place, the shopping centres of Delhi and visiting places for people, not only from Delhi but from around the country and the world. She never went to cinema or a theatre. She gave birth to ten children. Some died at birth, but she continued to produce to replace them. Her world was narrow. She did not know how to deal with relatives or the extended family.

She was often annoyed, when Nakul invited a relative to their house. She was thick headed but heavy weight. Whenever, she spoke to others, it sounded as if she was shouting. She could never engage into a quiet conversation. Nakul was a college graduate but light weight. Rather than attempting to lift his wife in social strata, he himself went down in status with her.

He did not behave like a middle class educated person. His food habits and living standard were those of a working class. They both had limited understanding of the universe and the society. That could be the reason that Nakul's wife shut the room's door, for

Jay's wife and children, when they were standing in the rain at night.

Many people questioned; how could someone make the young children stand in the rain at night? This was, however, like a scene in a Hindi movie displaying poverty and bad days. Jay's father took his family from Delhi to the village, but some younger members of the family made their life miserable.

Reena and the children had to return to Delhi, to face the same affliction and hardship. They had to live in a small kitchen, which was the only place available in that big house. Jay was not aware of any of these happenings. His wife never wrote of the adversities, or the problems, they encountered, in his absence. There was a saying that when the problems come, they come in trains and never alone.

Jay had sent enough money for his family to live comfortably. He, however, deposited this sum with Nakul because Reena did not have a bank account, or a safe place in the house to keep the money. He had written to Nakul that he should pay Reena, every month at least the same amount, which he was receiving as a salary, when he lived and taught in Delhi. Reena should not ask him for funds, because it was her bucks.

Nakul did not do that. Reena had to ask for her own rupees of him. Nakul often questioned, why did she need that much cash? As if he were lending his money to her, but feared, whether he would receive it back or not. He, however, sent an account when Reena and the children came to join Jay in England. It provided details of all money received and the expenses occurred over the two years.

Nakul was an amazing man who pretended to be a nice person in the community, but he was shrewd, cunning, controlling and a covetous character. Jay was aware of Nakul's narrow outlook. He started to analyse his character. He found Nakul selfish, greedy and distrustful. Selfish people tend to be excessively and exclusively concerned with their own interests. They look for their own advantages, pleasure and welfare. They disregard the interests of others. They are self-seeking, egocentric and exploitative.

Nakul was also jealous of Jay's accomplishments and success. Other traits of a jealous person were suspicion, possessiveness, aggression, and manipulation. They tend to be friendly from outside but bitter inside. They harbour envy and exhibit hatred and hostility. They even hold a grudge and work to crush others and bring them down. Jay saw all these characteristics in Nakul. In his psychological analysis, he would not offer or propound, Nakul as a narcissist, but he had a borderline personality disorder.

Such people think that whatever others have gained was unfair. They did not deserve it. Their achievement in wealth, education and status was unfair. They attempt to control their near and dear and would not let them express themselves. They were often told to keep quiet. "We will deal with your situations and circumstances." About others' property or wealth, they would say that "they do need that much" or "they do not deserve it".

Jay tried to avoid and evade Nakul who would not give up on him. He often returned to his old tricks of greed, bullying, self-interest, egoistic, jealousy and parsimonious. His neighbours and relatives told Jay that whenever, they visited him, he talked about him. He was surprised that Jay has made so much progress. He wanted a share of his earnings as he had done in the past. Nakul had no role in Jay's life. He was living in a different country and had faced enormous problems about which Nakul did not want to know.

Nakul did not care about the effect of his actions on others, either socially or psychologically. In one sense he had developed an inferiority complex without realizing it. Still, he wanted to be treated as a conspicuous person, without displaying any remarkable features. Jay did not owe him anything. On the contrary, he had done a great deal for him without making it public. He also forgave him and his family for their unforgivable demeanour. He, however, did not forget their conduct and undertakings of the times gone by.

At one stage Jay thought that rather than being Jealous of his achievements, Nakul should have worked hard and earned wealth in order to meet his family's demands. He should have attempted to rise in society by undertaking good and constructive work. He should have set out to help the needy who would have shown some respect and social regard for him. He did not do that.

His attributes and behaviour reflected his utter enviousness and resentment. His accomplishments had been minimal. He asked Jay to send goods for his family and friends and never made any payment. He even cheated their dad who felt very hurt. Nakul was an amazing man who pretended to be a nice person in the eyes of the relatives and neighbours, but he was a shrewd, cunning, controlling and covetous character. He lost all respect from his siblings and relatives who closely observed him. In this sense, he was an unsuccessful person whose accomplishments were negligible.

It has been noticed that selfish people tend to be greedy and distrustful. They want everything for themselves and are excessively or exclusively self-centred. They look for their own advantage, pleasure and welfare. They are self-seeking and megalomaniac. They look for their own gain.

"Greed leads to envy, anger, resentment, inadequacy, helplessness and disgust, which could lead to break up of relationship". Lord Krishna made a logical interpretation, when he wrote in the *Bhagwat Gita*, "An ignorant man sees another person with more objects of enjoyment than he has, the fire of jealousy gets kindled in his heart and it begins to burn him."

Jealousy often stems from low esteem, high neuroticism, and a feeling of possessiveness. There was no cure for this trait. It had been compared with craving. Jay concluded that Nakul might have these attributes. A jealous person resents another person because of his success. Some other traits of a jealous person were suspicion, possessiveness, aggression and manipulation. They harbour envy and exhibit hatred and hostility. They even hold a grudge and work to crush and bring people down.

After considering many characters, Jay asked himself a question as to why people become wrapped up in themselves, in the first place? It could be the consequence of their upbringing, social norms, their firsthand experiences, and psychological features. Individualistic behaviour could be caused by their insecurity, fear, or lack of empathy.

Such people think that they could do no wrong, which makes them hypersensitive. They could not comprehend any positive suggestion. Still, they think that they would bring good values to others. Jay believed and observed that such people tend to be less successful than those who help others. They would not realize the importance of supporting people around them.

During a short visit to India, Jay's dad expressed a desire to spend some time with him and his family in London. Jay, however, did not have enough time to obtain a passport for his dad. Their dad tried to seek help of Nakul's who flatly refused to fill in a passport application form and obtain any other documents. Jay's dad's wish to visit England remained unfulfilled.

Jay and his dad, however, continued their correspondence, as in the past. For a few months his dad moved to live in Delhi. He, however, wrote to Jay, that he found it difficult to live in Delhi with the family who mistreated him and cheated him. They did not look after him. He had to return to the village. He stated that he had many things to tell him (Jay) about the attitude of the family. "He would reveal everything, if they met and if he passed away, many explanations would go with him."

It was not the first time that Jay's dad missed him. He was told that about a decade earlier, when his youngest brother was getting married, there were rejoicings everywhere. His dad was surprised to see that none of Jay's brothers and sisters recalled his absence on that occasion. They did not miss him at all or thought that a member of the family was not present at the wedding rejoicings.

For Jay it was not new. He knew that for his siblings, he was not relevant. He had lived away from home for a long time. "Out of sight, meant out of mind". Yet they often sought financial assistance. Sometimes they asked for usable articles, both durable and for everyday use. They did not think, whether he had resources or not. He did not go into details about individual members of the family. Every one of them had their own distinctive quality, which could not be identified with good family affinity or consanguinity. There was no bond between them (Jay and his siblings).

<u>26</u>

Jay's room in London was not bigger than the kitchen in New Delhi. Jay's place, however, was close to certain amenities. There was a barber shop, a launderette, a newspaper shop, and a tube station, was nearby. The London Metro or tube was known as an underground, because so many trains run under the buildings especially in Central London. There were surface stations, and the railway track as well.

At the beginning, Jay's office was only three miles away from his room. He used to travel from his residence to office by bus. The bus service was direct from the office to the living place. The bus used to go through a small town in West London. One day he saw the name of the town on the front of the bus and thought that it was going through the same route. When he reached a new locality, he realized that it was an entirely different location.

It was a residential area with a park, large trees, and green grounds. The houses were big and beautiful with front gardens. He enquired about the position and discovered that he arrived at a wrong site. He wanted to go through a High Street, a shopping centre and then to Ennington.

He was given a choice by the man who helped him. He could go back and take a bus direct to the spot of his residence. Alternatively, he could walk through a local Road and take a bus from the High Street. Or he could take a train from the local Station to Ennington. He decided to walk along the road and scrutinize the area. He reached the High Street. From there he took a bus to his residence.

After three months of working in the department, he was moved to a bigger office. He received a promotion. It was still an office work. The difference was that he had to travel by Metro train. From his residence, it took him an hour to reach the office and another hour to return to his room. He always sat near a window in the train compartment, gazing through it and contemplating London from the moving train.

He saw beautiful Edwardian houses, which were built at the beginning of the 20th Century and had excellent architecture, beautiful front and back gardens with flowers, shrubs, and trees. There was sufficient open space with parks and tall trees in that inner city. He thought that eventually he would like to live in such an area. It reminded him of the open environment of his village in India.

Those who migrated from the Indian sub-continent in the1950s and 1960s, told him that up to two people lived in a room or twenty in a house. It was not easy to find accommodation in London. They also wanted to save money to purchase their own houses. Later, Jay discovered that in the Bengali community, residents rotated the use of bed. They worked in shifts and slept for eight hours, then another man would come and sleep in the same bed.

Not many families had migrated to England from the Indian sub-continent at that time. Only men came in search of jobs. Their families joined them afterwards. The Indian community decided to settle in Southall, a suburb on the out skirts of West London. Many had jobs at a rubber factory there. A few shops and restaurants were opened for Indians to buy their food supplies. Others could also dine at the restaurants and buy food at shops.

Jay never considered living in Southall. It was not convenient to travel to central London from there. Though there was a British Rail station, no direct underground train service existed from Southall to central London.

He had never worked in an office, yet he settled down well at a Government Department. He received two weeks training. One day, he went to see the computer room and was fascinated with the machine. In 1960s, the computer was exceptionally large and stuck along a wall. It used punched cards. A kind of code was required to work on it.

He, however, realised that he could not work on such a machine and would be happy to deal with files and fellows. He continued his commission at the Head Office. The office was overcrowded. Far more people were employed there, than were required. He had an eight-hour duty. He could, however, finish his assignment in three hours.

There was a tea club. Colleagues made tea themselves, rather than to go to canteen. They used to buy buns and butter from the canteen. Jay made some good friends, and he enjoyed his undertaking. The Head of department was an elderly lady, who was impressed with his moil and attitude. She asked him, how he was and did he like the office work.

He gave her positive feedback and told her that he was also interested in studies and wanted to attend evening class. She was glad to know that and encouraged him to study. At the end of one year, she thought that he should gain experience in other fields and expand his horizon.

She transferred him to another Section, where he kept records and prepared monthly returns. There were no word processors in offices in those days. It was a routine work, which he used to finish quickly, then sit at his desk and read files and books. Sometimes he used to type reports.

Jay wrote to his friends in New Delhi, about his life in London since he arrived there. "He faced some fundamental problems, both – financial as well as social. He suffered a few setbacks but soon, he began to feel at home. Life was not a bed of roses for him in this big city. Yet, he did not regret in leaving the places, where he had spent his childhood and boyhood."

"He could not make any permanent friends in London, because of different ways of thinking and approach in solving problems". He had learned his lesson in dealing with Naresh, Nahar and Prashant. They all had different attitudes and ways of thinking as well as demands.

After ten months, Jay moved to live in South London, where he lived in a small room on the top floor. A two room flat became available on the ground floor. Jay asked the caretake to keep the rooms for a few weeks because he was expecting his family to join him. He would rent the ground floor rooms. But his family did not arrive soon.

The caretaker told him that he could not keep the place for long. The landlord wanted to let these rooms. Jay could not ask for any more extension of time. He was frustrated. After staying alone in

London for more than two years, his family joined him from India. They all lived in Jay's small room for a week.

He asked his landlord, if he could suggest an accommodation for his family. The landlord said that his nephew had a big house. "He could allow you to live there." The nephew, however, had another property, which he let to tenants. This house was in partnership with his friend, whose family lived in the basement. It was a four-floor building. Jay's family moved to live on the top floor, two room flat in North-East London.

In that multi-story house, the family in the basement agreed to look after Jay's children, when Reena started a part-time job. They, however, asked the children to play on the stairs, rather than in a room or in the kitchen. Jay was not aware of this situation. His children did not tell him anything about that family's behaviour. On the other hand, their children used to come to the top floor, where Jay and his family lived. They played there and stayed there for hours. Reena used to provide them food as she provided to her children. There was no discrimination.

Jay noticed two contrasting behaviours by two families. The other family did not know that their children were having food at the top floor. They should have shown some culture and good manners. Reena did not care about all this. She was large hearted and understanding. Jay did not like separate approaches towards his children.

This locality had facilities for shopping, school for children, a big library, bus, and train service to travel to office. Jay had no problem in going to work. They lived there for twenty months. Jay took his family to visit different parts of London. They went to see the museums, the bridges including the Tower Bridge and the London Bridge, which had a story of its own.

A Californian American was keen to buy the famous Tower Bridge, because it could be lifted to facilitate the ships moving from and to the London port. He thought that Tower Bridge, was known as the London Bridge. He entered a legal contract with the Port of London Authority in order to purchase the London Bridge. The Bridge, he legally bought, was near the British Rail station. The London Port's authority dismantled, the London bridge and sent the stones, metal, and other material to the United States. It was a cheating because the American businessman wanted to purchase the Tower Bridge, but legally the British were right.

Jay tried to make his family's life as comfortable and as easy as he could afford. He did not ask them, how they spent two and a half years in India, without him. Did they encounter any problems or discomfort? He did not even talk about his early life in England.

They were keen to purchase their own house. They spent the summer weekends in search of a property. Jay's income did not attract a large mortgage. He kept his savings in his bank.

In the summer, they were burgled. The thieves stole their passports, the bank passbook, along with some other belongings. Jay reported the burglary to the police who came to investigate, and took fingerprints, but nothing could be recovered. Jay also informed his bank that his passbook had been stolen in the burglary. The bank Manager assured him that it would not be easy to withdraw money from a savings account.

By the end of the year, Jay and his family agreed to purchase a house, which they could afford. They received a mortgage offer. On the completion date, Jay needed the money to plunk as a deposit. The balance was a mortgage loan, which would come to his solicitor, direct from the landing bank, and it would be transferred to the seller's solicitor.

His bank, however, told him that he had no money in his account and that the entire sum was withdrawn a few months earlier. On checking the withdrawal date, they discovered that it was the burglary day. The signature on the receipt was Jay's full name which he did not sign.

A fraudulent had withdrawn the money from his savings account. He saw the Manager and told him that he had informed the bank about the burglary, and that his passbook was stolen along with his passport. He was assured at that time that no money could be withdrawn from his savings account.

He needed the money, to pay a deposit for his house. The bank Manager allowed to withdraw his money but statements in future months showed it as an overdraft. He went to the police again but there was no information about the passports, the bank passbook or the fraudulent.

He discussed the matter with a colleague in the office who had become his friend. The friend advised him to write to the bank's Head office and explain the whole matter. Jay drafted a letter and showed it to his office friend, who made a few alterations. He typed a letter and sent it to his bank's Head office. They solved the situation. The future statements did not show any overdraft.

Still, Jay did not like it. He had lost trust in his bank branch. He closed the account there and opened a new account at a different bank. He could never discover who withdrew his money and why the bank could not stop the extraction. The person could not be recognized. There were no cameras in banks in those days.

When Jay ascertained that his savings were withdrawn on the day of the burglary, he was staggered and stunned. It made a psychological impact on him. Consequently, he fell sick. He was ill for almost three weeks. His family was new in England. They did not know much about the area or the shops.

His wife Reena went out in search of special food for him. There was no one to support or help her at the time of need. Jay saw a doctor who gave him medicine, but it took him time to recover. He had fever for days. He could not speak. His voice plunged. He had memory loss for three weeks.

By the end of the year, however, he started to recover and was fully well in the early days of the new year. He resumed his duties. The house purchase completed in the first week of the new year, and they moved to live in their new home. Jay did not tell anyone that they had bought their own house in a new locality. He simply told his landlord that they were moving to a new place, because of nearness of his office. A van man moved their belongings to their new house. That was the only assistance they ever obtained, though they paid for the removal. Nonetheless, they felt obliged.

27

Jay's new house was a three-bed room terraced property. They did not make any enquiries about the new locality and faced some problems. There were not many shops in the area, and they had to go shopping at the High Street which was about half a mile away. They all went to seaside in summer of that year. In the new academic year, both the children started to attend the local primary school, where they adjusted themselves well. When both the children were in school, Reena started a part time job. Jay used to drop them at 9am and Reena collected them at 3.30pm."

He did not have a telephone at his home. Children used to stay on their own during the summer holiday. At lunch time, he used to come home from the office to visit them. Sometimes he was at the house only for a few minutes, but he felt contented that they were safe, and they had no conundrum. He hardly felt tired. He used to run from station to home and back to reach office within an hour.

When Jay and his family settled down to their routine in the new house, he wanted to know all about the behaviour of Nakul's family in New Delhi and the extended family in general. He asked his children how did they like their new house in London? His son

268

said that the house was much bigger than the kitchen in New Delhi. Reena attempted to stop him from speaking about that, but Jay understood what he wanted to apprise. She also tried to brush aside Jay's enquiries about the children's life in his absence. He did not insist for any clarification or elaboration. He had already discovered from a confidante, because the bitter truth never hides. There was a difference in points of view, towards money in India, the Indian communities overseas and the European people. In poor countries like India, money was a symbol of prestige and status. The rich obtain respect and happiness from their high earnings and business profits. On the contrary, Jay was more inclined to live the British way of life. In European countries, where necessities have been met, money did not necessarily provide happiness. They look to health, social help, welfare of all. Families like to go on holiday and eat out.

Along with doing his job, Jay was studying for a degree course. In order to take the first- year examination, and to prepare for it, he applied, for study leave at the office, through his section in-charge. It was customary in the civil service that employees, who wanted to enhance their qualification, were provided financial assistance and time-off to take the examination.

269

When Jay applied for leave and reimbursement of examination fee, his Section- in- charge questioned him, "how did he find out about this facility and why should he be given financial assistance and time off." This showed his frame of mind and prejudice.

The Section-in- Charge was an old man who had served in the British Indian army in South-East Asia, during the Second World War. He was fed information about imperialism and colonialism. The British had ruled India for ninety years and looked down upon the Indians as defeated people. He saw Jay as an Indian and not as a resident British citizen, who paid tax to the British government. He, therefore, did not support his application. Consequently, he (Jay) did not receive time-off or reimbursement of the examination fee.

He, therefore, took his own annual leave to take the examination and paid the fee by himself. The head of department asked him whether he wanted to appeal for the fee-recompense. Jay brushed aside and politely said that there should have been a reason for the decision. In his heart, however, he felt that a man belonging to a country, which robbed India for two hundred years or more, stole 45 Trillian dollar worth of wealth, at the current rate, was asking a proud Indian by birth that he should appeal for an eight pounds' financial assistance.

He did not care for that, but he wanted to follow the administrative system in the civil service, which provided aid to enhance education to its employees. Some of his office colleagues asked him, what was he going to do after finishing the degree course? Jay saw education as an investment and one day it would bring dividends by acquiring qualification.

He explained to his colleagues, some of whom had become his friends, that "people study to improve their status, better job prospects and because of ambition and interests". "Activities could be divided into two categories – one to enjoy and the other for the sake of doing them." He continued his explanation, that "life was, what you want to make it."

"Smooth living was not very progressive." "People ought to work hard and concentrate on the goals, they wish to accomplish." "For that a quest to succeed was essential." "This would require peace of mind, stability, discipline, humility, and constant effort. These were the essential ingredients for good human existence."

After passing his First-year examination, Jay decided to study full time for Part 2 of his degree course. He did not resign his post but took study leave without pay. His Local Education Authority provided him a study grant. He enjoyed his course where he learned new subjects and gained new knowledge.

271

When he applied for study leave without pay, the head of Section was not present. He saw the Deputy Head who told him that "we should send the leave application-form to the Personnel Department, immediately because the head might not support it." The study leave without pay was granted, because it had the support of the Deputy Head of the Section.

Jay started his Part Two of the degree course as a full-time student, which he enjoyed. He was always busy studying and reading books at home but sometimes at the University Library or at the local library. He did not go on holiday in the summer but worked to earn money to pay his council tax. His education grant was sufficient to meet the other expenses and pay bills.

After completing the degree course, he decided to change his career. He could not have used his skills and knowledge in a government office, which dealt with routine work. He thought of returning to teaching profession, after a big gap. Jay could teach Economics, Mathematics, and Geography. He started to make applications to schools and education authorities.

An Inspector of Schools, at a local education authority, invited him for an interview. He did not ask any questions but suggested to Jay that "he could easily teach Mathematics and Geography at school, because Economics was not a school subject." Jay accepted the suggestion.

A few days later, he received another letter from a School Secretary, who asked him to come to school. On reaching the school, he was seen by the Head of Mathematics who said that they need 1.8 teachers in the department and asked Jay to teach 0.8 in his department and 0.2 in Geography department. Jay told him that he wanted to teach only one subject at that time.

The Head of Mathematics agreed to take him full time in his department. Jay found the department well organised, and the other teachers looked friendly. He started to teach at a comprehensive school, where there was no selection procedure, based on achievement in Primary school. Students were of all abilities and many races, who attended the institution. It was a boys' centre of learning.

Girls attended this place for the Advanced Level subjects, where the number of students was small. Separate classes in all the disciplines would have been expensive and resources were not available in specialist subjects. It was understandable and a step in the right direction.

Jay was asked by his friends in India about his teaching job and other aspects of life in Britain. He did not want to criticize any system or country. He had lived in two countries, with distinct levels of economic development. He wrote, that "these were his personal views, which he had not discussed with anyone." Britain was an industrial country, which faced the problems of industrial relations, inflation, discipline, delinquency, and congestion.

While India was an agricultural nation, facing transformation. It was confronted with the concerns of over-population, malnutrition, unemployment, and the standard of living. It was attempting to find solutions to overcome the traditional chains of social customs and to modernise without giving up essentials of the national spirit, cultural and social institutions.

Because of Imperialism, colonialism, and occupation of the land by sword swirling invaders, India had been misrepresented, and her real virtues and cultures had been suppressed. The invaders always felt that their systems were better than those of the original residents of India, who had been overwhelmed. Many residents in Indian states and provinces, were rooted out from their ancestral homes. They had been forced to live in other parts of the country and sometimes in other parts of the world.

The previous invaders were defeated by the British, but when the British left, the rulers and the people in power returned to their old tricks of grabbing land from the poor and other residents of India.

274

Jay's family was no exception. His ancestors had to leave their homes, move out from North-West Sindh to West Punjab and again to Central Punjab. They settled in Lahore and the surrounding districts, but the fate would have it differently. They had to pack up and march again to Delhi, Uttar Pradesh, Haryana, Himachal Pradesh, Rajasthan, Madhya Pradesh, Iran, Greece, United Kingdom, Canada, and the United States of America.

Jay's colleagues and friends in London, wanted to know about India, as he was of Indian origin. He, therefore, pondered over the Indian system. "After all it was the largest democracy in the world." The success was still to be seen. There had been political upheavals in the developing countries, even across the borders in China and Pakistan. How did democracy survive in India for more than thirty years since independence in 1947?

Despite mass ignorance, immense poverty and vast unemployment, India's major achievements had been visible in the field of education. Primary education was provided to fight ignorance. The Secondary Education was geared to produce talents. The Higher Education had been designed to produce professionals and administrators. India had twice as many engineers as Western Europe. "She was supplying a pool of Engineers, Doctors and Technocrats, to the United States of

275

America, Canada, Australia, United Kingdom and the Arab Countries." The brain-drain has impeded economic progress in India.

In the 21st Century, the Indian governments, both Central and State, have made efforts to become self-sufficient and export orientated, in manufacturing sector as well as in the field of Defence. Jay stressed, that "the developing countries should utilize their resources, both human and natural, for the benefit of their people. Because of feudalism and imperialism, India's economy had suffered for hundreds of years. The Indian cotton industry was brutally destroyed by the British in the 18th and 19th Centuries.

<u>28</u>

The independent India, however, reposed emphasis on industrial development and agricultural improvement. In the early 1950s, steel plants were set up. Dams were built. Electricity generating system commenced. From the mid-1950s, emphasis was also ascribed to defence production and moving towards self-sufficiency in manufacturing of weapons. Ordnance factories were established to produce armament for the Nation's army. They embarked upon manufacturing of fighter jets, high velocity guns, anti-aircraft guns, high calibre bombs, small and medium size ammunition, and trucks for military transportation.

Light naval craft dredgers, harbour tugs, river steamers, water boats, and the barges were concocted in the country. Pontoons and whales were fabricated in India. The Indian government continued to import other equipment. They instituted to purchase the much-needed defence material from the Soviet Union. They did not want to depend on the West for their deterrent supplies. Moreover, Soviet weapons were cheaper compared to the Western prices. The standard was the same.

India continued to import, as well as to manufacture weapons in the country, which was vital to guard and shield the nation combatants and military offences. India had been a prey of foreign invasions for centuries, due to lack of preparedness in the field defence and border security.

Apart from the manufacturing sector, social reforms were equally essential to accomplish economic growth. Jay identified that people should be open-minded. "They should be prepared to give up some of the old customs and traditions, while preserving the religious tolerance and folk-life". He emphasized that the solutions should be found, in the areas of agriculture, industry, economy, education and society. There was a need for more understanding, mutual communication, fair mindedness, and large heartedness. People still intrigued against their fellow citizens and the nation.

After living for a few months in their new house and joining the new profession, he felt relaxed and was ready for any other adventures. He asked his wife Reena, about the family next to her father's house in their village. They had four boys. One of them called her, an honourary Rakhi sister (Rakhi is a red thread tied by sisters on the wrist of brothers on Raksha Bandhan, a festival which falls in August), because she used to tie a Rakhi on his wrist."

Reena narrated a story. "The boy thought that he was different, from his brothers, in the family, and friends in the village. He won a five-rupee scholarship in the Primary School, as he scored 100% marks in Mathematics and good marks in other subjects". "He went to the neighbouring town to study for the High School examination." "After passing his examination, he continued his study for the Intermediate Level at the same school."

He thought of joining an Engineering degree course at Kanpur University in Uttar Pradesh. He had to take an entry examination, which he cleared. He prepared himself to study at the university. His father also agreed to support him. The boy applied for a loan and a Scholarship at the University. The authorities agreed to provide him both. They wanted students from poor families to improve their educational and social status.

He worked hard for his degree course and passed the first-year examination. He and his family were encouraged. He, however, started to remain aloof from his brothers and friends. He visualized himself, superior to them. He forgot the sacrifice, his family had made in saving every rupee to educate him, feed him and clothe him. He was to spend three more years at the University.

In the final year of his degree course, however, the authorities changed the financial regulations. They wanted more students

279

from backward and poor communities to study for the Engineering degree. The Kanpur University decided that "a student could receive either a scholarship or a loan. No student would be provided both." In the meantime, his father lost his job. The young man was in a dilemma.

He could not decide his mode of action. Without financial help, he would not be able to complete his Engineering course, and three years would be wasted. He contacted his Rakhi sister, who was now living in England, if she could help him. He wrote a confidential letter to her "begging not to reveal his plight to her family." Reena, however, discussed the matter with Jay who suggested that we were helped in our need by people who knew us. They were not necessarily related to us.

He advised Reena to assist this young man on humanitarian grounds. He himself arranged to send a bank draft to his university address. It took time for the cheque to reach India. The young man had lost all hope and decided to pack up and return to his village, where he would start a bicycle repair shop. He, however, stayed for another day at the university campus.

After putting his belonging in a suitcase and bags, he bent down to pick up some papers near the door. While he was kneeling, an envelope fell on his head from the letter hole. He felt that it was a blessing from Laxmi, the Goddess of wealth. He opened the envelope and discovered that there was a cheque from his Rakhi sister in London. He changed his mind and stayed on, at the University to complete his degree course.

After completing the course of study, he was accorded a Certificate of Engineering degree. He danced in his room. He has got a Sanad (a certificate) and now he would have an Engineering position. First, he returned to his village and told his family and friends that "he was a qualified engineer." He went to visit one of his dear friends, who had never left the village. His friend said that if you are a qualified engineer, "you should come to my farm and check out my tractor. Its engine has stopped to propel." The engine has stopped, "I will make it work in no time," said the qualified engineer.

Both friends reached the farm. The engineer saw the tractor. He said, "it is made of metal." "I have never seen an engine made of steel." "I have dealt with paper engines only." "I have drawn many times and altered their shapes and designs". He did not use his knowledge to repair the engine because he did not gain any practical experience. He learned theories and paperwork. To work on an engine, would have been a working-class job, and he was trained as a sahib.

When Jay heard of the incident, he was surprised and shocked to know that an engineer could not help his friend in the village in repairing the tractor because of lack of contact with machinery. In the United Kingdom, Jay had observed engineers repairing the engines and even servicing them. He, therefore, maintained that an emphasis should be laid on practical education, which could be used in real situations.

The State government of Uttar Pradesh, nevertheless, provided him an employment of an Engineer and an office to operate from. It did not want to waste its money, which it spent on his education. They paid him a monthly salary, a house to live and pampered him in many other ways. A couple of years later, he decided to get married. He asked his uncle to find a graduate girl for him. His uncle replied, "who would give a graduate girl into your family"? The young man insisted that he wanted a graduate girl as his wife, who could accompany him to parties.

His uncle suggested that a girl was studying at a college in another district. She would complete her degree course in a year. She was, however, six years younger to him. The engineer's father advised him not to insist for an educated wife and live within the family frame. Eventually he married the girl when she completed her education. But she could not adjust in their lower middle-class family system. They both got cut-off from his brothers and sisters. He was also disrespectful to his honourary Rakhi sister who restored him to his university place. Once his father suggested to him that he should write a letter of thanks, to her, on receiving his degree and a good employment. He retorted, "I do not like people who change their plans." "Save money for their own needs, then ignore their expenses and commitments to their children and family".

"They seek out to help others to gain respect and admiration." He continued his conversation with his father, "I understand, they saved money in order to procure a house, but they postponed that acquisition and sent their money to me and continued to live in a rented accommodation." It was his opinion about the help which he desperately needed only a few months earlier.

Nevertheless, he worked as an engineer for more than thirty-five years. When he retired, he received a pension to live a comfortable life but endured loneliness. He attempted to analyse his accomplishments and discovered that his siblings and their children were more sociable and happier. He had become an out-caste. He received a degree because of a charity cheque from his honourary Rakhi sister, whom he ignored and showed no appreciation or approbation. He was a pauper by heart, despite his education and social mobility.

<u>29</u>

One of his colleagues invited him to his Christmas party. Jay considered the invitation carefully and discussed it with Reena who declined to go to the party. She said that the children were young. There was no one to look after them. She would not leave them on their own at night. Jay also thought that the party would end after midnight. There was no convenience for travelling. He did not want to travel by public transport after midnight and would not trust a private taxi. He, therefore, decided not to go to the party. He turned down the invitation and resolved to celebrate Christmas at home with the family.

A couple of years later, another of his school colleagues invited him for a Diwali party, which was to take place at night. Jay evaded to go. It became his habit not to go to parties at night. It happened again, when two of his colleagues, who were also his close friends, approached him to celebrate the publication of their book. This celebration party was to take place at night.

Jay was frank and told them that he does not attend night parties. There would be travelling problems, especially in returning home at night. His colleagues understood the situation and thanked for his openness and decision. Notwithstanding, whenever there was a gathering during the day, Jay attended it. He did not consider the distance or inconvenience as a hindrance.

He went to West London, South London, Southeast London, Southwest London, Essex or Surrey, wherever his friends lived and invited him. If any of his colleagues was sick, he used to visit them. He would take flowers, food, and a bottle of wine. He enjoyed their company. His friends and colleagues respected him for that. They enjoyed his presence and company.

Wise people have often argued that "one should not put all the eggs in one basket." In social behavioural terms, it could be suggested that "one should not depend on any one person, one system or one institution". He should consider and investigate the pros and cons of all aspects, and weigh their advantages and disadvantages or alternatives, before taking a decision or accepting the counsel.

A person's information or views could be subjective and may contain the advisor's self-interest. It could be contrary to the well-being of the person who was seeking the guidance or taking a decision. The public level decisions were taken for the benefit of the majority of people, if not for the betterment of everyone. Private individuals should be careful in considering a verdict and look at their own circumstances and situations.

Jay took certain resolutions, which were contrary to his nature and benefit. These accords were, however, taken by others and imposed on him. He was an innocent soul. He was easily persuaded to take quick adjudication, which proved detrimental. He realised that these people did not have his welfare in their minds and attempted to control him for their own interests.

He changed his course of action and even broke connections with such individuals. They were unable to understand him and his ways. They lacked experience in certain fields. Jay was determined not to hearken or follow them without weighing and scrutinizing the subject and never to lose the plot. He sensed that trust was vital in social relations. He watched those people who could damage his interests.

After living in Britain for more than five years, Jay and his family decided to visit their families and friends in India. In New Delhi, they visited markets, shopping centres, historical places, and newly developed residential areas. One day Jay's brother Nakul asked to accompany him to his office, where he saw Naresh's ex-colleagues. They enquired about their old friend. They wanted to know about his nature and conduct in London. Jay did not believe in criticising any one in their absence. He told them that Naresh was fine.

Then they asked Jay, when did he see him last? Jay replied that he saw him recently. One gentleman insisted on the time, month, and the year. "He told him that he met Naresh for the last time, more than four years ago." Naresh's ex-colleague laughed and said that "he (Jay) was a real diplomat." He did not reveal that Naresh was not his type. They could not become friends. They both had different approach towards life and society.

Jay had a comparative mind. He started to compare the British and the Indian systems. He perceived that the western education system had been planted into non-western countries. The European languages had been introduced there. The economic and political institutions had been designed on western patterns. Even religious beliefs had been accepted as superseding their own. In other words, the world has moved towards unity with the leadership of the West. He discussed his ideas with his friends in London and briefly expressed his views in a letter to his cousin Nitin who asked Jay what was he doing, those days? He wrote to Nitin that "Copying the West has not been a successful attempt because of geographical and historical reasons". "It has led to differences and deviations and sometimes conflict." It was difficult to change the mind set of men and women.

Jay advanced the view that after the collapse of the Indian political power in the form of the Mughal Empire and the Maharajas, the British took over the administrative reigns in India. Thereafter, western influence started to penetrate, in the Indian society and polity. Obviously, the host community resented, but with the loss of political power, India was in a weaker position. Indian reformists attempted to eradicate the frailties and looked to the ways to revitalize the nation.

Most western people thought that India was a deeply religious country. Yoga Guru Maharishi Mahesh Yogi visited the United States and the United Kingdom. He had many followers in these countries. On occasions, there were chanting of Hare Rama, Hare Krishna, on the streets of London. Some famous British singers became his followers and helped him in setting up ashrams (settlements) in India, and a Krishna Temple was constructed near Watford in England.

Jay, however, believed that Religion should be confined to the values of spiritualism and rituals in a person's life. The Rituals should not be treated as real. Every day need should be fulfilled by technology and by developing social, economic, and political institutions.

He had been teaching in London for a few years by now. His cousin Nitin asked him, how he would compare the teaching at a London School with the teaching, in schools in India, where he had taught in two places, in Delhi and Somanpur. Jay replied to Nitin, "In London school, there was very little teaching in the way, he was trained, or he had practiced in India". In his school in London, the children were of mixed ability. Some of whom were determined to study, while the others felt that they were being forced into the school system. They were not only anti-academic but also noisy and disruptive.

At-times, he was dismayed and disappointed at the class-room atmosphere and considered that the concept of education was miles away from the practice. The school was like a child-minding place. The education system was child centred. The child had to take the initiative and had to undertake his class work as well as homework. Every child was afforded individual attention, encouragement and sometimes punishment. There was, however, little scope for talking sensibly in a classroom atmosphere, where the teacher could explain the theme. The children could, nevertheless, copy anything from the board and answer questions from textbooks.

The whole resolve of schooling was not to produce intellectuals but to provide education as a social service and to educate children for citizenship, where they could play their part in social and economic life of the country. Sometimes he was amazed to see that a child, who stayed at school for about eleven years, yet he/she entered his/her adult life, as an uneducated person.

Some children could not read or write. It was not because of any language problem but because they had either escaped the attention of the teacher in class or were not encouraged to learn the three R's, reading, writing and arithmetic, at an early stage.

Jay continued that "a host of subjects were taught at a Comprehensive school. The main aim of the comprehensive education was to provide a choice". The entire system was geared to achieve "uniformity and equality of opportunity." Some young people, nevertheless, knew that as manual workers, they could earn more money than the educated folk. There was, therefore, little incentive to acquire formal qualifications.

Jay noticed some prejudice and discrimination towards students by some teachers. He advised students not to worry too much, but to maintain their cool and work hard to improve their educational standards. There was always a silver lining in every cloud.

He also thought about happiness. How could people be happy and maintain a good life. A job satisfaction, fulfilment of necessities, healthy environment at home, a good social atmosphere and even changes in behaviour in accordance with the circumstances, could make them happy. He apprehended that one should be happy with what he has, rather than be unhappy, for what he does not have?

Individuals and groups should seek happiness by spending time with their family and friends. It advanced sociability and heightened satisfaction in life. One should undertake a hobby which could provide pleasure and avoid negative deliberation. Jay believed that the society was an organic whole. Every person was important and had a role to play. Any parochial cause should not degrade humans.

In India happiness and enjoyment materialize at the time of weddings of children, grandchildren, and the ceremonies which come with these functions. Jay always loved the lavishness of Indian weddings, decoration, music, gatherings and of course the food of all varieties. There was no other country in the world which had such a vast variety of food.

In the summer, Jay went to see the English countryside. The villages were small with about ten to fifteen houses. Most of the population was elderly, retired people. There was a shop with post office in it. The retired men and women collected their pension at the post office on Thursdays. They bought their food supplies and other essentials there. The village environment was relaxed. The residents saw the city people with curiosity.

At the school, Jay's teaching room was on the fifth floor in a multistorey building. Students used to come to attend lessons in his room. After each lesson, another class would come. Jay used this room not only for his teaching commitment, but also as his office. He prepared his teaching material there, saw his personal tutor group and marked the students' scripts. However, he used to go for tea-break in the staff room on the ground floor.

Teachers used to line up for their cup of tea and snack and pay for it. Jay liked hot tea, but the tea lady used to pore tea in cups in advance to save time. She would, however, make hot tea for him, because once he refused to have the already made tea which was quite cold.

<u>30</u>

Like any other day, he sat down with his cup of tea. An Asian teacher, Arif, came and sat down next to him. He looked a little perturbed and confused. He said to Jay that the Head of Physics, with whom he taught his subject, "has told him that all inventions, and new research has been done by the Europeans and white people. There has been no contribution by the other races and countries in the field of science and technology."

Jay laughed at the ignorance of the Head of Physics and told his Asian colleagues that "you should have explained to him about the Indian contribution in various fields, especially in Mathematics". He added, "I could not fight your battle but ask the Physics teacher to discuss with me about the achievements and contribution, to Science and technology, by people, apart from the Europeans, who had sometimes stolen the ideas and presented as their own which was pure plagiarism."

There had been a great deal of misconception about the Indian contribution because of foreign rule for many centuries. India was politically and militarily controlled by the British for almost one hundred and ninety years. "Moreover, ignorance was non-excusable." "If the Physics teacher was ignorant about India and other countries, it did not mean that their achievements did not exist." "He should have attempted to explore and ascertain their contribution, before expressing his views or displaying his unawareness and oblivion."

Jay reminded Arif that "Arya Bhatt, an Indian mathematician wrote the first book of Mathematics and Calculus." "Egyptians gave algebra." "Bakhshali manuscript showed that the symbol Zero (0) evolved in India in the 3rd Century AD". "This manuscript was now deposited at the Bodleian Library, Oxford, England. He could go there and verify it."

In the early 20th Century, Srinivasa Ramanujan Aiyengar, who lived from 1887 to 1920, was a great Mathematician. In 1913, he taught at Cambridge University with G H Hardy who invited him as a visiting Lecturer. His contribution was in theorems. Ramanujan Aiyengar compiled 3,900 identities and equations. He was the youngest Fellow of the Royal Society and the first Indian to be elected as a Fellow of the Trinity College, Cambridge.

Jay continued to explain that India was not only a religious country and had a religious philosophy, but it also has made enormous contribution to the growth of Natural Science and Astronomy. He added, that "Acharya Kanad (also known as Kaushik) was the father of the Atomic Theory. Nagarjuna gave Chemistry, Bhagyan gave the Theorem of Pythagoras." "Acharya Chanak provided Ayur Ved, the Health Science." "Bhaskar Acharya researched on the Law of Gravitation." "Bharadwaj was the father of Aeronautics".

"Indians built aeroplane many thousand years ago". "They sent rockets to other planets. A dilapidated factory was found in the Western Indian state of Gujarat, which built aeroplane to fly across the country and to other nations. Seven thousand years ago "The Puspak Vimana (an aeroplane) brought Ram, Sita, Lakshman, Vibhishana and Hanuman from Lanka (Now Sri Lanka) to Ayodhya in Uttar Pradesh, India."

A bridge was built from Rameshwaram in Tamil Nadu, South India to Lanka. The NASA verified in the later part of the 20th Century that stones used to construct the bridge were seven thousand years old, though the sand could be just over three thousand five hundred years old.

"Arth shastra (the treaties on political economy) was written by Kautilya Chanakya". It describes the theory of taxation and the systems to maintain all kind of records in the state. Poet Kalidas wrote *Shakuntala, Kumar Shambhav*, *Raghu-Vansh*, *Meghdoot*,

and many other plays and poetry books which had no parallel in other languages or country."

"Vatsayana wrote books on Judicial and Legal system". "Rishi Patanjali gave Yoga to the world. He also authored a book on the *Interpretation of Mathematics*". "In ancient India, all researchers and Professors were called Acharya, Rishi and Maharishi".

India's two great Epics were well known all over the world. "The *Ramayana* by Valmiki was a Biography of Ram, in poetry form. It had all the characteristics of literature, dealing with Anger, Chivalry, Affection, Love, Laughter, Comedy, Compassion, Mercy, Disgust, Aversion, Horror, Terror, Amazement, Peace, and Tranquillity. It also explains and expresses that people should show respect to others, and the king should address the problems of the State as well as look after the interests of the public in the state.

"The Mahabharata" was a treaty on politics, discussing the Social Contract Theory. It emphasised the rules of warfare and the use of weapons in war, policies for Administration and Providing justice to people. It also considered the teachings of Hinduism. "The *Bhagwat Geeta* is an integral part of this epic". *The Bhagwat Geeta* had been translated into one hundred and forty languages and more.

297

In the 20th Century, quite a few Indian scientists have made contribution in the field of natural sciences. Sir C.V. Raman discovered that "when light passes through a transparent material, some of the deflected light changes in wavelength." He was the first Indian to receive Noble Prize in Physics. Homi Bhabha was a nuclear physicist. He argued for peaceful use of nuclear power and its use for industrial development. Sir Jagdish Chandra Bose was the father of radio. He was the first, to use semi-conductor junction to detect radio waves. He invented various microwave components and studied metal fatigue. He also showed to the world that plants breath, grow and are sensitive to climate change.

Vikram Sarabhai was Astro physicist and astronomer who initiated space research in India. He fabricated a satellite. The Indian scientists put their first satellite "Aryabhata" into orbit in 1975. Sisir Kumar Mitra made contribution in the field of Radio Physics and Electronics. Meghnad Saha was an astrophysicist who devised the theory of Thermal Ionisation. He invented an instrument to measure the weight and pressure of solar rays.

Har Govind Khorana (born in Peshawar) demented and broke the genetic code, which translated DNA Sequences, into protein molecules that carry out the functioning of the living cells. He did all his research in the United States of America. The contribution of Indian Scientists continued into the later part of the twentieth Century and in the 21st Century.

They contributed through the United States projects in NASA. It would be good to recall Ashwin Vasa Nanda, for the mars curiosity mission; Sharman Bhattacharya examined the effects of radiation and altered gravity on living systems. Kamlesh Lulla helped astronauts to land safely through remote sensing. Other scientists of Indian origin working at NASA included Sunita Williams; Kalpana Chawla; Meya Meyappan; Anita Sen Gupta; Madhulika Guha-Thakurta, and Suresh Kulkarni. They all have made significant contribution in the space research and in space exploration.

Jay explained that the highest peak in the Himalayas, was known as the "Everest, after the name of George Everest, who was the Surveyor General of India" during the British rule. After his retirement, Andrew Waugh was appointed the Surveyor General of India. He wanted to know the height of the peak of the mountain-Himalaya. "In 1852, Radha Nath Sidkar, an Indian mathematician and surveyor of Bengal, was the first to identify the Everest as the highest peak".

He used trigonometric calculation based on Nicholson's measurement for this purpose. It was designated as the peak XV, at the height of 8840 metres (29002 feet). Andrew Waugh called this peak, after the name of his predecessor, Everest. Sikdar's contribution had remained unrecognized because of the British imperialism in India. Sikdar was considered as a subordinate to the British Waugh. "You must not forget that in 1953, Tenzing Norgay a Nepali Sherpa but Indian citizen reached this peak along with Edmund Hillary of New Zealand".

Because of various invasions in the Middle Ages, India lost its visible contribution. The Nalanda University in Bihar (India) had nine million books. These were burnt in 1192, on the orders of Bakhtawar, a Turkish zealot. Bakhtawar questioned, "how could a nation have superior culture, when it had been defeated by foreign warriors"?

The Indian civilization was, moreover, philosophical and respected all faiths. Her culture and history had mostly been one of learning and diversity which had been damaged by persistent aggression, imperialism, and foreign rule in the last eight hundred years. India lost a great deal during this period.

Jay stressed that India's Gross Domestic Product (GDP) was the highest in the world in the First one thousand and five hundred years of the era. It was Second in the 16th and 17th centuries in the world. It, however, declined with the takeover of Indian administration by the British, who started to loot and drain, the Indian treasury and the wealth. India provided 46% of world Groos Domestic Product (GDP), when the British took over in 1757. It was 1.7% of World GDP, when they left India in 1947. They made India poor in just one hundred and ninety years because of loot and plunder.

The loot was counted equal to 45 Trillian US Dollars in today's price. Kohinoor Heera (Diamond) was taken from Maharaja Ranjeet Singh of Punjab and given to the British Queen Victoria as a gift. The British still have to return it to the Indians.

<u>31</u>

Despite all kinds of loot and suppression of people in India and Africa, the British people were very fond of praising themselves and wanted to be identified as the most tolerant and civilized society with innovative ideas. Many Indians came to live in Britain after the Second World War due to shortage of labour in that country. They worked hard and built properties and shops in London and in other cities. Damages were, however, inflicted to Asian properties in the 1970s. In 1980s. On a Friday night, two students were attacked and killed in London. After a week, a youth was brutally knifed and killed in Southall, Middlesex.

A black student was stabbed and killed in South-East London by a local gang. The police made every attempt to protect these offenders but after much publicity and efforts some of them were sent to prison. But the student's family lost their son, and the community lost a young man.

Even though the Indians and other visible minorities were invited to work in the National Health Service (NHS), the other public services and in private sector, they were often questioned by ordinary British people, when were they returning to their countries? They, all behaved like the Immigration officers. Perhaps, the British government did not explain its policies to the public that these people were in the United Kingdom on their invitation and on being given a work visa.

This did not reflect Britain's tolerance towards the racial minorities. When Adil Amal had a dream that he had been asked by Allah, to throw out the British Asians from Africa, many of them decided to come to Britain because they were British passport holders and had a right to settle in the United Kingdom. British politician Ernie Pickering made a speech. He visualized rivers of blood in British cities if Asians were allowed to come to the United Kingdom and blossom here.

His vision was no different from the dream of an African dictator. It portrayed Pickering's racial hatred and racial prejudice. There had been no rivers of blood in England. The British government of that time showed statesmanship and expelled Pickering from the ruling party. Efforts were also made to improve race relations, especially by the socialists, the Labour party, and the trade unions. Jay enjoyed teaching at the school. He also continued to improve his qualifications. A few teachers were against his furtherance in the school and hindered his career progress. His Head of department approached to discourage him from applying for an advancement. He was blunt and told him, "You must be kidding, if you think that you would attain that job." His right to think was taken away by this racist thug. Jay found it strange and repugnant. People, who had been associated with the school, found it repulsive and repellent. It was incompatible with the school system and the laws of the country. They maintained that an injustice had been done to Jay. He did not make any official complaint to the authorities against the teacher who conspired with the headmaster and stopped his promotion. The information, however, reached the Education Authority. The CEO made the headmaster, an Inspector of schools, in another borough. It was a promotion.

A few months later, Jay learned that his old headmaster had been sacked from his new position. He had done wrong not only to Jay, but he did the same thing to some other teachers at the school. He considered the school as his fiefdom. Yet, racial prejudice continued in the United Kingdom and the United States and in many other countries. Some teachers advised Jay to find a job at another school. He, however, was not going to leave the school without a good reason but moved to another Department at the same school.

There he excelled and made enormous contribution to students' education. The number of students soared in his new Department because of good public examination results, which were always above national average. Jay had an excellent teaching method. He could relate his subject matter to students, who enjoyed their studies. He was a father figure to some of them. He had his own children of the same age group. He knew that many students needed reassurance, sympathy, and support.

Jay and his family continued to live in London, where they had been comfortable. Jay wrote to his cousin Nitin about the area and explained its beauty and the facilities that were available, "the Bus services, railway stations and supermarkets, access to central London shopping areas. Accessibility to libraries and archives, which were to become his second home, where he instituted his research on several topics to author books."

He had hardly looked back to his early years. On the insistence of one of his mature students, he, however, talked about it. "How he left the primary school and his village, at the age of nine and took his degree at eighteen." There was nothing fascinating about it. He sensed no excitement or trepidation. Others drew some encouragement from such an account. It was difficult to recall those scenes and incidents. Only a few major happenings re-occurred onto his mind.

One student was particularly keen to know more about him. He thought that he would like to make progress like Jay and improve his status through good education. Jay was delighted to know that, and he encouraged him to study.

Jay was always eager to do something new. He had multifarious ideas. He observed that the world was economically dominated by the capitalist countries. Nations had moved towards secularism and multiculturalism. Yet, after the Second World War, the states of Pakistan and Israel were created on religious grounds.

In India, some people were not allowed to enter temples, because of their caste, which was unjustifiable. In course of time, he noticed that such discernment had started to recede. Legal actions were taken against those who stopped worshippers from gaining access to temples or for not being employed to higher positions. He thought that there should be an equality of opportunity for everyone.

Indians living outside of India, worked hard and were mostly highly qualified. These people had shown their Mattel and were being appointed to higher positions in all fields. Indians had been identified good at figure work. They were working as Accountants, Auditors, and Investment Bankers. These citizens had brought fame and proud to their country of origin. Yet, India was not a

306

Permanent Member of the Security Council of the United Nations. Many Indian bureaucrats worked at this World Organisation and provided good administration.

The Indian politicians have proved their abilities and skills and have shown their progressiveness and determination. The economic progress has been visible. Jay hoped that they would continue to work for the welfare of their countrymen and the world, with a belief in **Basudhev Kutumbhkam** (the entire world is like a family).

In India, the demand for education has increased many folds. The government could not meet this demand especially for medical studies and for higher education. The middle-class parents had started to send their children to study abroad in the United States of America, Australia, Canada, and the United Kingdom.

Some students had gone to study in China, Russia, and the Ukraine. Others were attending courses in Nepal especially in Medical Studies, even though it was an underdeveloped country but had more places in medical colleges than they could recruit locally.

Jay was in demand to talk about India and its ancient cultures. people thought that he might provide knowledge about the sub-continent. At a meeting, he acquainted his audience of the two great civilizations, which sprang up in India seven thousand years ago. "One of them, the Indus-Valley civilization was famous for its trade, administration, and architecture.

The excavations of Mohan-Jodaro and Harappa towns in the states of Sindh and West Punjab, suggested that people of these cities were fond of art, painting and sports." They had good drainage system, swimming-pools, and squared-houses. They had started to build two storey houses in cities. "The Indus Valley people (called Indians) were business minded."

They did trade with Rome and sold expensive jewellery, silk cloth, rice and high-quality cotton cloth to the Roman Emperors and their household. The Silk Trade Route was used to carry goods to Rome and other parts of the empire. (some people argue that this should be identified as spice route and silk route as a great amount of spices was sold to the Romans). There were stories that Indians sold expensive jewellery and silk cloth, which emptied the emperors' treasury. Their economy declined, which lead to the end of the Roman Empire.

The other Indian civilization flourished in the plains of the Ganga and Jamuna rivers. "The people of these areas were literary minded and created the Vedas, Upanishads, the famous epics of the *Ramayana* and the *Mahabharata*, and of course the *Geeta*." Many philosophers, poets and mathematicians contributed to this culture.

308

The Taxila University in the Punjab, Banaras (Varanasi) and Prayag (Allahabad) Universities in Uttar Pradesh; Ujjain University in Madhya Pradesh, along with Pataliputra (modern Patna) and Nalanda Universities in Bihar; were the great seats of learning and research."

"Sanskrit was the main language of these people". They followed the teachings of the Vedas and attempted to seek a reality of life through discussion, thinking and meditation. Jay continued the discern at the meeting that "the recorded history of India, however, began with the founding of the Mauryan Empire. Prior to that, city states and village republics existed."

The villages were not isolated from the mainstream of social and economic life of the nation. Apart from the political unity, a common culture prevailed from Kashmir in the north, to Kerala in the south. From Gandhar (now in Afghanistan known as Kandahar) in the west, to Assam in the east. Chandra Gupta Maurya, the founder of the peacock throne, was the first Emperor of the united India.

His grandson, Emperor Asoka, was an excellent administrator. He turned to Buddhism in the later part of his life. He sent missionaries to South-East-Asia, West-Asia, Sri Lanka, Mongolia, China, and Central Asia. He dedicated his wealth to spread Buddhism and to work for the welfare of all human beings across the world. He also laid a sound foundation of economy, which remained the highest in the world for more than one thousand and five hundred years.

Hinduism, however, remained the major religion in India. It was not just a religion; it was a way of life. Any one person or a group of people did not establish it. It has existed since the dawn of civilization. It was Sanatan Dharma (an eternal religion). The Buddhism and Jainism had made India passive.

The land and climate of the country required people to work hard and not to waste their energies in lethargy and laziness. In the Third Century AD, Adi Shankaracharya started to revive the ancient Vedic Hindu System. He appealed for cultural unity of the nation. He travelled across the country and realized that there was a need for continuous guidance of religious teachings.

In a large country like India, one Shankaracharya and one Math (temple) would not be sufficient to cater for the spiritual needs of the whole nation, and to continue with the teachings of Hinduism. He, therefore, set up four Maths, in four corners of the country. One Math each was established at **Dwarka** in the West, at **Puri** in the East, at **Badrinath** in the North and at **Kanchipuram** in the South. One Shankaracharya each was appointed to run these Maths. They were to communicate with one another and travel in their designated areas. Later a Shankaracharya was appointed at **Sringeri**, where a new math (temple) was set up.

In course of time, however, many organisations sprang up with their own agenda for social reform and to look after the interests of the communities. The Shankaracharya still exist. Their role was, however, limited. The government of independent India adopted a secular system in 1947. India, therefore, remains a multi-religious and multi-cultural country, though majority of people are Hindus.

The ancient Hindus thought that Hinduism was a religion because it had values and rituals. It embraced social customs and traditions. All aspects of human life from birth to death and beyond were discussed in it. "The main beliefs of Hinduism included cosmology, the **doctrine of the Karma**, the concept of **varnashrama-four stages of life** (the Childhood and Youth, the household age, the retirement and the vanaprastha, living in the forest or returning to villages from the cities), and the philosophy of the competence". The people at the gathering appreciated Jay's invocatory.

<u>32</u>

Subsequently, Jay became interested in psychology, which was the analysis of human behaviour. He identified that since the Second World War, the study of 'personality' and knowledge of the 'self'' had become important themes in the academic world. The Self' was the product of social interaction. A person perceived himself/ herself as the others saw him or her.

Personality had been considered in many ways, traits, and types, by classifying it into introverts and extraverts, neurotics and stable. Division of attitudes into conservatives and radicals, tender-minded and tough-minded had been advocated. The classification of character into choleric, melancholic, phlegmatic, and sanguine, appealed to him most.

He had also been looking into the attitudes, their formation and adoption. Anxiety, drive, and motivation lead to academic achievement and personality development. Those who had high self-esteem of themselves, tend to be adjustable. People with inferiority complex, low-self-esteem, and self-rejection tend to be mal-adjusted. He attempted to analyse his own self-conception and thought that "he was perhaps an introvert but creative."

312

He was in touch with his cousin Nitin in India. Nitin wanted to study for the Bar Final in London and become a barrister. He already had a law degree and a master's degree from an Indian University. On arrival in London, he stayed with Jay for a few weeks. He was accepted to study for the Bar at the Middle Temple and completed his finals within a year. After his examination, he was offered a job, at a Law Firm, which he accepted, in order to gain experience. He decided to stay in London and rented a flat in Hariandom, North London.

He was always busy and became friendly with Susan McIntosh, who worked at the same firm as a secretary. After two years of friendship, they both started to live together. Susan McIntosh felt that they know each other well. It would be a good idea to develop their relationship. She suggested to Nitin that they should get married. Nitin became nervous with the notion of marriage. He did not want to get married any way. To marry a white woman would be very demanding. He, therefore, did not proceed any further.

Susan McIntosh felt hurt. She stopped eating food. A kind of Gandhian fasting. With the result, she fell ill. Nitin also resorted to fasting. He did not eat anything for two weeks. A reciprocity. Nitin used to talk to Jay at every weekend. He, however, did not come

313

over or phone him for two weeks. Jay became concerned about him.

He went to see him at his flat in Hariandom and found him sick with high temperature. Jay took him to local hospital. He asked Nitin the reason for his sickness and why did he stop eating food? He did not fully explain and attempted to make excuses.

Jay, however, found out the reason for Nitin's illness, both physical as well as psychological. He advised him to solve the problem with Susan McIntosh by discussing sensibly and if he could do anything, he should have conversation with him.

He returned home and explained the matter to his wife Reena who understood the situation and said that they both were educated and sensible persons. They should attempt to seek a solution to their plight. Jay, therefore, did not do anything and felt that Nitin and Susan should solve their problems, in accordance with their circumstances and thinking.

Jay had been in England for more than a decade. His younger brother Vikram asked him to write about London. Vikram could not come to visit him in England. Jay himself wanted to write something about London and let his relatives know about this beautiful city. In a long letter, he wrote, "London was stretched many miles from North to South, and East to West. It was divided by the river Thames".

The various gates show that the Londoners lived within the city walls, which was now known as the City of London. The old Tower and the markets, surrounding it, were the witness of this truth. The example, he gave was that of Aldgate and Aldgate East which were very close to the Old Tower and the Tower Bridge.

Delhi also had its own gates, the India Gate, the Lahori Gate, the Ajmeri Gate, and the Kashmiri Gate. These places were now residential areas, but they had kept their names. Jay explained all that, because he wanted his younger brother to comprehend that a Gate did not necessarily mean an entry place with pillars. Of course, he stated that there were many other parts in London which had their own identities and names.

All localities in London, had open space and parks for the benefit of residents. Some parks had become famous and were recognizable across the world. "The Hyde Park, the Kensington Gardens, the Regents Park, St. James Park, Richmond Park and the Kew Gardens, were prominent and popular". The, the Greenwich Park, Osterley Park and Gunnersbury Park were quite big, where local people walked around every day. Jay himself had had picnic and walked around these parks many times over.

He also mentioned some popular museums, especially the "British Museum, the Albert and Victoria Museum, the Natural History Museum, Science and Geological Museums". People line up to visit these places every day. These were the tourist attractions for people from various parts of the United Kingdom and from abroad. London also had famous bridges, the Tower bridge, The London bridge, Westminster bridge, and the Kew Bridge were just a few. Not many Indian or other Asian families lived in Jay's locality. Some, however, ran small businesses there. There was an electronics repair shop at a walking distance from his house. He became friendly with the owner, Guru Nam. He had his video recorder repaired at his shop. During a conversation one day, Guru Nam asked him about his job. Jay told him that he taught at a university but did not reveal any further details.

Guru Nam asked him, whether he could help his daughter with her course work. Jay asked him to bring the work, she has done. He would have a look at it. Alternatively, "she could email her work to me." The next day Guru Nam brought the course work and delivered at Jay's house. He read the work and made necessary suggestions.

Guru Nam's daughter needed further clarification in other subjects. Overall, Jay spent four to five hours in correcting the work and in oral discussion. Guru Nam's daughter suggested to her dad, that he should not charge for the repair of Jay's video recorder. Alternatively, he should pay for her tuition.

Jay suggested to the young lady, "your dad's earning depended on his repair work." "I, however, get a salary from my university, which looks after my expenses and bills." "There was no need to pay me any money or give me a discount on the work that Guru Nam has done for me." "I could not charge for a few hours of help with her course work."

The father and daughter were happy. That was an enough award for discussing her projects. Jay pointed out a few ideas and amendments that "perhaps you wanted to write this sentence or express your views like that." The girl said to her dad, "how did he know, what was I thinking or planning to write"? Jay told her and Guru Nam that "it was a natural way of writing and expressing views by students."

He was not a psychologist or an astrologer to enter a person's mind. A teacher's experience could suggest, what a student wanted to write but sometimes, could not express herself\himself. Like any other student, "she was clever enough to reach the required standard but needed a little guidance." Jay considered it as a social work.

He noticed that Indians were ambitious. They respected their culture and social values. They had also become a part of the British society. The younger generation had adopted some aspects of the western way of living. The Asians have made a valuable contribution to the British economy, especially in small-businesses and in running the corner shops.

A House of Commons Report revealed that the Indians formed only 2.9% of the British population, yet they contributed 10% to the United Kingdom Revenues, through taxation. Many Indians were encouraged by the British government to emigrate to East Africa to help in the running of the colonies. After their independence, changes started to take place in these countries.

The African leaders became anti-British and anti-Indian, who had helped the British in colonial administration. They were asked to leave their countries. Many of them returned to India. Some went to live in the United States. Some, however, moved to live in Britain because they had British passports. The British government had created a pool of workers overseas, who could be allowed to come to Britain, when needed. On moving to reside in Britain, many East African Asians (as they were called) became shopkeepers and businessmen.

In retail shops, all members of the family gave their time by standing at the till and the check-out. They hardly employed outsiders because they could not afford to pay wages, and the employees would not be careful, as the owners themselves, in dealing with customers who needed personal attention. There were, however, examples, when a shopkeeper or an employee was on his own at the shop, and damages were inflicted to their properties, and windows were broken.

One shopkeeper in Jay's locality received so much damage to his shop that he had to close it down. He was not an educated person. He did not speak fluent English either. He had to seek employment at the Heathrow airport, where quite a few Asians worked as cleaners, porters, baggage handlers, shop assistants and bank clerks. The wages were low. They were paid only the national minimum wage.

Nevertheless, there were two other retail shops near Jay's house. He sometimes bought goods of them. They both were friendly and polite to their customers. Sometimes they delivered shopping at elderly people's houses. Their working hours were long and tiring. They both ran family businesses. One of them, named Rajat, got tired and looked older than his age.

He never went on holiday for twenty years or more. He decided to retire at the age of fifty-five. That was the consequence of his working fifteen hours a day. There was no social life for him and his family. Nonetheless, he managed to send both his children to Study at Universities. One of them became an Accountant and the other studied Information Technology.

The other shop keeper in the area was Shahid. He and his family also worked fifteen hours a day, Shahid had no time for his family. He had only one daughter. When she was young, she wanted to become a doctor. As she grew older, she realized that her dad had no time for her and the family. They never went to seaside, or any other visiting places or on holiday. With the result she lost interest in her studies.

Shahid's wife was very depressed. One day she told Jay, "If her husband did not change his working times, she would not live with him and divorce him". She emphasized that he does not spend valuable time with her and the daughter. He was always involved in his work and business. Expanding it, diversifying it. They did not have a social life. She stressed that work ethic was good but there should be a balance between social life, family life and business.

No progress could be made, if family members were not happy, and they did not support each other. Family dinner and family outing was an essential part of social life. If parents and children were close to each other, there would be less deviation and more openness and understanding. It would lead to progression and proficiency in all dimensions.

Any kind of narrow attitude would breed dissent, misapprehension, and ill-judgement. It would be grossly unfair to limit the scope of success. The customs and traditions should remain alive and therefore, subject to change.

<u>33</u>

Jay noticed that there was a division of labour in the United Kingdom, based on colour or race. The Black people worked in transport and the National Health Service as nurses, porters and in the kitchen. There were very few Indian nurses. Indian doctors, however, counted for 14% of all doctors and surgeons in the United Kingdom. A greater proportion than their population in Britain would suggest. In research and technical department more Asians, particularly women could be found.

It looked as if the white people still held the senior positions. If the British society became multicultural in the real sense of the term, it would be easy for people to manifest themselves and make progress. Otherwise, a struggle for advancement and existence would continue.

Jay attended a conference which considered multiculturalism and the teaching of multicultural education in English Schools. The aim was to introduce Black and Asian culture, literature, and other aspects of education, in school and college curriculum. He maintained that non-white people were in Britain because of the

Empire and the colonies and her relations with India, Africa, and the West Indies.

After the Second World War, there was a need for doctors, nurses, and transport workers in big cities of Britain. It was considered that the families of new immigrants, who looked different, had diverse demands, should feel comfortable and be able to assimilate in their new country.

Their children should not feel alienated. They should know their own culture, history, and literature of which they should be proud. They should not feel that there was still white domination through education system and subject curriculum, which would impede their intellectual and social advancement. Everyone recognized that Black and Asian writers should be studied along with the English writers.

The role of trade unions, views of political parties and the inclusion of ethnic people in social and political activities should be examined. Small businesses should be investigated, along with big corporations and big trades. The teachers should interview local businesspeople and residents. Many of whom had come from South-Asia and the West Indies. Their contribution should be recognized.

It would benefit the whole community and the entire country. Jay authored a report, about the discussions on multiculturalism. He sent a copy to the headmaster, a copy to the Inspector of Schools at the borough education department. He presented a seminar to his colleagues at the school. There was rich literature available by the Afro-Asian and Caribbean authors and writers.

The Afro-Asian-Caribbean society invited him to talk about the new project and conduct a seminar at Leicester as well as in London. He was keen to advertise this new programme. He agreed to go to places wherever, he was invited to. He not only talked about the Black and Asian writers, but he also emphasized that people from these communities, had actively participated in politics, trade unions, health services, social services, football, tennis, and other sports.

The Central and local government administration, public and private sectors of the economy. Schools, Colleges, and Universities had persons from the minority groups and communities. There was hardly any field, where people from racially visible communities, were not employed.

They brought new culture to Britain, which had enriched the nation, economically as well as culturally. Practical examples exist. The festival of Diwali had become a popular event in Britain. It was celebrated in the Houses of Parliament, at the Trafalgar

Squire, and other places. The Carnival festival originally started by the Caribbean community, had become a yearly event for everyone in London. It had gained international importance and recognition. In the month of August, people from many European countries come to watch the procession in London and to enjoy the variety of food.

The School of African and Oriental Studies appointed Jay, a visiting fellow in the Extra-Mural Department, to develop Multicultural Education which would be a popular and useful subject. It would benefit minority groups and help them to gain good education. He ran classes for all to promote multicultural education and inform of the necessity for such courses.

Questions were often asked about the method of informing, of the available facilities and how could they be encouraged to study relevant subjects and find good employment, to suit their interests and talents. The Black students were still lagging in employment and professions, even though there had been an equal opportunities policy for many decades.

An educational qualification was a medium for progression and to elevate people socially and economically. Other things would follow. He argued that access to education should be unlimited, regardless of age, race, gender, disability, or other needs. There was a requirement to provide information about such courses. It could be channelled by sending leaflets to households, Youth Centres, Libraries, Job Centres, Community groups and by advertising in local Black and Asian newspapers and periodicals.

The education institutions should identify areas where improvement could be made. Student's participation on different courses ought to be monitored. These courses must sustain relevance for employment. Students should be encouraged to study for professional jobs like Accountancy, Engineering, Architecture, Nursing, Management, and Medical Education. The education system should be geared towards practical side of employment. The students should be guided towards these courses.

It was an important method of promoting equal opportunities for all. The colleges and universities would play their role in creating a chance for Black and Asian young people. Jay maintained that the staff of these institutions would have to take practical steps to increase the number of Black and Asian students, on work related courses and progression to higher level courses and employment.

It was essential to identify good practice in marketing, recruitment, and continuation strategies to attract a higher number of Black and Asian students, in order to accomplish these objectives. Vocational courses could be relevant and beneficial for such groups. Both employers and students' needs, should be considered and met. Conducive to making progress in such areas, Jay organised seminars for staff in colleges and departments.

He argued that colleges could be asked to maintain statistics of number of students entering courses, making progress, and gaining employment in different areas. Employers' contribution was essential by affording finance and furnishing employment in their organisations.

People in parts of Britain were against multiculturalism. They wanted to maintain one culture and argued that the Black and Asian youth should conform to the existing British way of education and system. Jay expressed the view that it would restrict progress and identity of Asian and Black youngsters. It could lead to alienation rather than to mingle by accepting a different culture.

He suggested that special courses, should be designed, which should be targeted to these communities. There was a need for "Access to Mathematics and Science" to bring them to the level of entry required for degree courses. "Access to Accounting and Banking," along with the "Access to Law" and the "Access to Build Environment", courses should be brought into the system.

It was realized that more Access courses were needed in vocational areas like Construction and Engineering, where Black people were underrepresented. These courses could also be used as feeder routes to mainstream studies. The itinerary like "Leisure and Recreation" could be taught at colleges. Efforts should be made to help Black students in achieving their potential by encouraging them to acquire adequate education which would help them to obtain a right employment.

It was felt that the equal opportunities perspective and the issues of racism and gender should be included in the information provided to students and in the curriculum. Adequate resourcing and staffing were required to achieve these objectives. Teachers should be provided enough time to review the teaching areas and to prepare their teaching material. Good education should be provided to all.

Jay suggested that extracurricular activities fostered self-confidence and sociability. Students should be trained to meet the demand of business organizations. Some entrepreneurs provided, on the job training. Jay discovered that several courses had links with local businesses. They organized regular meetings to discuss the course curriculum. These links would help students to find employment at the end of their course. The employer-led programmes provided a guaranteed assignment which would benefit both, the employers, and the students.

It ensured that after completing their syllabus, students would have jobs, and employers would have decent quality work force. The careers advice and counselling were important aspects in the education system. Deliberating could reduce the drop-out rate and foster successful completion of courses. Work experience during studies, could assist students in making decisions, about their future education and employment plans. Monitoring of progression was inevitable for institutions to provide relevant information to future students.

Undergraduates, however, faced financial difficulties. Jay suggested that there should be a provision for bursary to pay their rent, buy books and other expenses. They could be inspired to find part-time employment over the weak-end or in the evenings. It was important to guide youngsters to ensure that their education did not suffer They should plan to balance their work and studies.

It was essential to investigate and foster the interests of Black and Asian students, who could have equal opportunity in education and employment and continue to make progress. With improved education standards, they would find good housing and other facilities in order to live a better life than they would have lived without such a provision and guidance.

<u>34</u>

The Teachers' training Department at Kings College invited Jay to teach Methodology, also known as the teaching methods to trainee teachers and acquaint them with the system required to become good teachers and to contribute to society by providing excellent education in schools and colleges. He recognized that there were at least three fields, which were required for a good teacher. He argued that a subject teacher, should be a good conversationalist and communicator. He/she should have knowledge of his/her subject and should be able to explain the theme in a language which can be grasped by students.

For this he would have to repeat his terminology and dramatize his topic under study. He should look at students and observe that they were attentive and were following the theme. He should not waver his attention or look at the walls and the ceiling, because he was dealing with young people, who must meticulously listen to the teacher.

Both the theme and the students were essential in teaching profession. The teaching method should be changed according to need. Sometimes the whole class should be taught together. At other times, students must be divided into groups for discussion and brainstorming. They should report their discussion points to the whole class before the end of the lesson.

Some students needed individual consideration. The teacher should allocate time for such students, who require re-emphasizing the topic. Jay always did that. The teachers should encourage students to present a seminar or read a paper and then discuss it. The remaining students should be encouraged to comment and add innovative ideas but not to criticize student's work.

Positive feedback was good. Negative criticism could foster loss of confidence among tutees. He recognized that a good teacher was always a student. He/she should continue to acquire current ideas and new knowledge, with the aim of passing it to on his/her class. In Universities, it was identified as continuous research. Jay himself acquired his Doctorate Degree, while teaching. He was research minded and research active. He continued to seek new knowledge and parted his cognition in variant ways. Some experienced academics found Jay's ideas and writings, new which they had missed during earlier years or were not aware of the added information and the new facts.

Jay expressed the view that academic administration was a crucial feature in the teaching profession. He himself was an admissions tutor. He interviewed students for courses and advised them about the suitability of a course. He was a class Tutor and made sure that his students did not miss lessons, without good reason. He investigated the cause for their absence.

He was a personal tutor to look at their problems and find solutions. He referred students to specialist departments, like accommodation for a room, finance department for any financial support, e.g. bursary or students' loan. Other duties included, undertaking invigilation during examinations, preparing examination papers, marking examination scripts and attending examiners meetings to finalise the students' results.

Some of his mature students would have liked to join the teaching profession after graduation. They asked Jay, what were the qualities of a good teacher? He responded that they should improve their method of teaching and discover new methods that would emerge to communicate new knowledge of culture, literature, history of different countries. Contribution towards advancement of science and technology by people of different nations should be acknowledged.

The students should be revitalized to write answers to questions in essay form. They should read loudly to themselves to scrutinize the language and how the material sounded to them and think of the ways it could be refined. They could change words and phrases, if these were being repeated in the same paragraph. If possible, the students should read their paper to their relatives or friends and seek their comments to enhance skills and understanding.

The teachers' comments should be taken seriously, and the paper should be rewritten, as the authors do in their editing process. A good teacher would not enter classroom without preparing the teaching material. They should regularly review and revise their teaching notes. In education and particularly in teaching, it was vital to use technology and computers. In the past, films were shown on agriculture and industrial life and people's practical experiences. Jay encouraged group presentation.

Quality control was often identified with the manufacturing sector and safety regulations. Jay told the trainee teachers that quality control was an indispensable part in education. It was a requisite to accomplish a high standard in teaching, to make the best use of resources and to provide the best service to students and the community including businesses.

The quality assessment was not only concerned with the teaching material or delivering lectures of high standard, but it also included other areas of learning process from recruitment and selection of students to curriculum content, teaching strategies, responsibilities of a personal tutor and the evaluation of courses.

He stressed that it was important the Admissions Tutor looks for communication skills, both oral as well as written. Numeracy skills and analytical skills were equally imperative. A student should be able to make decisions independently, with sufficient information, which he/she would have acquired through study and research.

The course curriculum normally provided an excellent opportunity for quality control. This could be accomplished by a structured programme. It should reflect the aims and objectives of the subject. The curriculum formation would apprehend progression for students. They would improve their skills and knowledge. With all such information, the institution would be better prepared to help young people with their studies.

This new system would become a vehicle to combat racism and bias. It could become a focus for special initiatives to consider the ways in which various constituents of good practice could be introduced in courses. One gentleman asked Jay, what was the difference between the aims and the objectives? He explained that external bodies, set the aims, which were to be achieved by students and candidates. Candidates could accomplish the objectives themselves.

334

A student could set his objective to achieve a certain percentage of marks in the examination. He would work for it and try to obtain the grades. These could be done through learning process, involving seminars, class discussions, one to one tutorials and group work. The continual feedback from staff and students would provide a better understanding of the quality of tasks and assignments. The involvement of community was also felt vital.

Jay taught in different departments on specialist topics, where students and colleagues appreciated his contribution. Some students had handicaps in numeracy and expression. Jay laid emphasis on numeracy and communication skills and in providing extra classes to students who needed them. It would lead to an improvement of learning Mathematics, statistics, Accountancy, social sciences, and languages.

He further stressed that the study skills programme should focus on notes taking from books and lectures. They should also lay emphasis on essay writing, data collection and its interpretation. The students should decide their own learning process to develop originality. The course review at regular intervals was essential to attain a high standard in academic encompassment. These points were important for the would-be teachers to understand and practice in their schools and colleges.

<u>35</u>

When Jay lived in India, he did not have a radio or a transistor, which his age group people and the neighbours possessed. He had limited resources but unlimited responsibilities. Even if he thought of purchasing a small transistor, he knew that his extended family would not let him retain it and they would remove from him. They used to ask for everything that he tried to acquire and enjoy.

Once he bought a fashionable decent quality towel. His mother asked him to gift it to his youngest brother. He politely said that if he had two towels, he would have given one to him. He knew that his mother had money to purchase a towel for the youngest, but she could not bear to see a superior quality towel owned by Jay.

In the United Kingdom, he bought a transistor and a television. The transistor was to listen, Hindi songs. When Jay arrived in London, there were very few Hindi schedules. Initially, these were limited to twenty minutes bulletin on Sundays. In course of time, the Indian community started their own radio station, for songs in Indian languages and to advertise and inform the community of events, which were to take place in various parts of the United Kingdom.

After five years, the organisers started to invite singers from India and other countries of South-Asia. People liked that and attended the events in large numbers. Jay and his family went to these events. When Indian programmes were not available, they used to watch British and American serials. The British shows were comedies, but a few films were also shown, which were of some interest.

The American serials dominated the British television. Some people felt that American culture was being imposed in the United Kingdom through Television broadcast and production. Jay enjoyed the detective programmes, crime investigation and comedies. The British programmes were based on individual or small group appearances, which led to laughter and relaxation. The Mike Yarwood Show, Norman Wisdom, Two Ronnies with Ronnie Barker and Ronnie Corbett, Eric Morcombe and Ernie Wise, Bruce Forsythe shows, were very amusing.

Bruce Forsythe appeared in various roles as a presenter, actor, comedian, singer, and dancer. He was the longest engaging actor on the British television. Steptoe and Son, a comedy of scruffy life in the east-end of London, showed relationship between father and son.

Only Fools and Horses, was another family drama. Two brothers and an uncle engrossed the public, with their humour and action. These programmes were short lived, but some continued for decades or more. They left their mark on the minds of the British people. Z cars, Inspector Morse, Inspector Linley, Dixon of Dock Green, were soft detectives which did not impress Jay. They did not show any solution to problems that they set out to resolve.

On the contrary, he enjoyed the fast-moving American shows. A Man Called Ironside with Raymond Bur, NCIS, Hawaii Five O, the Streets of San Francisco were his favourites. Steve's order "Book him Dano" led to laughter at the end of the Hawaii Five O. Columbo, a homicide detective with the Los Angeles Police Department, starring Peter Falk, who was famous with his shoddy coat, was laughable.

Apart from comedies and detective's programmes, there were serials like The Dallas with JR Ewing and his brother Bobby Ewing, the oil barons, and businesspeople. JR Ewing used to manipulate and extort people to accomplish his objectives. Larry Hagman, Patrick Duffy, Linda Gray, and Victoria Principal were the main actors in dominating position. Cliff Barnes was on the receiving end in this saga with feud.

The Roots was immensely popular. It was a story of slavery and how the slaves were treated in the United States. It was the dramatization of Alex Healey's book. It won nine awards. The Holocaust also showed, injustices done to the Jews in Europe and their extermination. Jay was terribly upset at the behaviour of people against other human beings. A community was mistreated only because of their colour and/or different religion and culture.

The Persuaders with Tony Curtis and Roger Moore, a detective programme, was full of action, adventure, and comedy. The Australian television drama, The Neighbours was immensely popular among the youth. It continued for almost thirty years. Some actors changed and found distinct positions. But some continued to the end of the series.

A few historical films were shown on television. Ben Hurl, Spartacus, The Roots impressed Jay, because of their stories and artistic performance. Some American films, whether they were about the Romans or the European settlement in the United States, did not make much impression on him because of their content and brutality shown on a different group of people.

A change occurred in the 1980s. Jay bought a video player and watched Hindi movies with his family. He used to hire films every week to enjoy the songs and the acting in Hindi cinema. They must have watched more than one hundred Hindi, Punjabi, Gujrati, and Tamil films. They were all entertaining with a message. Raj Kapoor, Rajesh Khanna, Dharmendra, and Manoj Kumar were his favourite heroes. Indian movies were full of songs with good music and lyrics.

Several song writers and play back singers made their mark on Indian film industry. Manna Dey, Mukesh, Kishor Kumar, Mahendra Kapoor were male singers of the 1960s and 1970s. Some continued in the 1980s and several new singers entered the industry. Lata Mangeshkar, Asha Bhonsle, Suman Kallyanpur and Kavita Krishnamurthy, were well known female singers. A few singers came only for short periods. Play back songs were an essential feature of Indian films.

Folk dance, village dance, regional dance like Bhangra and classical dances- Bharatanatyam and Katha kalam, played significant role in Indian Films. They displayed the Indian culture in many forms. Indian films were made in studios in Mumbai (Bombay), but certain other locations were also sought for songs. Kashmir and Parts of Tamil Nadu and Kerala were chosen. Some songs were filmed in Switzerland, Paris, London, Scotland, Budapest, and other locations in Europe and in India.

Jay was a busy man. He could not go to watch films in theatres. Distance and time were also factors. He did not like going out at night. Most films were shown in evenings. Visiting Indian singers also did their performance in evenings in various parts of London. He, however, stayed connected with the Indian culture.

He read hundreds of Hindi novels and English novels on Indian history and society. The local libraries in London started to keep books in Indian languages, as well as on the Indian philosophy and history. He read these books by borrowing of the libraries. He was a member of at least six libraries, where he could borrow books.

<u>36</u>

Jay felt that it was vital to remain vigilant in order to exist in adverse circumstances. Life was full of struggles but there were alternatives. If one road was not smooth and it was full of potholes, wisdom suggested, seeking a different route and to attempt a safe and secure drive-in order to reach the destination. The same principle applies to a life's journey. If one field or area could not provide progression, there would always be an alternative.

In the absence of opportunities to progress, Indians sought alternative routes and diverted their energies to undertake their own businesses, rather than to work as employees. Indians were very independent minded. They remained quiet and refrained from unnecessary confrontation or dispute but pursued their own path.

They worked in all professions. There were Asian Lawyers, private college owners, they ran medical practices in private sector and Chemist shops and stores. It should be recognized and appreciated by the authorities and the society as whole. Jay observed that similar trend was taking place in International Relations and on the world scene.

When Europeans and Americans ignored the Indian argument, they setup their own organizations for political, defence and trade relations. India had an educated young generation and 1.4 billion population with a democratically elected government. On the economic front the World Trade Organization, The International Monetary Fund, and the World Bank, were all controlled by the Europeans and the Americans.

They were still suffering from imperialism, colonialism and superiority complex. They became rich nations from the loots from India and Africa followed by a large settlement in the United States of America, South America and of course in Australia.

India became politically and administratively free in 1947, yet the imperialist civil servants and the British army personnel, who worked for the British Empire, continued to receive pension from the Indian treasury, throughout the 1950s and 1960s. The Indian contribution during the First World War and the Second World War was recognized by the Indian government. The British did not fully acknowledge their sacrifices for the defence and victory of Britain. The Indian contribution was enormous in personnel as well as in financial terms.

India and other countries had created an alternative to G 7 (a group of rich countries). It was known as G 20. The G7 became redundant, because it could not solve the economic and financial problems of the world. BRICS and other organizations have emerged to augment trade between nations. The climate change, the world Food problems, had not been fully addressed by the United Nations and other organizations. It led to bi-lateral meetings and relations between nations.

In 2023, India hosted the G20 Summit of Heads of State and Government. Meetings were held in New Delhi. Prior to the top gathering, meetings were also held in various parts of the country, to consider, special areas of administration and life. These conventions investigated economic and financial situations, education, trade, culture, sports, food, and objects of concerns of international importance. Indian leaders had shown their tenacity and spirit to lead the country out of troubles. Manmohan Singh as Finance Minister solved the 1998, Asian crisis very tactfully in his country.

When many countries witnessed the melt down and suffered economic and monetary crisis, India's economy continued to grow. There was no financial problem in India, during his Prime Ministership, from 2004 to 2014. He and his financial advisors continued to steer the economy and maintain high economic growth. It also included outsourcing and computer programming.

After winning the election in 2014, the Bhartiya Janata Party (BJP) provided an alternative to the Chinese production. It appealed to "make in India." It developed infrastructure and manufacturing sector. Factories were set up for weaponry and in many other fields, like motor industry, two and three-wheeler production for exports. Foreign investment was encouraged in manufacturing sector. Indian foreign reserves rose as her exports grew. It achieved self-sufficiency in defence production. Still, it continued to import aeroplane for its Air Force.

India had continued to have good relations with her neighbours including Iran and the Arab countries. Seven percent of Saudi Arabia's population was of Indian origin. They do all kinds of jobs and live peacefully there. It had been recognized and appreciated by the Saudi authorities, who suggested that they did not interfere in the Saudi internal affairs. They earn their living by working hard, send money to their families in India.

One thing Jay appreciated very much was that India maintained good relations with the United States as well as with the Russian Federation. No one had been able to pull India towards one or the other bloc. She has attempted to improve political relations with China but with little success. Though their trade had grown enormously.

India had continued to maintain her independent foreign policy. It had appealed to Russia and Ukraine to stop the war which started in February 2022. However, it did not intervene or interfere in their actions. Pakistan remained a headache for India. Without stopping terrorism, India would not converse with Pakistan.

Jay believed that if a person wanted to accomplish one's objectives, he/she should not give up but should continue with his efforts. His last effort could lead to success. The public decisions were taken for the benefit of most individuals and families. Trust was vital in social relationships. If we like someone, we should respect them. People should be careful from exploiters and those who were determined to harm others.

Some people were unable to understand Jay and his thinking because of their lack of experience or education in certain areas. Jay was not going to listen or follow them without proper consideration and reasoning. He did not want to be influenced by ignorant persons or to lose the plot which could go against his welfare and progress. He wanted to maintain the same principle in personal life as in society.

After teaching at a Secondary school for twelve years, Jay was advised by one of his colleagues from another department, that "it was time, he moved to teach at an institution of Higher Education."

Jay was also thinking on similar lines, that he had nothing much to contribute at the school. He, therefore moved to teach at a college of Higher Education and in a few years to a university, where he made enormous contribution in academics and multicultural education.

At the time of his departure from the school, his addition to the school welfare and academic achievement by students was admired by the headmaster. His colleagues told him that this school would not survive without him. One of his friends called him, "the fourth pillar of the school". In fact, the school closed, five years after Jay's departure from that place. There was, however, a different reason for that and not Jay's leaving the secondary school teaching.

At the University, the demand for him to speak about multiculturalism increased. Jay participated in Politics and History Department, Economics and Business Studies Department and Sociology Department. He wanted to tell people that Britain was bigger than just an Anglo-Saxons nation. Other people, who lived there were faithful, law abiding and worked hard at all levels of society. Jay's input to multiculturalism was valued by authorities. He thought that the situation in Britain was improving, and it was much better than they were twenty years earlier or when he arrived in London to start a new life. But he was proved wrong. During the summer months, violence flared up in various parts of London. The real cause of this act was never discovered. It was, however, argued that the police's mishandling of this latitude, coupled with the prevailing economic and social grievances led to violence.

The setting spread to outer London areas as well as to other cities of England including Liverpool and Manchester. At one stage it looked like a concerted action. It was repeated over the weekends, throughout the summer months. The police and the youths affronted each other. A great deal of damage was inflicted on public property including the police cars.

The government set up a Commission of Enquiry under the chairmanship of a retired Judge, to enquire into the causes of disturbances. People called this a delaying tactic because no immediate action was forth coming. Racism was on the rise in England. It was not only the police which displayed heavy handedness towards the Black youth, the Black children also faced racism at school. "The white teachers did not fully work for their welfare."

Jay's school in London had a substantial number of black students, who were not making much progress academically or socially. In the wake of the Judge's enquiry, the Education Authority appointed a new Headmaster who was highly qualified and intelligent, but he had afro hair because of his Afro-Asian origin.

The white teachers refused to accept his leadership. They often clashed with him at meetings and refused to implement his policies. They did not cooperate with him, even when he had promising ideas to improve the condition at the school. Many teachers turned up to meetings when he wanted to see only the Heads of Department. They were noisy and tried to annoy him. He, however, kept his cool and smiled. When Jay discovered of such activities, he was incredibly sad.

"Jay found subjective criticism bad and the rejection of the headmaster's ideas, unhelpful." All teachers did not oppose him but those who, were critical of him, were very vocal. At the school, no progress was being made in any direction. Obstruction and impediments continued, which looked like withstand and flout. One teacher called him "black Hitler." Another felt that he (the headmaster) would crack one day. The Education Authority considered acting against the rowdy and disruptive teachers.

The headmaster did not allow any action against his staff. He was very forgiving. He, nevertheless, could not achieve any cooperation from the teaching staff. The Education Authority decided to close the school. The headmaster took an early retirement. The students and staff were allocated to other schools and other boroughs. Certain teachers also took early retirement.

<u>37</u>

Jay was born in a village, where most people knew each other. They tried to assist one another, whenever it was possible and in whatever way, they could support their neighbours and acquaintances. He was convinced that small communities were the right basis for a good society where an individual could flourish and realize his potential and could contribute to its progress. He was not against big cities, where most jobs existed, or jobs could be created. People flocked to cities in order to seek employment, education and to improve their lives.

Several cities had, however, developed slums, where life was miserable. It was better to live in villages with less amenities but good natural and social environment, than to face conundrum in slums. People maintained that big cities in India depended on slums. The rich were rich, only because they took advantage of other people's poverty and made them work at lower wages.

He believed in reviving cottage industries in Indian villages, where more avocations could be provided. With changes in social and economic structure in the 19th Century, the harmony between the agriculture and trade was subverted. With the result, the foundations of village and village life deteriorated. In the Middle Ages, villages were richer than cities.

He wanted all education to be imparted in Indian languages, which were very flexible and rich. Indians, especially the middle-class people felt proud speaking in English language, even at home and talking to their family members including young children. Unfortunately, some middle-class parents had been sending their off- springs to English Medium schools. This divided the society and created apartheid within the camaraderie. It also hampered mental growth of youngsters, who could easily learn subjects in their own vernacular and express themselves better in local terminology than in a foreign language.

After migrating from India, Jay did not return to live there permanently. He, however, kept visiting his country of origin and went on holiday to various places and states. He could not visit India every year but went there, whenever it was feasible. He continued to write to his relatives and received correspondence from them, His writings, books, and articles reflected his thoughts on India, and concerns about Indians overseas.

Socially and physically, he became a part of the British society and adopted the British way of living. Still, his thoughts were based on Indian philosophy and culture. Of course, when a person lived in a country, he was influenced by the laws and customs of his adopted nation. His food habits also changed. From time to time, he celebrated the starting date of his new life in Britain.

He reflected over the period and the changes that have taken place. The problems he encountered and his accomplishments, especially in education and employment. He also brooded over his sufferings and losses. How he was rebuffed and looked down upon, discouraged from undertaking constructive work, he would have enjoyed doing. Yet, he struggled on and continued with his own pursuit.

He was not prepared to accept negative attitudes and intrigues or the blueprints of others. He altered his tactics and hoped for better times in the future. He observed that he was successful in several fields, be it honour, academic accomplishment or in other sectors of the economy and finance. He had a cheerful home and a happy family. His family members were not visionaries. Neither did they live an unrealistic life. They had a comfortable and dynamic sustenance.

People had asked him about the partition of India. He was incredibly young when the partition took place. Now he was keen to discover the reasons and the circumstances which led to the country's division on religious grounds. He set out to ascertain the real causes of partition and whether it was a separation of areas of India to form a new country or a unification of Princely states and other parts of the nation. It was both. Writers from different countries have written according to their thinking and experiences. The British authors had maintained that the two major religious groups could not reconcile and were fighting for their rights and privileges in India. The Pakistani writers have argued that Muslims would be in minority against the Hindu majority in an undivided India. In a democracy, where majority rule prevailed, the minorities could be suppressed and would be unable to express themselves, live freely and would not be able to practice their religion independently.

The Indian writers have written that after the Second World War, the Muslim League failed to work with the Indian National Congress. In late 1940s, violence flared up in various parts of the country. The Muslim League started a day of action, which became uncontrollable. The minorities in the Western states and Eastern states of the country, became worried about their safety and security. They, therefore, started to move to places and states, where their religious majority lived.

In the 21st Century, an experienced Indian politician- Jaswant Singh, who had been India's foreign minister and Finance minister, published a book. *"Jinnah, India's Independence and the Partition."* This title brought uproar in the Bhartiya Janta Party and the Sangh Parivar. Jaswant Singh was expelled from the party. Even though he was a senior leader and a minister in the Atal Bihari Bajpai administration in 1990s.

It was suggested that Singh had praised Jinnah in his book, while Nehru and Patel had been criticized. They also stressed that Jinnah was responsible for the partition of India in 1947, which dislocated twelve million people. Over one million people were killed in communal violence. In expelling Jaswant Singh from the Bhartiya Janta Party, nonetheless, the party leaders behaved like village feudal elders and not as a modern political party.

In Jay's opinion they were like the Lohanas (a particular group of local Hindus) in Gujarat, some one hundred years earlier. He argued that Mohammed Ali Jinnah's grandfather Premji Bhai Thakkar had started the trading business of fish, within the coastal town of Veraval, to support his family. His business, however, clashed with the ethics of the Lohana Hindu community, to which he belonged. They, therefore, ostracised him from their fraternity. Premji Bhai Thakkar (Jinnah's grandfather) earned a great deal of money in fish business. He attempted to rejoin his community. He also discontinued the fish trade. Still the local Hindu group and their leaders rejected his request. They did not allow him to become a member of the association of people in the area. Premji Bhai's son, Punjan Lal Thakkar was infuriated at the humiliation of his father. He left the community, and he gave up the Hindu religion.

He adopted Islam as his new religion, whose leaders embraced him with open arms. He changed his sons' names including that of Mohammed Ali. He also dropped his surname Thakkar. Mohammed Ali's father Punjan Lal was a slim man. People called him Jino, which in Gujrati meant "skinny".

Mohammed Ali decided to change his family name to Jinnah (children of Jino) and adopted his father's nickname as his surname. He aimed to be associated with his father's nick name. The other members of Mohammed Ali's also family also became Jinnah. His sister was known as Fatima Jinnah.

Jay argued that if the Hindu community had permitted Premji Bhai Thakkar to rejoin the community, Punjan Lal would not have been exasperated, Mohammed Ali would have remained a Hindu. He would not have insisted on a separate state for India's Muslims.

For Jay, a fundamental question remained, "whether a single person was responsible for the creation of the state of Pakistan"? And, therefore, partition of India became inevitable. He expressed the view that no single person could be held responsible for a historical phenomenon.

There were several parties in India's freedom struggle. The British imperialists wanted to hold on to power as long as they could. When it had become impossible to rule India by force, the British government led by Clement Atli decided to relinquish the country in 1947. The British Conservative party led by Winston Churchill and quite a few retired ICS officials, who were members of the India Defence League, however, wanted to continue to control India and remain in power. The British rulers created mischief and disorder in the country, with a belief that the Indian leaders would ask them to stay on to maintain peace and to continue their administration.

In June 1947, Gandhi offered Jinnah, the Prime Ministership of the united India and he agreed for the sake of avoiding the partition. It was, however, Jawaharlal Nehru who made a political justification and expressed the view that the Muslim League of which Jinnah was the leader, was a minority party in the Legislative Assembly. He questioned "how could its leader become Prime Minister, when the Congress party was the majority party"? Nehru himself wanted to become the First Prime Minister of free India.

The same month the Indian leaders including the Viceroy went to London to draw up a final settlement with the British government. During this period, Mountbatten who was the Viceroy of India, went to see Churchill who asked him to keep a part of India under British control. Mountbatten promised to fulfil his wishes. Despite this promise, Mountbatten often insisted and wrangled that he could have avoided the partition of India, if he had known that Jinnah was suffering from cancer and would die within a year.

The British government and the Indian leaders decided to create the state of Pakistan with Baluchistan, Sindh, West Punjab, and Northwest Frontier in the west, and East Bengal in the east of the nation. At that time, all the governors of these provinces were British who created fear among the people. Consequently, disturbances flared up. The British civil administration and the army refused to stop the violence. People of different communities started to move from one part of the country to another part, depending on their religion. The two communities, who had lived peacefully for centuries, were killing each other. It took time to stop the carnage.

Initially, it was thought that the **partition** would be temporary, and the two sides would come together, when sanity returned. Because of geopolitical reasons and short sightedness on the part of both, the Indian and Pakistani leaders, partition became bitter and permanent.

The two power blocs led by the United States and the Soviet Union created their areas of influence. The United States and Britain indirectly controlled Pakistan. They provided defence and financial support, which was often used against India. Indians also did not seriously attempt to improve relations with its neighbour and the new state.

Surprisingly, in course of time, India's relations with the United States and Britain improved, but her affinity with Pakistan did not become cordial, when they should have been better because of geographical, historical, and cultural reasons. Jay thought and hoped that Jaswant Singh, through his book might have attempted to recognize the role of Jinnah and the Muslim League in the independence movement. It, nevertheless, blew onto his face, because a substantial number of people blamed Jinnah and his intransigence, not to join the Indian Constituent Assembly in 1946. The Muslim League, nevertheless, joined the interim government led by Prime Minister Jawaharlal Nehru with Liaquat Ali Khan of the Muslim League, as the Deputy Prime Minister. Indeed, Liaquat Ali wanted to prolong this administration because there was no central government for the new state of Pakistan. It was essential to have a working regime in place, before the new state, could start to function and implement policies. If that situation existed, the carnage of killings and the unplanned movement of population, could have been avoided.

It had, however, been the policy of the British imperialism to divide the country. The division of a nation left behind many problems, as it had been experienced in the partition of Ireland, Palestine and indeed India. No single person or party could be held responsible for the consequences of history and political judgements.

<u>38</u>

Jay had studied about the British rule in India. He started to investigate and scrutinize the real facts of history. In the past the Hindus and Muslims had lived together. They lived in villages and in towns and cities. There was no state where people of both religions did not dwell and abide. So, what were the real and hidden reasons of violence to have exploded? There were four parties at the time of the start of partition process. The Indian National Congress, the Muslim League, the British imperialist government, and the Indian Princes (Maharajas and Nawabs).

After the Second World War, Britain had become financially a weak nation. It was impossible for her to maintain an Empire in India. There was also a shortage of administrators and army personnel. Indianisation of the Administrative Services (IAS) had started at the beginning of the twentieth century. There were two million Indians in the British Indian army, and only about fifty thousand British soldiers in India. Britain had to quit India.

They, however, took advantage of the religious rivalry among Indians. They decided to divide the country on religious grounds. The British Conservative party leader Winston Churchill thought that if the Indian National Congress under Jawaharlal Nehru took over the administration and policy formation, it could contravene with the British interests in the Indo-Pacific region.

He held the view that Nehru had leftist leanings. He would introduce communism in India. If that happened, Britain would be cut-off from Australia and New Zealand, which he considered Britain's outposts. India, under the Congress party rule, might not allow British ships to obtain fuel at the Karachi port. Churchill, therefore, impressed upon the Muslim League leader Mohammed Ali Jinnah to insist for a separate state of Pakistan. Churchill agreed to support the Indian Independence Act, only if India was divided.

The last Viceroy of India played a significant part in this process of apportionment. Two months prior to granting India independence, Indian leaders came to London when Jinnah saw Churchill, several times. Churchill convinced the Muslim League leader that it would for his community's advantage to have a separate state. Although he had the British interests on his mind.

Thereafter the partition of India had become inevitable, and it was engraved in the Indian Independence Bill and the Act. It was the consequence of the British Imperialist rule in India. It had never happened in the past, either under the Muslim rule or under the

Hindu period. India was always a united nation geographically, politically, and culturally.

Indians not only faced the **imperialist rule** by the British, which they never accepted and kept on fighting to rid themselves of the foreign rulers, who made decisions from overseas. They also had to deal with the **Indian feudalism**. Apart from the British India, there was also an Indian India. This part of India was ruled by a motley group of Indian rulers who called themselves the Maharajas and Nawabs. There were more than six hundreds of them. They ruled the City states. Some rulers had only a few miles of land area and a small population.

The Feudal rulers who were in the Pakistan territory, opted to join the new country. The independent India had 565 Princely states within its boundary. They were protected by the British, during the imperialist administration. The Independence of India Act gave them freedom to join India or to remain free states. A few rulers did really consider remaining independent.

The government of Independent India created a Department for States, to amalgamate them **within the India Union.** The Princely States ruled over 40% of the land area and the population was also almost 40%. Some of them had their own army, railways, currencies, and stamps. In bringing the Indian states into the Union of India, Home Minister Sardar Ballabh Bhai Patel, Home Secretary Vappal Panguni Menon (commonly known as VP Menon), and the Governor General Lord Mountbatten, played a significant role.

(After India's freedom in August 1947, Mountbatten was appointed as the first Governor General of India in order to maintain the continuity of administration. Invitations were sent to all the Maharajas and Nawabs. They were offered Privy purse, for their expenses. They could keep their palaces and the wealth. Through an Instrument of Accession, Indian rulers were asked to give up their control over defence, foreign affairs, and communications, to the government of independent India, which was under the control of the Indian National Congress party.

The Maharajas and Nawabs were also given position of governor or lieutenant governor of a state. Their Principalities were amalgamated into the existing states or new states were created by bringing geographical areas together. Within a period of two years, the 565 States or so, were brought together into 14 States. Most of the States accepted the conditions put forward by the Indian government and they joined the State of India.

There were problems with the state of Hyderabad. The Nizam wanted to remain Independent. The government of India had to act.

It sent an army. The Sardar himself went to Hyderabad and argued of the advantages for Hyderabad in joining the Indian Union. The Nizam joined India. There was no need for military action.

The Maharaja of Jammu and Kashmir had a similar dream. He wanted to keep his kingdom as a separate state. It fell between India and Pakistan. Within six weeks, however, the tribals, supported by the Pakistani army and guided by British soldiers, attacked the North-Western part of Kashmir. The tribals and the Pakistani army were only a few miles from Sri Nagar, the capital of Jammu and Kashmir. The Maharaja was unable to defend his kingdom. He, therefore, requested the Indian government for help. Home Secretary, VP Menon flew to Srinagar and received the signature of the Maharaja on the Instrument of Accession. The state of Jammu and Kashmir joined the Indian Union on 26th of October 1947. The next day, the Indian government sent army to stop the invasion by Pakistan. The Pakistani intruders stopped, where they were on 27 October. But India could not vacate them.

Mountbatten argued that the two new States should not start their lives by fighting among themselves. Nehru believed in the United Nations. He referred the matter to the United Nations, which asked Pakistan to withdraw its forces. The Maharaja of Jammu and

Kashmir had acceded the entire territory to India, but it has remained a divided state. One-third part is under Pakistani control. Even though the British India was partitioned into two countries, India and Pakistan, India was also unified by bringing the Princely States into its fold. It, therefore, remains a story of Division and Unification. People do not consider from that angle, but for Jay it was vital to discuss both aspects of independence and its impact on the Indian population and geography.

While India lost a vast area of land and resources to Pakistan, it also gained land area and population by uniting the scattered states across the country. Jay was keen to put forward his views on India's partition and unification, because most authors and politicians had laid emphasis only on the apportionment of the country and the creation of the new state of Pakistan. The Unification of India provided a strong, central government, which was essential to achieve economic growth and for defence and security of the nation.

39

Jay had wide variety of interests. He was sometimes requested to talk to young people on these themes. They wanted to know the distinction between an Individual and Society, and who was more important? Where and in what situations could an individual make progress and prosper? For Jay individual freedom was paramount. A controlled human being could not thrive or make advancements in his/her life. They would not be able to contribute a great deal to the community, as they would like to do.

An individual could not make progress under restrictions. He was also aware that a framework of rules was needed to endure a civilized life. Man was a social being. Other people were required to communicate with, to live and to work together. Eastern and Western philosophers have maintained that unity was required between individuality and society. Both were vital for survival and upward mobility. Certain facilities were needed by a person, which could be provided only in a society or by specialized groups.

The Hindu Upanishads had also argued for a unity between individual freedom and the community. It had been suggested that "he who sees the one in the spirit of all, could look with contempt

367

at no creature." Jay maintained that the interests of an individual and the community were not contradictory, because people tend to identify themselves with each other. People saw themselves as members of the community where they lived.

In the 21st Century, people had observed that development of an individual's self, was possible only in a free environment. Of course, some people attempt to create. obstacles in other people's progress. It could, however, be caused by jealousy, contempt, or any other psychological or social factor. Groups or individuals might attempt to control their fellow citizens and residents in the vicinity. Communality and individuality, nevertheless, were reinforcing. It was only by developing his own individuality that a person could contribute to amplifying other people's personalities. It was in society that a man could find possibilities of manifestation and forward movement. Jay suggested that an individual should be able to take his own decision, without any restrictions and hindrances from any outside pressures. Society could unfold an exchange of ideas, make suggestions to facilitate and promote advancement. The final decision should, however, be left to an individual. It would be in his/her interest and for his/her welfare. It was only by conforming to his own will that a person could feel free. They should not give up their own moral principles and values.

No individual could flourish without the breakthrough of the nation. Temporarily, the achievement of individuals might look brighter, and that should be good enough for others to follow. In this process, education could play an imperative role and could lead to efficiency and save time and resources. He sustained that self-consciousness enriches personality and strengthens the self of an individual. Without the individual's development, the elevation of society would not be possible.

With liberty, however, there was a need for equality of opportunity to share the same social environment. If people were unequal socially and economically, they would be disruptive in the overall headway of the nation. Members of society might display superiority complex and attempt to control others. Outside the society, however, development of individuality and of the "self" could be obstructed. When people work for the welfare of all, they also work for their own welfare.

In a communal society, people defend the interests of each other. There was no clash of interests between an individual and the society. The self-evolution by an individual was consistent with the society's advancement. When a person makes progress, others also tend to elevate themselves because they are part of the nation. Individuals and society are, therefore, interdependent, and indivisible. Their interests are identical, supportive and reinforcing.

There was, however, a need for mutual understanding and cooperation between the communities. There should be no richness and no poverty, no superior or inferior in a society. It has been argued that society helps individuals to realize their moral and economic existence. There should be nothing abstract. All tend to play a positive role.

It was, therefore, imperative to provide an apparatus, a system to regulate the society for the sake of defending an individual's interests and freedoms. It was important to stop any conflict. Change was the law of nature. Society and individuals should adjust with the changing circumstances. Still, it would require simplicity, freedom, equality, and social justice in contemplation of individuals and society, for a contented living and prosperity.

Jay was often asked to talk to scholarly groups to share his knowledge and experience with them. The International Institute of Comparative Studies, in Somerset, Southwest England, invited him to speak on economic relations between the North (Advanced countries) and the South (Developing countries). They thought that

Jay might have knowledge of both. He was born in a developing country and had lived most of his life in an advanced nation.

He spoke for about twenty-five minutes to half an hour. He was then open to discussion. He started by saying that the world was one and he believed in cooperation between nations. Indeed, he expected both the North and the South to work in partnership with each other. He said that the developed countries had capital and technology.

There could be capital investment and transfer of technology from the rich countries to the developing countries, to increase the use of their resources, for the advantage of their compatriots and indeed the world. Every nation would gain by the expedient use of their assets which will benefit the whole humankind. Jay was aware that the capitalist advanced countries had skilled -workforce and managerial talents. The Southern countries were waiting to develop expertise, knowledge, and education, which could be provided by the rich advanced nations.

They could open colleges and institutions of technology, in the developing regions. They could also provide scholarships to students to study at their universities. As a matter of fact, the North- South divide was the consequence of imperialism and colonialism and exploitation of the natural and human resources

371

by the European countries in the eighteenth and the nineteenth centuries. It led to stagnation of economies in the colonies. India an industrialized nation until the 18th Century was turned into an agricultural country by the British.

His study had shown that the British industrial revolution grew out of the decline and ashes of the Indian Cotton Industry in the 19th Century. While the Indian cotton goods production and exports declined, the British cotton industry grew and prospered. Its exports rose.

On many occasions the British cotton goods were given preference in taxation, in place of the local cotton goods in India. Import subsidies were provided for the British goods sold in the colonies and the empire. Heavy duties were imposed on home produced goods in these countries.

Jay expressed the view that it was essential for the advanced nations to invest capital in human resources in the developing countries in order to help them in achieving economic growth. Both, private and public sectors could play a significant role in developing the manufacturing sector in the Southern countries. This investment would trigger expansion that would lead to further growth and employment. The purchasing power of local people would increase which would spur further job creation. Invention and innovation could assist the Southern countries.

Foreign investment could be tricky. The advanced countries invest in areas which benefit them. Consumers goods industries, assembling of smart mobile phones and smart televisions and washing machines, had attracted financing in the advancing nations from the rich countries. The manufacturing of these goods would still provide employment to local youth and other workforce.

Domestic savings and investment could lead to development. The economies would accelerate in the countries of the South. The problem was that these countries had little savings to invest in the manufacturing sector. They do not have a large entrepreneurial class to set up their own businesses. They could, however, produce agricultural goods and start food- processing industries, along with some manufactured goods industries. Trade could also be developed between the nations of the South themselves.

They could specialize in their fields of expertise. South- South trade would benefit the developing countries. It could be for their mutual benefit because these countries were at the same level of technology usage. There had also been an argument, "whether the developed countries should provide aid or develop trade with the less developed nations." In Jay's opinion this had been a dilemma since the end of the Second World War, when most of the colonies were freed. All the rich countries, however, did not provide the aid of 0.7% of their GDP, which was suggested by the United Nations. It was, therefore, essential to develop trade between the nations. International trade should take place without tariffs or with low tariffs. He told his audience that the rich developed countries should realize that they could not dictate the terms of trade to other nations. In the past everything worked for the interest of the European states. The developing countries had realized that they would have to stand up for their people' rights and their economic welfare.

He argued that the rich countries had often used the environment and social concerns as a means for protectionism. They had proclaimed against industrialization in the developing countries. The labour laws and pollution created by factories were the main reasons against industrial development in the South. Although it was the European countries and the United States of America, which created most pollution and disfigured the world environment.

The Southern countries, nevertheless, started to develop industries by the end of the 20th Century. They manufactured goods as their import substitutes and later started to export their products. Self-help was considered vital. They also recognized their own interests and knew what was economically advantageous for them. Jay argued in favour of the developing nations. Industrialization was the only a route to achieving economic growth, for providing employment to their people and take away some burden from agriculture. Far too many people worked on farms in these countries.

The agricultural yield was not sufficient and in accordance with the resources put into this sector. It was sometimes less than half of the output, provided by the United States of America. Jay examined the problems confronted by the developing countries. Many of them could not pay their loans borrowed from the IMF and the World Bank or the Regional Development banks. The economic productivity was low. The work force was inefficient. The politicians were corrupt. To set up a factory or another business, the investor had to bribe the local politicians and administrators.

Without prior payment of what was called a commission, the files would not move forward for decision making by the relevant officials. Surprisingly, the commission demanded, by the decision makers in these countries, was to be deposited in Western banks.

This did not help with investment or creating employment. The money was not even transacted. Yet, it was considered as a loan to the nation.

This part of the loan never entered the country. Jay was disgusted with this kind of practice and conduct by the decision makers. He considered it utterly disgraceful. In course of time, some politicians and administrators were caught, especially in India, but the money could not be chased. These politicians and administrators did not realize that an investment was coming into their country, which would create employment for their people and their constituents.

They thought that the investors wanted to start business in their countries to make profit. They, therefore, wanted their share of that gain in advance. Some western investors, indeed, returned home without even discussing the projects or the level of investment.

Jay felt that depositing the bribe money in western banks was a transfer of resources from the developing countries to rich countries rather than the other way round. The interest and profits were being paid on loans, which never came to the nation. The transfer of profits to the investing country was also a withdrawal from the developing countries. If these profits could be ploughed back into the economy of a nation, it would have led to growth, employment, and further expansion. It was being denied by the selfishness and greed of some politicians and civil servants.

Nevertheless, cooperation between the rich and the developing countries had been profitable in the 21st Century. India has developed its computer software industry to meet the demand of the United States, Britain, Japan, and the European countries. The advanced rich countries were genuinely interested in helping the less developed nations. Jay established that economic growth could be achieved through exports.

If the rich countries wanted to assist the underdeveloped nations, they should purchase products from the latter. They had, however, criticized the goods manufactured in these nations, as the products of cheap work force or sweat labour. Still these cheap goods have penetrated the markets of rich nations through the "Dollar shops" or the "Pound Plus stores."

He discovered that in the 20th Century, there was hardly any progress in transfer of Technology or Investment from the advanced rich nations to the developing countries. If there was any transfer of technology, the old redundant technology, which had become unworkable in the rich states, was being disposed-off to them. No modern technology was passed on to the poor nations. These nations were despised and neglected.

377

Some countries were, however, making efforts through education which was to become a vehicle for economic and social progress. In course of time, the advanced developing nations decided to increase trade and investment among themselves. It became feasible after the fall of the Soviet Union, when all the states of that Union became independent.

<u>40</u>

After Reena's demise, Jay's life and living system changed. He lost all interest in his country of origin. There was no social attraction. Both his parents died much earlier. Some loved ones, who were close to him, also passed away. He could have gone to visit places of interest but due to health conditions, it was not realistic.

His immediate family was divided over two continents. A few members had moved to live in North America and the others continued to live in Britain. Jay loved them equally. He had lived in London for six decades; it would not be easy for him to live in a new country. He once visited his doctor and got involved in conversation as two social beings. The doctor was aware that Jay loved his children and grandchildren, who lived in the United Kingdom and North America.

She suggested that he should move to live in Iceland, which was at an equal distance from Britain as well as from North America. Jay circulated the idea to his family, who had their own views. One of his grandchildren wanted him to move to live with them. The other suggested that "it was grandpa's choice", where he wanted to live in his old age.

He tried to please everyone and divided his time between the United Kingdom and North America. He was very well looked after at both the places. His grandchildren took him on holiday and short breaks. They accompanied him to doctors and hospitals. They did his shopping. When he had his knee replacement, they slept at his house and looked after him. They moved his bed to the ground floor and had a shower built. They provided him hot meal and tea, whenever he wanted. He continued to watch news and television programmes and films.

Still his life was restricted because of imposition. He did not want to go far and preferred to walk locally and in local parks. When he recovered from the knee operation, he did his own shopping. His grandchildren were there to bring bulky items, especially spring water. Though he enjoyed the company of his children and grandchildren in North America and had acquired a Permanent Resident Status, he realized that he could not live there permanently or stay away from his home in London for a prolonged period. He loved his house and the surrounding areas. His neighbours started to miss him.

He enjoyed visiting the supermarkets and small shops. Touching and picking food items, especially fruits and vegetables. Every now and then he visited shops and stores in Southall, the centre for Asian food and clothing. He also went to Hounslow in the Middlesex County, whenever he could and needed to buy articles for daily use. These places also have good restaurants of world standard and provided food and sweets of his liking.

Yet, he did not visit these places, as much as he visited with his wife Reena. After her death, there was a void in his life. There were several reasons for that. They had lived together for half a century. They understood each other and respected each other's views. Jay let Reena win in decision making.

Gradually, as Jay grew older, he started to lose his hair, began to use a walking stick, developed health conditions, like diabetes and hypertension. He had hernia operation, prostate operation, knee replacement and abscess removed, on a few occasions. He suffered scope many times when his blood pressure went down. The lack of blood circulation led to his unconsciousness. Pollution has increased in Britain and around the world, which has affected people's living and health conditions.

Jay's children grew up and moved to live their own lives. He was in touch with his grandchildren. He sometimes imagined, if he became a great granddad, how would his great-grandchildren act and react. What would they say? How would they speak and laugh? He tried to examine from the child psychology point of view.

There was hardly any social contact with his siblings. He, however, was in touch with his colleagues and friends, whom he had met in the past fifty years or so. He sent and received Christmas cards every year from them, reviewing the year just passed and changes that have occurred in their lives. Some of them attempted to meet once or twice a year, for as long as they could.

He joined a local gym on the advice of his doctor. This gym aimed to provide physical exercise for people of all ages. Personal touch, individual attention, friendly environment, and other aspects of socialization made an impact on him. It brought smiles and laughter on the faces of those who came to use the facilities. He noticed that the whole environment at the gym was geared to fraternize and mingle with other participants, who were strangers only a few days earlier. The group practice in the studio was designed to bring them together for multiple activities, where elderly people walked sideways and did pushes against the wall.

The instructors provided individual attention which brought pleasure and happiness to those who came to take part in different physical tasks. It led to fun and friendship. Involvement in conversation increased pleasure. For most partakers, activities were identified to meet needs based on their health conditions. The instructors endeavoured to assist everyone. The improvement in conditions was monitored, as was the lack of amends. It was the social and psychological factors which brought amelioration and betterment in their physical well-being.

This was accomplished by creating an environment conducive to establishing trust and understanding between the instructors and the participants, who achieved their personal best through encouragement and motivation. Emphasis was laid on regular exercise, which augmented self-confidence, prevented depression, and reduced stress. It led to control of emotions and increased focus. Meeting others without personal self-interest was the foundation for establishing friendship and developing mutual respect.

He lived a simple life. He used to get tired because of diabetes. His memory was still sharp. He could remember minute details of earlier years. He noticed that in this changing world, some people's behaviour and dealings hardly ever change.

CONCLUSION

In the twilight of his life, one evening, Jay was lying in his bed near the window, overlooking the front garden of the house. He indulged in reminiscence and dwelt upon the past seventy-five-year span, since leaving the Village Primary. He thought that if his father had paid five rupees to the teacher, his life's journey would have been different to the one he travelled. All his adult life, he had contended that money was not everything. Yet, five rupees changed the course of his mode of living and pursuit.

He could have stayed in his district, if not in the same village. He would have moved to live in another city, in his state for his career and to make his sustainment. He might have at least spent his life in the country of birth and would have done something good for the country's citizens, the district community, and his village folks, whom he so dearly loved, and they loved him back.

The tussle, between two grown up men for five rupees, however, altered all that. They threw him into a life of turmoil, where he had to grapple with problems, and face obstacles. On occasions, he starved, slept on bare floor, was bullied, his cheek was made red, where he had visible finger marks of a slap. He, nonetheless, survived the stormy times and adversities. He never felt defeated or disorientated. The challenges became a part of his routine and his personality. He was conscious of the fact that humankind had to compromise between the conflicting interests.

As a child, he was not allowed to start his Primary Schooling, because he was not yet five years old. When he went to village school, he was kept in the reception class for two years, even though his teacher asked him to teach oral arithmetic to his classmates. On non-payment of five rupees, he had to leave his school and the village. His talent and skills were not recognized in his early years.

Yet, he ended up scoring qualifications, leading to the Bachelor of Arts degree; Bachelor of Science (Honours) degree in Mathematics with Economics. A Master of Arts Degree; A Master of Philosophy (M Phil) Research degree and in the end the Degree of the Doctor of Philosophy (Ph.D.) by published work.

Jay had gained sufficient knowledge in Psychology and understood the traits, attitudes, and human nature, which was also a biological factor. He once read a letter from a man and analysed his character and attitudes, which turned out to be correct.

As a teacher, he never entered the classroom without preparing the teaching material. He knew what he was going to deliver in his lectures and class teaching. He provided notes to his students, when needed, marked their work and homework, advising them to improve their standard. He checked their examination scripts objectively.

He was available to students whenever it was essential for them to see him. He looked at their interests and supervised them at lunch break, so they could enjoy themselves and develop sociability. One afternoon, he was in the company of a colleague and friend, John Ferguson, who expressed his observation and said, "Jay, knowing you, it looks, you are not going to stay at this school for long. What is your desire and ambition"?

Jay replied, "John, if I had a choice, I would like to teach and retire at a university and then write my memoirs with a title "From Factory Floor to University Chair, the story of an Immigrant in Britain". This he really did. He became a teacher and taught at all levels, using his academic qualifications. He started to teach at a High School. In the course of time, he moved to teach at a college of Further Education, then at a college of Higher Education. Moved to teach at a Polytechnic and finally at a university. He taught full-time for thirty-five years and part-time to earn some extra money, in order to fight his poverty, and to seek financial security for his old age.

He lived in slums, in a big house in Northeast London, and in an inner-city suburb, where beautiful parks and tall trees provided the green environment which reminded him of the natural surroundings of his village. He walked freely with the aim of breathing fresh air. He observed that a person's childhood played a significant role in the development of his personality and maintained that good memory was fine. Sometimes, however, it was virtuous to forget the bitter experiences.

Jay was a man of principles. He followed the social norms set by wise people, for smooth running of society and family life. He looked at the facts in dealing with people. In philosophical terms, it could be identified with the truth. Yet, he was misunderstood by people who could not discern or comprehend his point of view and purpose.

They created impediments and obstacles in his way. He contemplated that he wanted to live on certain axioms and tenets which were not easy to follow by everyone. Consequently, he faced enormous encumbrance and stumbling blocks. He had to struggle to survive and to improve his living conditions.

In the end, he felt exhilarated, when considering his achievements, especially in the field of education, progression, and peaceful living. He deduced that his life had been a race contrived by circumstances. It was not a sprint or a long-distance race, it was a hurdle engagement, where he had to cross barriers and jump fences. He had to go through flood plains, rivulets, farmland, and barren areas in order to reach his destination (goal). On his accomplishments, he acknowledged, that the purpose of his life has been fulfilled.

He was a happy man, despite many impediments. Many people helped him at various stages in this progression. He turned the negativity into positive actions. He mingled with all kinds of people and ignored the jealous and gloomy thinkers, who would create restrictions in his up-lift and work. He changed with time and with the changing circumstances.

He asserted that disagreements and physical attacks could find their roots in ideological differences. People thought differently in accordance with their social and historical background. There could be a genuine deviation between family members and neighbours who could find it difficult to accommodate each other's points of view.

These ideological disparities could be expressed through arguments. People could criticize each other openly or in private. This could lead to shouts, abuse, or verbal attacks or they could physically harm each other. It was, therefore, vital to uncover an alternative approach, and respect each other's culture, history, and philosophy. Cooperation and reconciliation were vitally important in society and in organizations.

He recalled that he had travelled by airplane, going to India and North America. As he grew older, he became scared of flying either within the country or going abroad. Big aero-plane and large airports terrified him. Queuing to get onto a plane or coming out of a plane was cumbersome for him because of walking difficulties.

He tried to avoid huge crowds. Even though he was, sometimes, provided wheelchair assistance to and from plane. The changeover at airports was uncomfortable and awkward, especially when he was left by attendants at unknown places to be picked up by another attendant. Sometimes, he feared missing his flight, which could presumptuously obstruct his journey.

Jay received enormous encouragement and hope from the life of king Harish Chandra and often considered that even a great Raja (king) had to encounter difficulties, but never succumbed to problems, always followed the path of the truth, Jay was just a simple villager who had to face enormous obstacles. He always looked at this story and continued his life's journey by confronting and solving his enigma.

There had been other people who always spoke the truth. The most famous person who was recognized to tell the truth in the dvarpar yug (The Iron Age), some two thousand years after Raja Harish Chandra, was Yudhistir, the son of King Pandu of Hastinapur. He himself became the king of Indraprastha and Hastinapur in course of time. He was recognized for his truthfulness and honesty from his childhood. It had been suggested that he never lied and was, therefore, called, Dharmaraj (a righteous man).

Still, Yudhistir had to confront hardship and hindrances in his life. He even had to live on alms (begging). He was exiled to the forest, with his wife and siblings, where they lived for twelve years, and were not allowed to work. Yudhistir believed in morals and virtues and was famous for speaking the truth. He lied in the battle at Kurukshetra on the instructions of Lord Krishna. He was instructed to pronounce that Ashwatthama had been killed in the fight, when an elephant named Ashwatthama was killed by warrior Bhim.

Ashwatham was also the name of the son of his teacher, warrior Drona, who was convinced that his only son had been killed in the combat. Yudhistir announced loudly that "Ashwatthama had been killed", without clarifying whether it was a man or an animal. Technically, Yudhister was not wrong and did not lie. He maintained his truthfulness.

His stepbrother, Karan was also the son of his mother Kunti but was born outside the wedlock. Karan was famous for giving arms, especially if he was requested, after his morning prayer. During the armed conflict between the Pandavas and Kauravas, he parted with his shield (Kavach) to Indra. This caused his death. He was aware that without his shield he would not be able to protect himself and survive. Yet, he kept his habit of giving anything, if demanded after the morning prayer.

All his life, Karan encountered problems. He was abandoned by his mother after his birth. His teacher, guru Parshuram took away all his skills, when he discovered that he was not a low born but a warrior. Bhisma refused to have him in the Kauravas army because he was not brought up as a warrior but was recognized as the son of a charioteer. His biological mother queen Kunti accepted him as her son in the end, but he refused to return to her fold.

He had promised to fight for Kauravas, for prince Duryodhana and king Dhritarashtra. He was famous for keeping his promise and never renounced his habit. He was a good warrior, a good friend and believed in dharma (righteousness). He could be recognized as a truthful person who believed and practiced honesty and kept his promises, as well as making sacrifices for the benefit of others.

391

Encouraged by such stories, Jay continued his life's journey, by removing the hurdles and crossing the barriers, building a life of his own, stone by stone; brick by brick, cementing it, with education and knowledge. Making it stronger with the adhesive of wisdom. Progressively, he strolled the path with determination, style, and good humour. He accomplished excellence in thought, acquired excellence in internal and external ideology and sought goodness in other people. He maintained self-restraint, modesty, and politeness. He continued with his service to humanity through generosity, cooperation, and virility.

It all provided him happiness and contentment. For Jay, struggle and happiness prevailed side by side. He realized that the aim of life was to seek happiness. It saved people from depression. Though humanity had to struggle and attain satisfaction and make progress. It was human nature to seek comfort and pleasure.

Happiness, nevertheless, was not rare in his life. Happiness sprang from the understanding of basic values. It came from within. One should seek it within oneself. Of course, folks seek happiness through their performance and profession. Jay concluded that happiness was the result of people's actions, which they did not receive in any physical shape. It was a symbolic posture. They tend to blame society for their failures or lack of happiness. If people gave up selfishness and arrogance, they would have the feelings of happiness.

When a person reads a book, it may not provide him with systematic pleasure, but at an interesting reference, he would burst into laughter expressing happiness. Pleasure and satisfaction were important in life. Human beings should maintain and keep their thoughts pure. There should be no smell of sadness or dejection. They should not overdo anything because it would lose its significance and diminishing returns would start. Without continuous effort, the community would not accomplish contentment.

An all-round development of interests was vital. Be it physical, mental, educational, or spiritual. If we ignore any branch of life, it could make people unhappy, incomplete, and dissatisfied. They should, therefore, continue their physical exercise, literature reading.

Jay felt that "elation was not a house which could be built by human hands. It was like a song, which people murmur at night or early in the morning". He discovered that it was vital to control human demands to achieve their well-being. People should not become slave of their wishes and desires.

Jay found his life's journey, like a motorway with meanders and curves, hills, and valleys. Slip roads and side roads joining the main route. New travellers came in and joined the peregrination. People changed lanes for the sake of avoiding problems or for saving time to make progress. They had to negotiate the track to avoid hindrances and obstacles. Smooth driving was like a smooth life without conundrum.

Some individuals exploit and take advantage of others' gentleness, modesty and later call them fools. In certain circumstances, individuals could confide with family members. There was a need for courage, confidence, and commitment with the aim of making progress in life and happily contributing to the advancement and improvement of commonality.

Printed in Great Britain
by Amazon

59702508R00218